MW01169908

Self and Motivational Systems
Toward a Theory
of Psychoanalytic Technique

Psychoanalytic Inquiry Book Series

Volume 13

Psychoanalytic Inquiry Book Series

Self and Motivational Systems
Toward a Theory
of Psychoanalytic Technique

Joseph D. Lichtenberg
Frank M. Lachmann
James L. Fosshage

THE ANALYTIC PRESS

1992   Hillsdale, NJ   London

Earlier versions of the following chapters have been published elsewhere and appear by permission of the copyright holders: ch. 2 in Lachmann, F. & Lichtenberg, J. (1992), Model scenes: Implications for psychoanalytic treatment. *J. Amer. Psychoanal. Assn.*, 40:117–138; ch. 7 in Fosshage, J. (1990), Clinical protocol. *Psychoanal. Inq.*, 12:248–274; ch. 8 in Lichtenberg, J. (1991), What is a selfobject? *Psychoanal. Dial.*, 1:455–480.

Set in 10 point Schneidler by Lind Graphics, Upper Saddle River, NJ

Library of Congress Cataloging-in-Publication Data

Lichtenberg, Joseph D.
   Self and motivational systems : toward a theory of psychoanalytic technique /
Joseph D. Lichtenberg, Frank M. Lachmann, James L. Fosshage.
    p.   cm. –(Psychoanalytic inquiry book series : v. 13)
   Includes bibliographical references and index.
   ISBN 0-88163-154-X
   1. Motivation (Psychology) 2. Self. 3. Psychoanalysis.
4. Psychotherapist and patient.   I. Lachmann, Frank M.
II. Fosshage, James L. III. Title. IV. Series.
   [DNLM: 1. Ego. 2. Motivation. 3. Psychoanalytic Theory. W1
PS427F v. 13 / WM 460.5.M6 L699s]
RC489.M655L533 1992
616.89´17–dc20
DNLM/DLC
for Library of Congress   92-49414
                                      CIP

Printed in the United States of America
10 9 8 7 6 5 4 3 2

Contents

Self and Motivational Systems
Toward a Theory
of Psychoanalytic Technique

1

Motivational Systems and Other Basics

We believe that the theory of the self and motivational systems calls for a revised theory of technique. Based on the concepts formulated in *Psychoanalysis and Motivation* (Lichtenberg, 1989a), this book provides a *foundation* for a psychoanalytic exploratory technique. Through clinical examples, we indicate the forms and methods of a technique based on self and motivational systems.

Reconsider briefly the theory offered in *Psychoanalysis and Motivation*. Psychoanalytic theory is, at its core, a theory of structured *motivation*. Five systems designed to promote the fulfillment and regulation of basic needs were delineated. Each system comprises distinct motivational and functional aspects. Each system is a psychological entity (with probable neurophysiological correlates). Each is built around a fundamental need. Each is based on behaviors clearly observable, beginning in the neonatal period. The five motivational systems are: (1) the need for psychic regulation of physiological requirements, (2) the need for attachment and later affiliation, (3) the need for exploration and assertion, (4) the need to react aversively through antagonism or withdrawal (or both), and (5) the need for sensual enjoyment and sexual excitement.

5 systems

During infancy, each system contributes to self-regulation in mutually regulatory interactions with caregivers. At each period of life, the fundamental needs and the wishes, desires, aims, and goals that derive from those needs in each

1

motivational system may be rearranged in different hierarchies indicated by different conscious and unconscious preferences, choices, and proclivities. From moment to moment, the activity of any one system may be intensified to the point where it provides motivational dominance of the self. The "self" develops as an independent center for initiating, organizing, and integrating motivation. The sense of self arises from experiencing that initiating, organizing, and integrating. Experiencing has an active (agent) and passive (receptor) mode.

Why do we need a new theory of motivation? Isn't the vitality of motivation guaranteed in the human by instincts or instinctual drives? [We] argue that motivations arise solely from *lived experience*. Based on the particular lived experience, motivations may or may not achieve optimal vitality. Whatever biophysiological urgencies and innate neurophysiological response patterns underlie psychological motivations, the vitality of the motivational experience will depend initially on the manner in which exchanges between infants and their caregivers unfold. Later, the development of symbolic representation enhances the potential for flexible, self-created reorganization of lived experience. A psychoanalytic theory of adaptive and maladaptive motivational functioning is about lived experience throughout life. Lived experience is about how we human beings consciously and unconsciously seek to fulfill our needs and desires by searching in potential events for affects that signal for us that experiential fulfillment [pp. 1–2].

The five motivational systems were derived from a host of empirical findings. They represent a way of clustering these findings so as to make sense from the vantage point of dynamic psychoanalysis. The five systems depict our vision of human motivation. We may ask, is that all there is to human motivation? Do these motivational systems capture the triumph of Liza Doolittle when she "got it?" Do they capture the agony of Richard Nixon when he "lost it?" Do they capture the ecstasy of an orgasm or the loneliness of the long distance runner? Our response is a modest "yes," but we would quickly agree that when motivations are looked upon with a cold, empirical eye they may not pack the wallop of Freud's rider-on-the-horse metaphor.

Follow our exploration of the motivational systems, and among your rewards will be an affiliation with a psychoanalytic community that values small, logically, observationally, empirically derived steps. We are not averse to the exciting metaphors of seething cauldrons or armies that leave provisions behind in case of retreat. But for us psychoanalysis is best understood and participated in when one's physiological requirements are quiescent and explorations are conducted into the affectively rich subjective life of the analysand. Then the uniquely individual imagery and metaphors, the unconscious fantasies and beliefs, the model scenes, are discovered and formed jointly by analyst and analysand. Descriptions of the moment-to-moment analytic exchanges in which these joint constructions occur lack the grandeur of Eros and Thanatos or other broad metapsychological speculations. In our pursuit of the specific determiners of the experience of motivation and their implications for psychoanalytic theory and practice, the feet of the empiricist may seem sometimes to stand on the soul of the poet.

As you read the chapters that follow, you may be surprised to find that familiar terms like unconscious, defense, conflict, and resistance have been redefined to be as close as possible to what can be experienced. With these terms redefined and the pillars of the tripartite structural hypothesis (dual drives, id, ego, and superego) removed, then, unlike the little boy in the famous story, we are saying, "The clothes have no emperor!" This book represents our ongoing effort to provide clinical psychoanalysis with a democratically elected "new emperor," an empirically, developmentally derived model of motivational systems.

We want to speak to the psychoanalyst-clinician and offer a way of moving between theoretical models and clinical phenomena without losing the rigorous constraints of the former or the empathically derived riches of the latter. We believe the terms we use to facilitate the back-and-forth interplay of theory and phenomena—systems, dimensions, perspectives, and regulation— are relatively neutral and are unlikely to shape technique into their own imagery. What is lost in the evocativeness of our language we believe the clinician can more than make up for through the creative discoveries of idiosyncratic subjectivity stemming from the analysand's associations, memories, and model scenes.

The five motivational systems are not a rock-bottom concept. The inferential steps between them and the analytic situation can easily be detailed. We propose, however, that the five systems all function to develop, maintain, and restore the cohesiveness of a self or self-organization. In delineating our understanding of the reciprocal relationship between motivation and the self, we are carving out the conceptual pillars that may eventually hold up a theory. This is our psychoanalytic-philosophical belief. We propose it. We cannot demonstrate it empirically. But, we hold, it provides a useful, overarching clinical perspective. The five motivational systems might conceivably fit into another psychoanalytic-philosophical system, but that is not our main concern. We are not advancing a new psychoanalytic theory. For that matter, we are not proposing a theory in any final form although we have proposed its motivational underpinnings. We are working toward a theory of technique, specifically a theory of technique that will provide the practitioner with a conceptual ally in the moment-to-moment work of psychoanalysis.

In the course of our explorations, we frequently confront theoretical constructs that are currently in vogue or backed by an accumulation of theory-derived treatments. In such instances, for example in our discussion of unconscious fantasy and interpretive "depth," we challenge existing propositions and advance our own perspective in combination with its clinical implications wherever we can. But our focus accents the clinical rather than the metapsychological aspects of theory.

In our more detailed discussions of the five motivational systems we provide the psychoanalytic clinician with a conceptual tool that both offers a set of primary motivations and leaves open the possibility that any motivation can be used in the service of limiting awareness of any experience to which the person is averse. For example, sexuality or attachment motivations may be used to avoid experiencing isolation and loneliness that are stirred up by exploratory possibilities. The five systems leave the relationship among the systems to be worked out uniquely and specifically in each case. With sexuality and aggression no longer as basic, irreducible drives or their pathology as always a product of a breakdown of the self, analysts can follow the patient's narrative freely without having to adhere to a preconceived and empirically unsubstantiated hierarchy of motives.

The debate among the adherents of the various psychoanalytic theories can be understood as a debate about which motivations are primary and which ones are derived or secondary. When the findings of the empirical infant researchers are sorted out, the hierarchies of motivations as proposed by various theories cannot be supported. All five systems operate at least from birth on, and all five interact and are instrumental in shaping experience and hence eventuate in the shaping of the sense of self. These findings make moot some of the acrimony found in theoretical disputes. We are prompted to claim that the clinical findings of any psychoanalytic theory should be explainable through the five motivational systems and the cohesiveness of the self. In addition, our proposal should provide the clinician with a vantage point through which explorations previously closed off by theoretical assumptions can be opened and explored. Our emphasis on organizing principles and themes and being open to our patients' stories maintains an ambience of exploration, investigation, and the joy of discovery.

The clinical prescription that follows from this freedom is that the analyst's empathic-introspective stance can be more consistently maintained. The analyst's interventions, however, will shift from the language of impulse-defense, wish-resistance, and need-frustration to an explication of themes, organizing principles, interpretive sequences, model scenes, and motivations in relation to self-cohesion and the pursuit of selfobject experiences.

Although we claim the mantle of the empiricist, we do not neglect the poet. Just as nature inspired the Romantic poets' use of metaphor, alliteration, and onomatopoeia, the clinical exchange draws our attention to the dynamic creativity of analyst and analysand at work. Both poet and analyst and analysand working together draw the origins of their creativity from those magic moments in childhood when, through symbolic play, a stick "becomes" a spoon and the teddy bear becomes the self being fed by the mother-self. In our rendering of the construction of model scenes, the unraveling of "unconscious" fantasy, and the elaboration of attributions of the analyst's attitudes and values as perceived by the analysand, we recognize the creative power of the collaborative effort. In the active process of communicating and listening, as one person speaks to the other, directs wishes to the other, we identify the subject–object dimension of the exchange. This points us to the individual subjectivity of analyst and analysand. We hold that what has generally been thought of as having been organized solely intrapsychically inevitably bears the stamp of the intersubjective context of assumed responsiveness and motivations of the other. Thus, we place the analysand's expectations of evoking a selfobject experience from the analyst at the center of the organization of the analysand's associations and communicating; we place the less often considered analyst's expectations of evoking a selfobject experience from the work with the analysand at the center of the organization of the analyst's associations and communications.

We have an opportunity here to address an important but often neglected issue. The analyst's endeavor when optimal is a product of the exploratory motivational system. When exploration is infused with aversiveness, the analyst's adherence to an empathic mode of perception cannot be maintained. Then the exploration may become side-tracked as the analysand's motivation is no longer attended from the analysand's point of view. Explicit or implicit accusations of resistance often follow, with the effect that the analysand feels put off and communications become limited. Any motivational system may coopt the exploratory endeavor of the analyst. The analyst's alertness to these shadings and nuances in the encounter with the patient provides a built-in signal to disruptions in optimal responsiveness.

Our plan for the book makes for a challenging presentation. Principles of technique, such as model-scene construction, sequences of interpretation, disruption–restoration sequences, the path to awareness, and the empathic mode of perception will alternate with presentations of research findings and conceptual frameworks that provide the foundation for the technical recommendations. We offer the reader recommendations about the methods we espouse mixed with theoretical underpinnings to these recommendations. Methods of approach have in the past had to be intuitively related to a dual-drive theory that we believe is outmoded. Because we regard motivations to be organized in five systems that form in response to basic needs, we are forced to ask new questions about technique and suggest new answers. Our suggested answers to questions about technique oscillate with proposals of developmental principles that are in keeping with our motivational hypothesis. The developmental principles, in turn, lead us to reexamine a long list of familiar psychoanalytic concepts: unconscious mentation, conflict, defense, values and morality, and transference. We also extend an ongoing exploration of the development, maintenance, and restoration of self-organization. In a chapter that is a cornerstone of the book, we present our view of the central importance of the pursuit of selfobject experiences and the link this understanding provides to the treatment of addictive disorders. We suggest that the traditional method of exploring any clinical finding from an intrapsychic or intersubjective perspective is inadequate unless equal significance is afforded to an assessment of state. The importance we place on an assessment of state derives from our study of dreams and particularly self-psychological studies of self-state dreams, state transitions in infancy, and state alterations in pathological conditions. We apply the concept of state to describe the optimal mind set of analysand and analyst during an analytic session and to the pathological conditions of disturbed self-cohesion, panic, abuse, and hatred.

By taking as our starting point the conceptualization of self and motivational systems, we are compelled to explore developmental events through the intrapsychic organizing principles of self-organization, self-stabilization, dialectic tension, and hierarchical rearrangement. Our view that intrapsychic development is intrinsically intertwined with an intersubjective perspective requires us to place considerable emphasis on the analyst's contribution to the therapeutic process. We will provide the reader with a detailed presentation of verbatim exchanges that depict interpretation as a sequence of interventions made or not made by the analyst. This clinical presentation illustrates the process by which sequences of interpretation integrate patterns and relationships. We emphasize neither the analysand's associations nor the analyst's interpretations but rather the back-and-forth exchanges that coexist with the analyst's and analysand's alternating uncertainties and growing awareness.

How the analysis is deepened is a concern that runs throughout our book. Deepening of the analysis is inextricably dependent on the application of the empathic mode of perception and entry into the state of mind of the analysand. Deepening of the analysis requires the analyst to sense the motivational goals of the analysand that are dominant at any given moment. The focus on motivational goals directs us to an appreciation of affects as guides for our empathic perception and to the state of self-cohesion as recognized from a perspective of regulation and resilience (self-righting). The application of this focus expands self-experience and increases self-knowledge. Our discussion of unconscious and conscious mentation, the path to awareness, and changing symbolic representations or schemas of self and others provides the conceptual and empirical underpinning for our clinical focus. *The analyst, as perceived by the patient,* is the most significant "other" for the patient's deepened awareness of the pursuit of selfobject experiences. Thus, we stress the technical importance for analyst and analysand to construct (often by way of model scenes) the vision of the analyst that the patient experiences.

Our book is for the curious, self-reflective clinician. We believe that at times we pursue questions and challenges that have long been present but dormant in the analytic community. At other times we raise less familiar questions that need to be asked. We hope that we are opening psychoanalytic inquiries into areas hitherto closed by fidelity to early theoreticians and the sense of certainty derived from adherence to familiar theories. If we can challenge readers to challenge us in return, we will have found adherents and adversaries combined in the spirit of psychoanalysis at its best.

2

Model Scenes
Implications for Psychoanalytic Treatment

In the course of psychoanalytic treatment, analyst and patient construct model scenes to organize previously puzzling information, further integrate previous understanding, and initiate further exploration of the analysand's experience and motivations. The model scenes that analyst and patient construct and modify during the course of analytic exploration convey to each, in graphic and metaphoric forms, significant events and repeated occurrences in the analysand's life. The information used to form model scenes is drawn from the patient's narratives, unfolding transference configurations, or role enactments. Model scenes highlight and encapsulate experiences representative of salient conscious and unconscious motivational themes. Constructed within the patient–analyst interaction, model scenes convey and experience as a "picture" and thus are "worth a thousand words."

"Model scenes" (Lichtenberg, 1989a,b) refers to three constructs: (a) a conception that analyst and patient form that epitomizes significant communications from the analysand about his or her life; (b) a conception that analytic theoreticians and infant observers form that epitomizes significant developmental experiences; and (c) a conception (unconscious fantasy or pathogenic belief) that the analysand has that epitomizes significant past problematic lived experiences.

In this chapter we further develop the concept of model scenes as (1) a means of conceptualizing experience of any age; (2) providing a valuable clinical tool for moving from the general to the specific or particular experience

7

of an individual patient; (3) providing a theoretical construct that includes the contributions of recent developmental advances in psychoanalysis; and (4) an analytic illustration through which past and present, foreground and background, and empathic entry into transference and analytic responsiveness can be integrated.

A critical juncture in the history of psychoanalysis occurred when Freud recognized the Oedipus complex as a model scene in which the little boy possessively and erotically desires his mother and experiences intense rivalry with his father. We tend to think of the theoretical significance of the oedipal scene as a ubiquitous developmental vicissitude whereby Freud (1900, p. xixn) established the existence of infantile sexuality. We need to remind ourselves of the excitement of discovery when Freud recognized in his clinical work that associations and dreams of his own and his patients' could be understood through the pattern of relationships and desires in the myth of King Oedipus portrayed by Greek dramatists. Previously puzzling fragments of verbal associations, dream images, and transference configurations in particular coalesced into an explainable whole.

Freud's analogy to the drama of Oedipus lay not only in the depicted triangular relationship but in the fact that the "action of the play consists in nothing other than the process of revealing, with cunning delays and ever-mounting excitement . . ." (pp. 261–262) elements of Oedipus' history. From these elements, both Oedipus and the audience could piece together the mystery of his past and his destiny. Freud noted that the very process of revealing-with-cunning-delay portrayed in the drama "can be likened to the work of psychoanalysis" (p. 262) where analyst and analysand can explore the unknown. Because of the place the oedipal relationship holds in our schema of normal and pathological development, we may easily forget that Freud, in the clinical application of his discovery, worked out with each patient the particular configuration taken by the triangulation and affective mixture.

Model scenes that relate normal or pathological experiences in infancy and childhood may convey the essence of an adult's relationships and motivations. Lichtenberg (1989a) has described the model scene of a patient as a little girl tugging at her mother's leg or skirt while sensing the stiffening of her mother's body as she resisted the child's importuning. This model scene illustrates a specific pattern of repetitions of unrequited love and attention that continues into and characterizes the patient's adult life. Other examples of model scenes of childhood that analysts have used to organize and explain findings in adult analyses are those of toddlers straining to retain feces and resist toilet training (Abraham, 1923; Erikson, 1950) and those of toddlers moving away from their mothers to explore their surroundings and then, realizing the distance, glancing back fearfully to be reassured (Mahler, Pine, and Bergman, 1975) or excitedly to receive approval for their adventuresomeness (Kohut, 1984).

Model scenes capture and give conceptual representation to developmental experiences that occur during infancy, later childhood, adolescence, and current adult life. The representation may or may not be an actual, lived experience, since under the influence and elaboration of subsequent experience, early and later events amalgamate in memory. Model scenes include the fantasy elaborations and transformations to which all experiences are subjected. The concept of model scenes is broader than and includes screen memories (Freud, 1899, 1918) and shares certain functions of the processes of telescoping of events (Kohut, 1971).

MODEL SCENES AND SCREEN MEMORIES

Freud (1899) described screen memories as well-remembered, often vivid scenes whose content or subject matter is of an indifferent nature. He distinguished two types of screen memories. In one kind, later events owe their importance to their connection with early, suppressed experiences; in the other kind, the significance of the childhood scene is accounted for by later experiences. A screen memory is equated with a manifest dream in that it points toward something important that it disguises. The memory itself and its "indifferent" content are to be discarded as the analyst recovers and reconstructs the significant, concealed childhood event or fixation. Like a film editor, the analyst would leave on the cutting-room floor the later accretions and transformations once their contributions to concealment had been nullified. Thus, the potential representational message in the memory in all its versions was treated as inconsequential, as a fingerprint or clue would be by a detective once the crime was solved. Furthermore, despite Freud's (1899) excellent example of the back-and-forth work of "analyst" and "patient" (of course, himself in both instances), the contributions of the exchanges between the two partners to the uncovering process came to be omitted. The contribution of the patient–analyst interaction itself both to revealing the suppressed childhood memories screened off by the indifferent manifest memory and to fashioning the childhood memory into an overarching theme is rarely considered. Kris (1956) pointed out that screen memories focus on reconstructing what *has* happened. In contrast, model scenes pay equal attention to what *is* happening.

Illustrating the typical usage of screen memories in analysis and the advantage of the model-scenes concept is a case described by Mahler (1971). In her analysis of a borderline patient, she described two screen memories that emerged:

> the helplessness and lonesome desperation when as a schoolboy he had been wheeled away from his parents into the operating room and another traumatic episode when he had been banished from the parental bed, (which) . . . he insisted occurred when he was not yet 3 years old [pp. 418–419].

By referring to the memories as "screen memories," Mahler was following Glover's (1929) and Greenacre's (1949) observations that traumatic memories may serve a screening function. She placed their importance not in their manifest appearance but in their function as a cover for earlier, pathogenic events. The patient recalled that prior to age three, his mother had allowed him to snuggle up to her and occupy his father's bed and then had banished him because he had become too big for such intimacy. In this screen memory, attention is directed to early, strong, overly gratified symbiotic longings that were precipitously frustrated.

Treating screen memories solely as "screens" or covers against the recall of prior pathogenic events, attributes the significance of both of the patient's memories to early specific disturbances in the separation-individuation process. The influences and subsequent transformations of this theme are given less weight in the preoccupation with the presumed causal precedent. The banishment at age three, aside from its implications for the separation-individuation of a toddler and regardless of a presumed prior overgratification, would also be relevant to understanding the structuring of later themes of seduction and rejection, wariness about intimacy, and the fear that growth could mean banishment, loss, and isolation. Furthermore, each of these themes would be relevant for understanding the current organization of the transference (Stolorow and Lachmann, 1984/1985). Typically, the analysis of screen memories leads analyst and patient backward along a time dimension and thereby downplays the significance of the interrelation of the various earlier and later themes, especially their relevance within the transference.

When viewed as a model scene, Mahler's description of her patient as helpless when separated from his parents and taken to the operating room first and foremost illuminates the potentially active transference configuration of aversiveness to the analysis. The patient's dread of being separated and injured is activated, perhaps because the analysis, and the use of the couch in particular, are equated with the passive helplessness of the traumatic operation. The banishment from the parental bed also described the anticipation of loneliness and isolation, the direction in which the patient feared his analysis was pushing him.

In summary, screen memories are created by *the patient* to depict an indifferent lived experience so as *to prevent* (defend against) the coming into awareness of something that is disturbing to know. In contrast, model scenes are created by *the analyst and patient together to depict,* from a reconception of what is known, something previously unknown. The purpose of screen memories is to conceal or obscure; the purpose of model scenes is to give full and complete affective and cognitive representation to obscure repetitive configurations of experience. By emphasizing that model scenes are constructed by analyst and patient, we are indicating that they are *not* relics found on "the lost continent of childhood" (Greenacre, 1949, p. 73) but are interactively constructed "models." Model scenes are in the spirit of Emde's (1981) statement that psychoanalysis "has placed far too much emphasis on early experience itself," even to the point of reducing and recasting later events into infantile prototypes, and far too little on "the processes by which [such early experience] is modified, or used by subsequent experience" (p. 219).

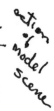

MODEL SCENES AND TELESCOPING

Kohut (1971) proposed that, in the course of an analysis, memories of genetically analogous later experiences that correspond to archaic ones may be analyzed without the earlier ones necessarily being uncovered. He proposed that these earlier experiences were contained within the later ones. He suggested that the telescoping of the earlier into the later memories was not necessarily in the service of defense but expressed an early trauma through the medium of analogous psychic content. Kohut's position coincides with ours that model scenes may use people, settings, and formal elements from any time of life as long as the model scene captures the affective intensity and motivational significance of the present and past experience being analyzed. While we believe that model scenes of some early experiences have the dual evocative appeal of depiction and a sense of causality, we argue against a restrictive use of the concept of model scenes for reconstructive purposes.

Besides telescoping affectively similar experiences from different time periods, model scenes represent the coming together of information from different sources. In the formation of the model scene, analyst and analysand draw on sources of information common to both and on sources that lie in the private domain of each. The analyst shares the information about the analysand's life experience and motivations built up throughout the preceding analytic work and especially through the crucible of their unfolding experiences with each other. The analyst alone brings to bear his knowledge of model scenes learned from studies of normal and pathological development. During the analytic work with the patient, the analyst processes in his internal monologue information gained through introspection (based on personal analysis and self-inquiry) and through resonance with selected theory constructs. The analysand brings to bear his knowledge of dimly perceived fantasies and pathogenic beliefs (Weiss and Sampson, 1986). During the analytic work, the analysand processes the analyst's effort to use a model scene to give order to experience by sensing the fit (especially affective fit) using knowledge of his inner life to which only the analysand is privy. As analyst and analysand articulate their developing understanding of the model scene, by the act of putting into words, of "naming" (Shapiro, 1970), they create a new set of meanings. Thus, the analyst's knowledge of theory, plus introspection, guided by the empathic mode of perception (Lichtenberg, 1981b; Ornstein and Ornstein, 1985; Stolorow, Brandchaft, and Atwood, 1987), becomes telescoped with the patient's introspective entry into a private domain of self-knowledge as increased awareness opens the way to exploration and assertion. In our explanation of the patient's contribution to constructing a model scene, we draw on the extensive psychoanalytic studies of the intrapsychic processes of unconscious fantasies and beliefs. Many analysts have conceptualized the unconscious contents whose revelation and exploration are crucial. Personal myth (Kris, 1956b), organizing fantasy (Arlow, 1969a,b; Greenacre, 1971), core conflictual relationship themes (Luborsky and Crits-Christoph, 1989), and curative fantasy (Ornstein, 1984) are examples. We regard the goal of the mutual enterprise in the work with model scenes to be to gain access to these vital intrapsychic precipitants and organizers of the patient's experience.

CLINICAL ILLUSTRATIONS

Two model scenes are particularly relevant in illuminating transference configurations. Each scene is derived from the complex interplay of a patient's early experiences, transformations and elaborations of those experiences and activation of themes from these experiences in relation to the analyst.

Ms. A

Ms. A, a woman in her early 30s, sought treatment because of her difficulty in sustaining relationships with men; those relationships which she was able to sustain were unsatisfying to her. In these circumstances she felt generally abused, unacknowledged, or shunted aside. She would keep her complaints to herself but then, to the surprise of all, would burst forth with rage.

The patient had grown up in a small Midwestern town. She was the third of four children, with two older brothers and a younger sister. When she was two years old, her mother became seriously ill just after the birth of the younger sister. When the patient was four, her mother succumbed to cancer. Her father was an energetic, physically active, successful businessman who, after the death of his wife, ran the family as a benevolent despot with the aid of a series of housekeepers. During the patient's early teen years, her father married a widow who came with a large family of her own. Describing the newly formed family, Ms. A stated that her parents had made sure that all the children would get along harmoniously although she felt far from "harmonious" toward the newly arrived mother and her children.

In her work, Ms. A functioned below the level her doctorate in her profession would entitle her to. In the course of her treatment, she described her cordial relations with her girlfriends. She generally assumed the role of the "good listener" and commented that in her analysis she felt awkward talking so much about herself.

The patient had begun analysis with another analyst (female), who after two years moved to another city. Understandably, the first issue to emerge was her sense of loss and its connections to the loss of her mother. Memories emerged about the illness of the mother, her gradual physical deterioration, and a general sense of hushed restraint that permeated her home. During the two years the mother was bedridden, the children were admonished to remain quiet and not burden or disturb their mother in any way since that would adversely affect her strength and health.

Toward the end of the first year of analysis, the issue of the loss of her mother receded and the relationship to her father, as well as its consequences for her relationship with other men, became central. With this shift in themes, an idealizing transference emerged in which the analyst was seen as one who could manage an ill person. Initially the analyst (as well as her boyfriend and other people in her life) had been cast as the vulnerable mother whom she had to take care of and treasure during the few precious hours they would still be available to her. She now began to experience the analyst as a competent adult who could be expected to relieve her of a precociously felt burden to look after others. A dream presented six months after the emergence of the transference shift further crystalized the precarious nature of her reliance on others:

> There was this small car. A man was driving, grey suit, plump, short, an anonymous man. The car was a two-seater, so small I was riding on the outside of the car, sitting on it, on the back of the car, holding on with my fingers. I thought that he really has to let me ride in the front seat, but I was resigned to my place.

The patient went on to describe her stormy relationship with her boyfriend. The mood of the session was friendly, with some shared laughter about the clarity of the dream images and allusions especially to the "anonymous" short, plump driver.

The transference that emerged centered on her admiration and idealization of the analyst. She felt "unworthy" and "childish." In particular, she was acutely aware of fearing that she would lose his interest.

In the course of this phase of the analysis, the analyst noted that during the sessions with this patient, more frequently than with other patients, humorously phrased interventions would occur to him. He thought of quips and cleverly phrased comments. He noted this reaction and, though he generally enjoyed such word play, thought he had been able to restrain himself reasonably well. In the dream, the patient felt that the analyst was in the driver's seat and that she was just barely holding on to the analysis with her fingers. In fact, she seemed ready to resign herself to this precarious position.

In a subsequent session, the patient discussed her relationship with her boyfriend and her annoyance that he was always beating her at tennis although she was an excellent tennis player. Further exploration revealed that in the preset warmup, the patient succeeded in placing the ball in just such a way as to give her boyfriend (and anyone she played with) excellent practice with forehand shots, backhand, net shots, and the like. He could smash the ball back to her, but she never had equal practice. Contained in this interaction was the patient's need to make sure that her boyfriend would enjoy playing with her, her fear that otherwise he might lose interest in her.

The analyst recognized that this vignette depicted a model scene and provided a perspective for understanding the organization of the transference. The patient was serving beautifully placed straight lines so that the analyst would enjoy smashing them back to her and would thereby want to continue to play with her. She obviously paid a price for maintaining this pattern, and it was not surprising to learn that her first tennis teacher was her father.

This scene can be described as the patient's carefully setting up the ball so that her father would enjoy himself while playing with her and therefore would want to continue to play with her. This scene was an amalgam of past experiences and impressions and was instrumental in shaping her current experiences as well. A synopsis of a number of salient themes is contained within it. After the death of her mother, the patient attached herself desperately to her father and feared she would lose him also. Her two older brothers were far more adept at maintaining their connections with her sports-minded, "macho-valuing" father than she was. In fact, she felt she could compete with them only by playing a supporting role.

The model scene, playing tennis with her father, was derived from experiences during her teen years, after her father's remarriage. She recalled that when her father played with her they would play on a back court at their tennis club; but when her father played with her brothers, they used the front courts where the "pros" played and spectators were present. At first, she had to strain to keep up with her father. We conjectured that the urgency with which she held her tennis racket reappeared in the dream as the kinesthetic experience of holding on to the outside of the car. That is, she was not in the front seat of the car, not on a front court, and she was barely able to hold on with her fingers. Later, when she became one of the championship players at the club, she had to walk a narrow line in relation to her father. With him, she still played on the back court, but she now tried to impress him with her skillful game and yet not beat him lest he give up playing with her. She had to play well enough to retain his interest, but not so well that he would criticize her for being "unfeminine." The theme of the model scene can be stated as: I have to serve others, especially men, by letting them display their skill to my disadvantage to ensure that I will be accepted, valued, found feminine, interesting, and therefore stayed with.

We can consider that model scene from the standpoint of motivational systems. The motivational system formed in response to the need for exploration and assertion normally facilitates the development of skills in games such as tennis or even in competition bantering. Exploratory-assertive motives dominate at moments when physiological requirements, need for attachment, and sexuality are quiescent and no strong aversive motive is active. At these moments, a child or adult is sufficiently disengaged from other needs to explore and function with problem-solving tasks posed by toys or other inanimate objects. If the task involves humans rather than inanimate objects, intimacy pleasure is a subsidiary gain, whereas the principal affect sought is a sense of efficacy and competence. For this patient, the capacity for exploration and assertion in games and conversation had become subsumed by the need to ensure attachment. Deprived of a personal sense of efficacy and competence and of assertion of self-formulated preferences, her sense of self-worth was imperiled. She would inevitably become frustrated with her sacrifices and with the person whose intimacy cost her so dearly. Then her aversive motivational system would become dominant in a burst of rage.

Understanding the shifting dominance of her motivational systems, and especially the coopting of exploratory-assertive motives in the service of attachment needs, provided a theoretical base for the creation of the model scene. The imagery came from the patient's memory of adolescence. The testing ground for sensing the affect state of the two partners in the tennis game was drawn from the transference. The model scene telescoped experiences with current friends, work associates, and memories of adolescent and childhood relationships. The explication of the model scene reorganized the hold on the patient–analyst relationship of "setting up" the other. It brought to a halt a continuing transference enactment of the "straightman"–witty-analyst interplay. It clarified the characterological stance of resentful resignation to adverse circumstances that had influenced much of the patient's adult life. She slowly reorganized her representation of herself as barely hanging on by her fingers to the one that placed her in the driver's seat of the analytic endeavor.

Mr. B

Mr. B, a man in his mid-40s, came for analysis because of intense anxiety verging on a state of terror. He also described intense feelings of shame that led to searing self-criticism. He anticipated criticism, hostility, and denigration from superiors at his workplace. This expectation prompted his withdrawal from coworkers and reinforced his sense of isolation. To entertain the possibility of professional advancement was intolerable. His self-consciousness was such that such everyday activities as shopping for clothes or food, going to a bank, even arranging for laundry or cleaning, were impaired. In general, he described himself as "afraid to make waves." His tension and anxiety could prompt him to shut his eyes, clench his fists and bang them against his legs, and leave the office during sessions. Aversive motivations appeared to dominate his life, triggering affects of fear and shame. Of the two primary aversive responses, withdrawal predominated, and antagonism was expressed in attacks on himself.

In contrast, he was able to speak in an eloquent, affectively engaged, articulate manner. He betrayed a dry sense of humor and a sensitivity for nuances and details in his associations. He enjoyed athletics, participated in his firm's soccer league, and was an avid skier and skater. His first marriage had ended in a separation just at the point when he began his analysis. He felt guilty about the end of his marriage, even though he and his wife had not had sexual relations for many years, an avoidance he explained as due to her "ticklishness." At the start of his analysis he was living with his girlfriend, whom he described as emotionally and sexually outgoing. He liked these qualities in her, but he could not understand how he could be their recipient and felt undeserving of her.

Mr. B was born in the United States; but when he was seven years old, a few years before the outbreak of World War II, he and his family returned to Sweden, the birthplace of his parents. Shortly after their arrival, however, war became imminent and his father returned to the United States. He had intended to bring his family back at a later date, but war intervened and the patient, his mother, and his two-years-younger brother were stranded in Sweden for the next ten years.

The war years were terrifying for Mr. B. He was overprotected and doted on by his mother, who bathed him, brushed his teeth, and slept in the same bed with him and his brother until they were reunited with the father. The patient slept between his mother and brother. The family was constantly on the move, relying on relatives to take care of them. The patient attended 23 different schools during his stay in Sweden. When he left his house, he was picked on and terrorized by neighborhood children who made fun of his shyness and his differentness.

He recalled the brief time before his father's departure from Sweden as a particularly happy one. He had just begun to learn ski-jumping and was practicing to participate in a competition. Excitedly and proudly he had looked forward to showing his father his jumping skill. But his father had to leave just before the competition took place and the triumph the boy anticipated never came to pass. Mr. B described his father as a "praise-depriving task master"; he had hoped that through the ski-jump competition he would finally be able to extract the affirmation from him that he so longed for.

As a consequence of his mother's overindulgence and intrusiveness, even with respect to his bodily functions, the patient seriously neglected his physical health into his adult life. A knee injury sustained in soccer had never been attended to and was causing him considerable difficulty. Only when this injury threatened to limit his ability to play soccer did he discuss his physical neglect in the analysis. Similarly, he had neglected his teeth, and major dental work was necessary to correct the consequences of the years of neglect.

The initial transference was understood as a dread of experiencing an intrusive mother who would, even with the best intentions, usurp his autonomy. Secondarily, his need to obtain affirmation and recognition from his father was noted.

The focus on these transferences, grounded in his fear of and reliance on his mother's intrusive care, enabled him to appreciate his deficit in regulating his own physiological needs. He arranged for knee surgery, began major dental work, and, with the impetus of this self-assertion, pursued a divorce. His relationship with his girlfriend progressed well. His work situation had reached some stability; but he had no intention of pursuing advancement, for to do so would require that he place himself in a more "visible" position. He summarily ruled out such a move, fearing that he would thereby subject himself to envy and criticism from his coworkers.

Dreams he reported after about a year of analysis contained increasingly more frequent references to water, ships, decks, and his initially described fear of "making waves." In one dream, dressed only in underwear, he felt embarrassed and awkward. He was with a lady who was attractive, but he did not want to have anything to do with her. He just wanted to get back to his girlfriend:

> This lady and I had to go on a dock to meet a riverboat, to meet her husband. Then we were in a large lavatory, like a gym with showers. I was with my girlfriend now and in my underwear. I was supposed to go out into a crowd, but I ended up in a token seller's booth in the subway. Other people were going about to their trains.

Combined with the material of the sessions, the dream was understood as addressing the sense of embarrassment with which he had accepted his mother's ministrations for as long as he did. The "sea" references were understood as his longing for his father's return so that he could be relieved of having to squire this "lady" about and return to his own agenda. The "token booth" remained a puzzle at this point, but the crowd he was expected to face was understood to represent the gang of mockers whose condemnation he felt he actually deserved because of his acceptance of his mother's overindulgent care.

In a dream reported four months later he recalled, "I was trying to avoid being found out by a girl. I was not afraid for my life, I was afraid of embarrassment." What was not clear then but did become clearer later was that he was ready to sacrifice his life to overcome his dreaded embarrassment.

In his adolescence the patient had read a story about an English sea captain whose ship had been torpedoed. The entire crew was saved in lifeboats. As they floated away safely they saw their ship go down, with the captain on the top deck. The captain took a golden cigarette case out of his pocket, lit a cigarette, and, as a ray of sunlight reflected off the golden case, smoked his cigarette until he was covered by the water as he went down with his ship.

The analyst recognized that this "captain" had become the embodiment of Mr. B's ideals. The details of the scene, the captain stylishly going down with the ship, were used as a model scene to explore the vitalizing experience the patient derived from it. It embodied the manhood he sought but felt had been denied him by his mother's overprotectiveness and the absence of his father. He was sensitive to the depleted sense of self his gender identity gave him. As the captain, he felt restored. The scene depicted a man who did not flee – as his father had – but stayed with the sinking ship. It contained the cool courage he wished he had had when faced by the gang of boys who persecuted him. In his latency years, when the patient attempted to test his manhood on the playground by feats of assertion – fighting and ski-jumping – he felt he failed. And the scene contained a standard of savoir faire to which the patient aspired but that, he believed, required a readiness to sacrifice one's life to stand one's ground in time of war and to stand up to a bully. Anything less than this readiness for total self-sacrifice (going down with the ship) he experienced as the shameful cowardice he evidenced and despised.

The way in which this model scene organized the transference could then be examined. As mentioned earlier, during the prior years of the analysis, Mr. B had experienced upsurges of excruciating terror that would prompt him to leave the analytic sessions before the end of the hour. The analyst had encouraged him to speak about his terror states and his need to leave. The patient felt that he should be able to live up to the analyst's reasonable expectations, but since he often could not, his frustration and shame increased.

Through his understanding of the model scene, the analyst could recognize that, in the patient's sense of him, he was the abandoning father who left the little boy at the mercy of both the Nazis (personalized as the gang of persecuting mocking boys) and his infantilizing, emasculating mother. Rather than rescuing him from this fate, the analyst, like his father, abandoned him to it by expecting him to tolerate the analytic situation. As he had with his father, the patient blamed himself and his "cowardice" for feeling so frightened. Like the captain, he would resolve his predicament by turning his cowardice and humiliation into heroism and give up his life in one daring, exhibitionistic act. He would stand at the top of his ski-jump for his one, final jump. But, as if in a "subway token seller's booth," he was trapped alone on the analytic couch while all those around him were able to travel to their desired destination without any manifest indication of weakness. His father's ignominious, life-saving flight had to be countered by his own proud, life-sacrificing act.

Exploration of the possibility that the analyst give him permission to leave when he felt too uncomfortable was experienced by him as a refining of the overly indulgent mother, whose sympathy would add to his self-condemnation for being a coward and not measuring up to male standards. The analytic requirement that rather than fleeing he associate to his desire to leave the session continued the enactment of the shame of his cowardly withdrawal but did not provide the vitalizing glory of the model scene. The terror he felt in the sessions (but not only in the sessions) was anchored in his sense of being doomed to be on a perpetually sinking ship, but without the glory of a noble, heroic, *self-determined* sacrifice "as the sun reflected off his golden cigarette case."

For a time, Mr. B tested his ability to decide whether or not to stay in the session when he felt frightened. He would leave sessions early, sometimes only moments after arriving, and sometimes he would arrive at his sessions only moments before the time was up. Along with the explication of the model scene, interpretations focused on his experience of attempting to reclaim self-determination over his motivations. The back-and-forth exploration stimulation by the model scene ranged over problems in each of the motivational systems as they appeared in the associations. He believed he was doomed to need others to regulate his physiological requirements. Attachment to a woman meant he had to be grateful for being taken in, lost, abandoned soul that he was. He experienced women as replicas of the mother who was able to obtain shelter for the family after they were abandoned by the father. Attachment to a man meant that he was certain to be humiliated because he would be unable to meet demands for masculine functioning. Exploration and assertion meant being bullied and tormented by peers. Aversive responses were most commonly triggered by his own failures. As a result, he seldom used instrumental anger, normally directed at frustrations from others, and often felt powerless. Sensual longings and sexual excitement would threaten exposure of his unsureness about his shaky male identity but could be experienced when he felt needed. He had to retrieve the initiation and organization of his motivation from both his mother, who had treated him as though he were "hers," and his father, who by default had placed him in his mother's hands.

The model scene of the heroic captain eschewing attachment to others and to life itself, although derived from a book the patient had read during his adolescence, may well have been remodeled by him to fit his own needs. But, as shaped, it served as an unconsciously organized theme that tied together his early yearnings, self-reproaches, and disappointments. He emerged with an ideal rooted in his experiences of shame. Once formed, his ideal, as depicted in the scene, afforded him some sense of pride to counteract his pervasive sense of cowardice and lack of masculinity. The pride he gained from the image of himself as a dying hero could be explicated in the analysis so that he could achieve a sense of pride from opportunities in his everyday life that did not require such enormous self-sacrifice.

3

Model Scenes and the Search for Clinical Truth

In this chapter we continue our exploration of the formation of the sharable imagic representations we refer to as model scenes. In particular, we consider the thorny question of validation of the model scenes constructed by analyst and analysand, an issue related to the distinction between narrative and historical truth (Spence, 1982).

For C, an adolescent patient, his analyst's silence or refusal to respond directly to an appeal for immediate help was experienced as gross, unforgivable neglect. On one occasion his hearing the analyst rattle paper precipitated a rage response that took weeks to subside. From dream images and the slow recovery of memories, analyst and patient, acting in concert, pieced together the model scene of his coming to the room where his mother worked behind a locked door. By insistent rapping, he could get her grudging attention. She would open the door but leave the night latch on. She would answer him perfunctorily and then, unseen, return to her work as he continued to speak. Her diverted attention was signaled to C by her rattling papers. The formation of this model scene helped to explain much previously puzzling information, helped to integrate bits of previous understanding, and initiated further exploration, especially of other disturbances of his attachment motivation.

The construction of such model scenes convinces both analyst and analysand that they are in touch with deep-seated, emotion-laden events they had previously shared only "through a glass darkly." Shared conviction, expanded awareness, and a sense of causal linking all contribute to what we call "clinical truth," which we define as any sought-for, coherent body of information and experience that moves a psychoanalytic investigative treatment forward. Like narrative truth and historical truth, clinical truth is a useful fiction, but we believe it has heuristic value for the validation of an hypothesis formed during an analysis. Lichtenberg (1989a) has suggested that progress in analysis results from two processes: self-righting and the reorganization of symbolic represen- tations. Both are the activation during analysis of processes that are key to normal development. Self-righting represents the resilient return to normal functioning that occurs when an obstacle has been removed. The reorganiza- tion of symbolic representations occurs at the transition point of every stage of development. It is the process by which the sense of self and the sense of others are reorganized and transformed into later versions while early versions remain. During analysis, empathic understanding and responsiveness ensure self-righting, while model scenes are often instrumental in triggering the reorganization of self- and other representations.

These definitions stimulate questions: If constructing model scenes is as valuable as we believe, what human developmental factors explain its signif- icance? What aspects of development and of the analytic use of model scenes facilitate confirmation or discomfirmation?

DEVELOPMENTAL FACTORS

Why do model scenes have the clinical impact we have ascribed to them? Our response to this question depends on the circular relationship between our knowledge of neurophysiology and observable, empathically discernible phenomenology. Model-scene construction must be aligned in a fundamental way with the manner by which the brain processes and arranges information; the way we can know how the brain organizes motivation and experience is by approaching the psychological realm by observation, hypothesis forma- tion, and testing. The studies of event knowledge reported by Nelson (1986) provide a basis that is essential to our understanding. She notes that "phenom- enologically the world is experienced as a series of ongoing events" (p. 4) and that "children as young as 3 years are sensitive to the temporal structure of events and are able to report act sequences of familiar events virtually without error" (p. 231). Children of three years can easily be tested about their experiencing of events, and strong evidence supports a conclusion that event representation occurs as early as one year. Moreover, as we can expect from the pragmatic requirements of information storage, young children form *general* representations of the events they experience. Asked to tell about making cookies, a child of three responds, "Well, you bake them and eat them," and a child of four years, five months answers, "My mommy puts chocolate chips inside the cookies. Then ya put 'em in the oven. . . . Then we take them out, put them on the table and eat them" (p. 27). These examples demonstrate the use of the timeless verb and the general "you" form and the accuracy of sequence. Older children progressively produce longer, more detailed accounts but the essential form and content are identical. "The generalization of an experience appears to be a natural product of the child's mind. . . . As more episodes of the same type are experienced, memories of them become more skeletal and general" (p. 232).

The essential organization of the generalized event representation is temporal and causal. In a restaurant event, "the action of entering the restaurant results in the new state of being inside. Being inside, in turn, enables you to go to your table. The succession of causal and enabling connections is what moves you through the actions of the event" (p. 51). Nelson notes the provocative finding that, in describing their event knowledge,

> young children use relational constructions and linguistic terms that reveal an understanding of logical relationships in advance of that usually attributed to them. Hypothetical and conditional relations are appropriately noted by forms such as "if . . . then" or "when x then y." Causal relations are expressed by "because" and "so." Temporal relations are expressed by "then" but also by "before," "after," and "first". . . . Adversative relations are coded by "but," and alternatives by "or" [pp. 232–233].

Consistency in mother–child routines is essential for establishing the child's event knowledge. The shared discourse of mother and child facilitates the child's language acquisition.

These studies help to explain how the consistent familiar experiences of everyday life are organized cognitively. They can easily be integrated with our concept that basic schemas underlie the events in which each of the five motivational systems is played out. The one big gap lies in the role of affect, which provides the salience for events. Nelson notes that in describing events young children consistently emphasize a sequence of events rather than descriptions of settings or of emotions such as likes and dislikes. Before we attempt to bring the basic organizing schema of event theory in line with affect-laden model scenes, we need to describe other aspects of the organization of experience.

Stern (1985, 1990) distinguishes between discourse organized in the form of an internal monologue of an experience world and discourse organized in the form of a spoken narrative of a story world. Both contain the theme or context of life events selected from the totality of daily exposure. In the experience world, the child constantly constructs what to attend to, what current themes to elaborate, and what new ones to design. Stern (1990) gives the example of Joey at four years elaborating an aggression theme from a day's experience of hitting a girl. "Joey relives the scene of hitting the girl and feeling himself seen by other people as dangerous and bad. He reexperiences his feelings of alienation, shame, his being put in his room, his making noise and loud music to express his anger and to comfort himself" (p. 148). In his experience world, Joey makes frequent references to his feelings. In contrast, in the story he tells of the same event, references to feelings are relatively few. The same event organization constructed in the experience world is now reconstructed into a story to be presented to an audience. He renders the story in the form of an action sequence: "I played," "He hides." He streamlines the events and makes the rendering more dramatic by a small change in the sequence. He also uses disguises, lion for himself as hitter to reduce his embarrassment and potential censure.

In summary, by the age of three, and probably much earlier, children organize experience in the form of event schemas. By experience, we mean moment-to-moment lived experience and the memory encoding of it. The schemas are organized by actions arranged in a temporal sequence with open slots for specific details. Once an event is experienced as such it becomes generalized, for example, as taking a bath or going to the store. Event representation tends to create two types of experiences. In one, the repetitive reexperiencing of similar events creates an easily constructed generalized schema with easy inclusion of small variations within the ordered temporal sequence. In the other, an event of greater variance becomes experienced as distinct, a novelty that either is welcomed for its vitalizing effect or is aversive because it breaches an expectation. Knowledge, once organized in events, forms the cognitive base for the different experiences of inner representation and interpersonal accounting. In the internal lived experience and the monologue about it, affect and sensations are more richly represented than in spoken discourse.

ORGANIZING EXPERIENCE AND THE ORGANIZATION OF MOTIVATION

How can we bring these findings about the cognitive basis for organizing experience in line with observational and clinical findings about the organization of motivation? In forming the motivational systems concept, we assume "that whatever infants do with observable consistency, they are motivated to do. Thus, infants are observed to take nourishment at regular intervals, the implication being that they are motivated to do so" (Lichtenberg, 1989a, p. 7). The parallel formulation for event knowledge would be that whatever infants experience themselves doing with observable consistency, they organize into an event schema. Thus, infants experience taking nourishment at regular intervals; the implication is that they form a generalized representation of the feeding event. The integral relationship between motivational schemas as we conceive them and event schemas can be appreciated from the intuitive manner in which infant researchers study videotapes in terms of *episodes* of feeding, or mother–infant conversation, or free play, or diapering. Event theorists speak of a change of state and of action defining an "event," such as sitting at the table and eating or sitting on mother's lap and talking to her. We speak of a change of state as defining a motivational system shift, such as going from the regulation of a physiological requirement for nutrition to a need for an attachment experience. The emphasis that event theorists place on action and temporal sequence in testable verbal renderings contrasts with the emphasis we place on the affect goal in the motivational systems as experienced in the inner world and the internal monologue.

Model scenes bring these two powerful trends together. They draw on the fundamental inclination of analyst and analysand to organize experience in terms of events or episodes. Because of the clinical purpose they serve, the events selected are those amplified by an affective response triggered when the needs of a motivational system are met or, more likely for the analysis, unmet.

EMPATHIC FAILURE AND ACUTE TRAUMA

Model scenes bring into fuller awareness the motivational significance of the two kinds of events that have the greatest salience for pathological development: repeated experience of an empathic failure and acute trauma. By empathic failure we mean a mismatch between the child's need in one or another motivational system and the caregiver's response. The encoded generalized memory of repeated mismatch experiences, commonly called stress trauma, may become the unspoken, even unthought-about expectation when a similar need is again experienced. This is especially likely with those analysands who practice the same neglect on themselves. In the case of C, the adolescent mentioned earlier, only the subtle events in the shared experience of the analytic encounter are likely to offer the opportunity for sensing the personal meaning of the analyst's "ordinary" silence and rattled paper.

The other kind of event encompassed by a model scene is an occurrence that markedly contrasts with the analysand's positively toned generalized expectations. This type of event, an acute trauma (Haynal, 1989), is the kind of experience for which Freud (Breuer and Freud, 1893–95) developed his original theory of abreaction. Freud saw the analyst as an interested physicianly (Stone, 1961), external observer helping the patient to discharge intrapsychic tension. In contrast, Ferenczi (1933) described the intersubjectively based exchange that characterized our approach to model scenes:

[margin note: Like Bollas]

R.N.'s dream . . . Dr. G forces her withered breast into R.N.'s mouth. It isn't what I need; too big, empty—no milk. The patient feels that this dream fragment is a combination of the unconscious contents of the psyches of the analysand and the analyst. She demands that the analyst should "let himself be submerged," even perhaps fall asleep. The analyst's associations in fact move in the direction of an episode in his infancy (a history of a nurse at the age of one year); meanwhile the patient repeats in dream scenes of horrifying events at the ages of one and a half, three, five and eleven and a half, and their interpretation. The analyst is able, for the first time, to link emotions with the above primal event and thus endow that event with the feeling of a real experience. Simultaneously the patient succeeds in gaining insight, far more penetrating than before, into the reality of these events that have been repeated so often on an intellectual level. At her demand and insistence, I help her by asking simple questions that compel her to think. I must address her as if she were a patient in a mental hospital, using her childhood nicknames, and force her to admit to the reality of the facts, in spite of their painful nature. It is as though two halves had combined to form a whole soul. The emotions of the analyst combine with the ideas of the analysand, and the ideas of the analyst (representational images) with the emotions of the analysand; in this way the otherwise lifeless images become events, and the empty emotional tumult acquires an intellectual content [pp. 13–14].

In the model-scene construct, analyst and analysand—talking, feeling, thinking, imagining together—sense their way into an event by constructing and deconstructing Rashamon-like variants of the analysand's lived experience. They continuously reexamine the issue in conjunction with the many aspects of influence that the event has had on the analysand's development. We view the goal of constructing a model scene as far more than sharing declarative knowledge of an event (its historical truth) or gaining insight into the analysand's participation in the episode or even a reexperiencing of the affect that may have been derailed. The model scene of a trauma, either chronic or acute, provides an opportunity for analysand and analyst to share their perspectives on the influence of the variant or repeated event. We emphasize *influence* because the way a motivational system is affected may appear in treatment not only as thoughts, feelings, fantasies, and beliefs (that is, as mental contents), but also procedural behaviors, such as somatic sensations, vocal tone, facial expressions, gestures, symptomatic acts, and transference enactments. Viewed in this way, clinical truth involves the joint search for the influence of experience organized as events having motivational significance.

Clinical Illustration

A female analysand, D, a health-care professional, had reached the conclusion that the events of her birth had influenced her preoccupation with the round breasts and bottoms of other women. Her mother had been ill while pregnant with her and then had had to leave the baby to the care of three men, her husband, his brother, and their father, while the mother was cared for by her family in a distant city. After returning to the husband's home, the mother was chronically unhappy. D felt that her mother had never developed a loving attachment to her.

The model scene she and her analyst constructed dealt with the little girl's craving for soft cuddling, a need spurred on by her observation of the mother's open affection for the patient's older brothers. Working within this construct, after a recurrence of her preoccupation with women's soft body parts, D wondered why she automatically responded with altruistic concern to anyone toward whom she became angry. As D verbally reviewed the now familiar model scene of her infancy, the analyst pictured the little girl's anger and frustration as she tried to pull responsiveness out of her mother, an enactment patient and analyst had engaged in numerous times. He visualized the mother's hurt, depressed face as, in her exhausted state, she could not meet the child's legitimate needs. Then, switching to the child's view (the base necessary for empathic understanding and framing interventions), the analyst thought, "How can I stay angry when my sympathy is evoked?" This was a familiar response of D toward her patients and others, but these feelings had never been considered in reference to her mother in the early years of their aversively tinged attachment. The analyst suggested how depleted and depressed her mother may have seemed to her and she agreed. He noted how difficult it must have been to remain angry with so sad a person even if that person failed to fulfill her wishes for the loving response. Yes, D acknowledged and added, "And the same with you now and especially when you are going away next week." She continued in an exasperated tone, "Oh why should I believe any of this?!!"

Why indeed! Why should any of us believe that, because of these early events, D was influenced in a variety of motivational systems? She experienced difficulties in the regulation of physiological requirements (as evidenced in occasional eating compulsions, a smoking addiction, and enuresis until age 11). She was unable to form lasting attachments with men or women and was ineffective in confrontations, swinging between hurt sad panicky desperation and brief episodes of rage. D also described many problems with sensuality and sexuality. Indeed, many later events can be associated with her difficulties. Yet along with Ferenczi (1933), we believe that through this model scene we are approaching clinical truth.

EVIDENCE THAT SUPPORTS THE "CLINICAL TRUTH" OF MODEL SCENES

1. Infants, from the beginning of life, are equipped to monitor contingencies: If I get my finger in my mouth, I experience a sensation of being soothed. If I push this button, a jack-in-the-box appears.

2. Because of this innate recognition of sequencing, a sense of causality is solidly established in the human experience, a causality that differs for each motivational system and lies at the core of the differentiating and overlap of systems.

3. Even with young children, lived experience, whatever form it takes, is not random or disordered, but is subjected to nonconscious processes of

> pattern analysis, categorization of similar elements (with similarity defined along several different dimensions), correlation of co-occurring elements, linear ordering (i.e., sequencing), organization into higher-level units (i.e., categorizing) and inferencing (i.e., filling in informational gaps on the basis of prior knowledge) [Nelson, 1986, p. 10].

4. Observation and extensive research on infants of depressed mothers (Zahn-Waxler et al., 1990) reveal the potent influences the mother's altered state has on the recurrent events that build the schemas of each system.

5. The onset of language usage has a double effect. Transformations permit further development, such as greater success in communication and therefore attachment, and thus may obscure or bury the early, more disturbed experience. Depressed mothers may be more responsive to verbal children, who are better company. The earlier experiences, however, will color linguistic choices, providing metaphoric evidence that weaves into the child's personal sense of an encoded, subjective sensitivity to the empathic failure. To quote Stern (1985):

> Language grabs hold of a piece of the conglomerate of feeling, sensation, perception, and cognition that constitutes global nonverbal experience. . . . [Core and intersubjective relatedness] lead two lives—their original life as nonverbal experience and a life as the verbalized version of that experience [p. 174].

As Lichtenberg (1983) puts it,

> The toddler of about 18 to 24 months is in a position similar to Pirandello's six characters in search of an author: The infant has memories, affect states (with transitions between them), preferences, and complex interactional patterns, all in search of a form of symbolic representation [p. 169].

6. The search for clinical truth repeats the process from early life to find inner and communicative representation for the poorly articulated and the aversively avoided traumatic experiences of every age.

EVIDENCE THAT QUESTIONS THE "CLINICAL TRUTH" OF MODEL SCENES

1. As Emde (1981) notes, "Discontinuities, with major organizational shifts, are prominent in development. [An individual] may construct from modes of

experience and aspects of reality we would never have been aware of if we were . . . on the spot" (p. 217). D's preoccupation with breasts and her postanger altruisms may be a complete discontinuity from the early infantile experiences, the product of, for example, her oedipal years alone.

2. "Although the cognitive system may analyze, categorize, and make inferences about the information represented, it cannot supply missing information" (Nelson, 1986, p. 6). D is not remembering information about her mother's attitudes but is stating conjectures that had to have been formed later. A child's powers of observation and of concept formation often tend to be paralyzed in the presence of adults, especially parents who have intense affective reactions. Thus, gaps of information in the scenes people reconstruct may be more representative of the actual experience, and the filler details that tend to attract our conviction are often liable to be retrospective additions.

3. Young children form rules that govern their conceptions of the way things should be from the way things are. Sometimes this results in a desperate need to retain a familiar unfulfilling pattern with a principal caregiver and regard the efforts of someone else, say, a father, to free the child as alien and aversive. To the child, the father seems an unwelcome intruder; to an observer, a parent offering help.

4. Although children are excellent recorders of episodic and procedural memories of lived experience, lived experience includes a large share of deception. Thus, it is not surprising that children of two and a half to four and a half are adept at manufacturing potentially disinforming clues well calculated to mislead others into believing to be true what the children themselves knew to be false (Hala, Chandler, and Fritz, 1991); likewise children of this age have a fundamental grasp of lying (Lewis, Stanger, and Sullivan, 1989). How much, then, of what we may believe about an analysand's childhood includes the lies they were told, the deceptions practiced on them, the lies and deceptions they practiced on others, and, most important, the lies and deceptions they practiced on themselves?

ASSESSING THE LIMITING FACTORS
TO CLINICAL TRUTH

What does the analytic experience contribute that weighs against these serious limiting factors to verisimilitude? To respond to this question, let us consider the special perceptual-cognitive-affective state that characterizes the optimal mode of awareness (see Chapter 6) during the analytic exchange. First, analysands are more apt to be in touch with a broad array of needs, wishes, and desires, as well as more tolerant of that recognition, than they are ordinarily during their active daily life. Analysands turn inward to delve into their private affective life to capture nonverbal imagery in all sensory modalities plus representations of motor activity and autonomic visceral and somatic experience. Second, analysands are more apt to monitor their internal monologue, which accompanies and supplies much of the contents of free association. The more diffuse bits and fragments of private nonverbal and partially verbal experience are linked with the communicative verbal code. Analysands embed their generalized emotional experience into the special details of an event narrative, including time and place setting. Bringing together the verbal and nonverbal through the specific details of an event replayed in the analysand's mind or an event in the session facilitates surprise and new connections. Third, analysands in the course of analysis become exquisitely sensitive to the context of the analysis itself so that they are continuously blending the cognitive and affective perceived "actuality" of the situation and the analyst's verbal and nonverbal contributions with their inner constructions.

What is the state of mind of the *analyst* that potentiates the ability to listen empathically and participate in the construction of model scenes? First, an analyst must be sensitive to his or her own needs, wishes, and desires to sense fully those emerging in the analysand; at the same time, the analyst maintains as a dominant motive the need for exploration and assertion. Second, the analyst monitors his or her own monologue, which is filled with contents related to the experiences the patient is describing, the analyst's linkages of these experiences to knowledge of the past, and the analyst's reflections on his or her own responses (Ferenczi's case) and the meanings ascribed to what the patient is conveying. Third, an analyst must share with an analysand an exquisite alertness to the context, both situational and affective, in which the analysis takes place, or many transference experiences and role enactments will be unrecognized.

We believe that patients are able to associate more or less freely with a self-assertive vitality when they experience themselves as being listened to in a supportive empathic ambience. When they experience an empathic failure, this openness to their inner world and to the free expression of it alters as self-cohesion is threatened, depleted, or fragmented. The perceived empathic failure may be the result of a technical error or a countertransference disturbance, but it may not. All transferences of empathic failures of the past as they approach awareness in the current analytic exchange seem to possess antennas to search out minor, even insignificant, cues to trigger an experience of failed responsiveness. We regard the occurrence of many disruptive episodes during an ongoing analysis not as undesirable regressions or unwelcome defensive postures, but as positive indications that the path to awareness of long-held needs and longings is becoming open to analytic work. The patient has established enough trust to be able to reopen old psychic wounds (Shane, 1989). Thus the analyst, probably unlike prior or present contributors to empathic failure, must be sensitive to a full appreciation of the patient's experience and recognize the altered affective and cognitive state in words. Gradually, the recognition of the disturbed state of being, as seen from the patient's point of view, encourages self-righting in the form of a return of a sense of cohesive intactness and openness to an exploratory motivation.

The key concept in this type of restoration, based on analytic work rather than nonspecific recovery factors such as the passage of time or a distracting event, is recognition by analyst and analysand of the triggering event *from the patient's point of view*. Generally, because of the sensitivity of both analyst and analysand to events and affects occurring within the analytic exchange, analysts often recognize their contribution to the disruption as experienced by their patients. Analysts' acknowledgment of their contribution often exerts a powerful thrust toward self-righting that suggests more motivational power than solely exploratory enrichment. Ernest Wolf (1989, personal communication) suggests that analysands experience a sense of effectiveness and competence in being able to influence their analysts to recognize responsibility. This sense of being influential may have been lacking when disruptions occurred with their caregivers. Ferenczi (1933) described his surprise that engaging in a frank discussion of what he recognized as his contribution to a patient's difficulty "instead of hurting the patient, led to a marked easing off in his condition . . . the admission of the analyst's error produced confidence in his patient" (p. 159). When an analysand gains confidence from having contributed to the analyst's seeing an experience from his or her perspective, the analysand may be more open to expansion of perspective.

Sensing this increased openness, analysts feel themselves and their analysands moving back together and able to share an imaginary "observational platform" (Lichtenberg, 1981b, 1983a, 1987a) from which both can exchange their awarenesses. This may permit the construction of a model scene that provides an integrative explanation for the experience of the disruption. Now, with the analyst's encouragement, insight into the source of the disturbance will not only complete the restoration of self-vitality (the self-righting), but also further understanding of the patient's vulnerability. The path to awareness in the form of freer associations has been restored and expanded.

If by clinical truth we mean a coherent body of information and experience that moves the treatment forward, we can usually be on solid ground in tracking the successful unraveling of the disruption–restoration sequence we have just described. When analyst and analysand share a sense of what triggered the disruption, what feelings were aroused, what view of the analyst was exposed, and what experience of retrieval of the lost sense of working together in an exploratory mode occurred, we feel a conviction of the meaning of an episode set in a causal sequence. In other words, when we isolate an event that unfolds within the clinical situation and ask clinically oriented questions we can usually find answers we consensually validate. Asking questions about a specific clinical event applies to Luborsky's (1976) Core

Conflictual Relationship Theme, which asks, what did the patient want from other people, how did the other people react, and how did the patient react to their reactions? Weiss and Sampson (1986) ask, what pathogenic belief has the patient formed; what plan does he have to disconfirm the belief; and does the analyst's intervention appear to the patient to fit with his plan, thus enabling him to feel safe enough to bring repressed contents to consciousness?

When we consider the use of model scenes, we are on less solid ground. The positive effects of self-righting can be confirmed by examination of a process recording of the exchanges between analysand and analyst. The positive effects of the reorganization of symbolic representations, the goal of the work with model scenes, is more difficult to assess and verify. The theory of the process is straightforward. Analyst and analysand are engaged in exploring inchoate, unconsciously determined shared experiences through a constructed, plastic model scene that integrates the experiences in an intelligible manner. Intelligible refers to an understandable motivation, an appreciation of the meaning of the experience and of its causal linkages. But the key to its power for positive change lies in the simultaneity of two contrasting subjective realms. In one, the analysand fully experiences the analyst as implicated in his distress (you rattled the paper, you ignore me, I hate you); in another: you are the person I am talking to, being open with, and having my point of view acknowledged and affirmed by. In the words of Atwood and Stolorow (1984), "Every transference interpretation that successfully illuminates for the patient his unconscious past simultaneously crystallizes an illusive present—the novelty of the therapist as an understanding presence" (p. 60). We believe the pathogenic representation embedded in the traumatic event illuminated by the model scene may be softened (derigidified) by the coexistent alternative sense of the analyst as empathic coexplorer. Thus, while analyst and analysand can achieve consensual validation of their shared experience as reflected in a model scene that combines past and present events, confirmation by research of approximations to historical truth is more difficult.

Arlow has expressed alarm at our premise that research and direct observation provide us with a set of model scenes closer to the living experience of the child and that these normal and pathological prototypes facilitate the analytic process (Lichtenberg, 1989b).

> To me, this represents a fundamental error in the psychoanalytic methodology of interpretation (Arlow, 1979, 1987). It is what I have called the phenomenological error, namely, foisting upon the patient's associations an interpretation based upon a model concept of pathogenesis [Arlow, 1991, p. 544].

Ellman (1991) has noted that Arlow is arguing that an analyst using the model scene proposal "interprets or reconstructs on the basis of theoretical concepts of development *rather* than on the basis of the patient's associations" (p. 273). After an extensive discussion, Ellman concludes:

> The important aspect of an interpretation is the way it integrates patterns and relationship and . . . how the analysis is deepened by the intervention. Arlow's argument against attempts to interpret preverbal experiences falls by the wayside if one takes seriously his differentiation between reconstruction and recall of actual events. [Analysts] can interpret from any theoretical matrix if they follow the guidelines of context, contiguity, and convergence (of themes). If they do then it may be possible to compare the effect of interpretations from different theoretical viewpoints [p. 279].

Zuriff (1992) argues that new psychoanalytic theories of infancy should be treated as postulates rather than presented as proofs that older theories are *proven* wrong.

> The model accompanying these postulates may also be helpful in supplying us with a picture meaning, if not a literal meaning of the subjective world of infancy. Some (Lichtenberg, 1989; Stern, 1989) suggest that this picture is useful in treating because it supplies them with additional "model scenes" of early childhood as they struggle to understand the patient's past. . . . Picturing the infant as having a primitive self may inspire the theorist to develop new ideas for both theory and research, ideas which may not have occurred otherwise [pp. 31–32].

These statements alert us to the need to be extremely clear in our proposals both about the foundations for a technique based on self and motivational systems and for the technical principles we espouse. We believe that Arlow's admonitions, while accurate, are misplaced as applied to us. We emphatically do not espouse "*foisting* upon the patient's associations an interpretation based upon a model concept of pathogenesis" (italics added). We not only agree with Arlow's demand that we follow guidelines of context, contiguity, and convergence of themes in interpreting patients' free associations and constructing model scenes, but we go beyond them in a number of ways. First, we consider the construction of model scenes in the clinical setting to be the activity of both analysand and analyst, not the assignment, however well grounded, of an interpreting analyst alone. Thus, becoming convinced about the appropriateness of fit to the patient's conscious and unconscious experience is not the responsibility of either the analyst or the analysand alone, but of each as it evolves in the back-and-forth creative work. Second, we broaden the network of data that goes into the model-scene construction to include not only verbal associations but subtle and overt affective expressions, gestural and other indications of ambience and relatedness, and the persistent bringing into awareness of role enactments of both partners. Third, we do not regard the construction of a model scene as the effort to re-create a specific event or relationship embedded in photographic fashion in memory. As both Arlow and Ellman state, the experience of recalling an actual event, especially from the preverbal period, is subject to many hazards. A model scene, even if it achieves a rigorous analogue to a past event, is never an "immaculate reconception" of that event. The mentation involved and the experience of the construction exist only in the present and are organized within the communicative and relational context of the analytic moment.

In an elegant statement of a similar conception, Poland (1992) notes

> that life exists in the present moment; (2) that like a crystalline drop of water mirroring the universe, the worlds of past and present, self and others, become visible by examining the reflections in the tiny and fragile drop of the immediacy of the moment; (3) that what we see when we look closely at those reflections are the lights of the present (that is, that the past does not merely repeat itself in the present, but that the present creates our pictures of the past); and (4) that it is the emotional sensations experienced in the moment which shine the light that makes possible our seeing and knowing the inner universe of buried dynamics and of the past [p. 186].

According to Stern (1985), "Narrative-making may prove to be a universal human phenomenon reflecting the design of the human mind" (p. 174). We view that design to combine in every account of any event or episode three factors: motivation, signification (the search for personal meaning), and causality (the history of contingent unfoldings) (Meissner, 1991). Thus, clinical truth and narrative truth involve "thinking in terms of persons who act as agents with intentions and goals that unfold in some causal sequence with a beginning, middle, and end" (Stern, 1985, p. 174).

4

Human Development and Organizing Principles

An account of human development requires an understanding of organizing principles. We place the development of the motivational system and self at the center of our account of human development. In this chapter, we select one system, the exploratory-assertive, for illustration and indicate the relevance of the organizing principles of self-organizing, self-stabilizing, dialectic tension, and hierarchical arrangement for the *formation and functioning of each system.* We consider also the relationship *among systems,* their dialectic tension and shifting hierarchical dominance. The sense of unity and self-awareness of experience and its continuity over the life cycle prompts us to conceptualize the hierarchical superordinance of self or self-organization as the initiator, organizer, and integrator of experience and motivation.

To begin with a clinical illustration, let us take the case of Mr. E. Mr. E had attained high scores on his LSAT but was in danger of failing in law school. After graduating from college, he spent two years living with his family while he daydreamed about being a rock music star. He knew the name of every popular rock band, the musicians in each, who had switched from one to another, and the gossip about their lives. He had problems in a variety of areas and had been diagnosed as having a borderline disorder. After a period of treatment in his home city, he was accepted into law school in another state and he resumed psychotherapy. During one session, when asked to give details about a law school problem with which he was having difficulty, he recounted the following fact pattern. A man had an automobile accident in a state in which he was not a resident. The problem was to determine which laws applied to the case. The decision about the law depended on the jurisdiction in which the case would be tried. That, in turn, depended on a particular principle of law governing interstate matters. After Mr. E had provided all this information in response to questions, the therapist summarized the problem through a sequence of governing principles. Mr. E instantly comprehended and was furious. How could the therapist, who knew nothing about law, solve the problem when he could not? This was a repeat of humiliations he had suffered all his life when others no smarter than he, often clearly less smart, could learn and he could not. After Mr. E became calm, the therapist suggested that perhaps he had a serious learning difficulty, an inability to arrange information in hierarchies of increasing or decreasing significance. Mr. E acknowledged that although he could absorb huge quantities of linear information – narratives about people – he could never make a successful outline. With much reluctance and wounded pride, he accepted this understanding and began to use law school study guides that were arranged in hierarchical order. With these organizers, he could compensate for his learning deficit.

Through this vignette we illustrate the enormous handicap for an individual, or a science, unable to conceptualize a hierarchical order of significance. But where does hierarchical ordering lie in the multitude of factors that govern human development?

To conceptualize the development of human experience and motivation, we advocate a systems approach (see also Rosenblatt and Thickstun, 1977; Rosenblatt, 1984; Stern, 1985). Following Sameroff (1983) we regard a developmental system as evidencing four attributes or properties: self-organizing, self-stabilizing, dialectic tension, and hierarchial arrangement. Guided by information gleaned from infant research and observation and from clinical experience, we have identified and described the five motivational systems, each of which develops in response to a basic need. Each motivational system has as *one* of its properties a hierarchical arrangement of its components or modes of operating. But what about the relationships among systems? We can easily observe among motivational systems dialectic tensions and shifting dominance, that is, hierarchical arrangements and rearrangements. And as if that weren't enough complexity we must answer the question, does a higher level of integration exist, one that constantly works to organize and stabilize dialectic tensions and hierarchical shifts between the five motivational systems? Such an integrative capacity, for which we borrow the concept of self (Kohut, 1971, 1977), self-system (Basch, 1988), or self-organization (Gedo, 1979, 1984, 1986), would constitute another hierarchical organizer.

We can illustrate the complex relationships among hierarchies and other organizing principles in one motivational system, the exploratory-assertive system. Specifically, we examine the formation and properties of the exploratory-assertive system as it self-organizes, self-stabilizes, responds to dialectic tensions, and forms hierarchical alignments.

THE EXPLORATORY-ASSERTIVE MOTIVATIONAL SYSTEM: SELF-ORGANIZING

Sander (1975, 1980), tracking infants through 24-hour cycles, noted their state changes from crying to alert-wakeful to quiet-wakeful to fussy to REM and non-REM sleep. He noted an "open space" that occurred when physiological requirements were satisfied (that is, when babies were neither hungry, eliminating, cold, nor needing sleep) and their mothers were not engaged with them in attachment play (eye contact, vocalization). Babies fill these open spaces in the daily cycles with spontaneously occurring exploratory activities. They eye scan and appear to work to bring objects into focus. They attempt to grasp objects near at hand. They use the mouth as an organ of exploration. These observations support the contention that exploration of the environment is spontaneous; that is, it is an activation of an innate neurophysiological system. Other observations lend further support. For instance, of all the positions in which one can hold a somewhat fussy infant, the most effective for calming is the front of the baby's body pressed against the adult's shoulder, the baby's head held firmly above the shoulder. Why? The answer seems to lie in the baby's eyes. Infants use the propped position to scan and thus to "turn on" exploratory motivation. Similarly a baby in the midst of feeding may become fussy because of gas. When the baby is propped, patted, and burped, the fussiness disappears because of the physiological relief from the air bubble. But often babies stop fussing before the air bubble is released. Again, in the propped position, the infant undergoes a brief shift of state from physiological distress to exploratory interest through eye scanning. Parents intuitively will try to calm distressed infants by offering them a rattle, toy, or finger to "distract" them, actually to use the object to activate exploratory activity and the calming effect that is triggered by it.

The trigger for a self-organizing motivation may arise through an internal or an external stimulus. Frequently an internally evoked exploratory pattern will activate spontaneously when conditions are opportune, when an "open space" exists. An externally evoked exploratory pattern will be activated by any object that arouses interest (in Dr. Seuss's words, "A shovel is to dig"). The experiential side of self-organizing lies in a remarkable double aspect of emergence. One aspect lies in the emergence of perceptual clarity as the infant's sensory skills (visual, auditory, tactile) and their cross-modal information processing form a perception of a face or a hand crossing the midline or a mobile. This emergence is akin in very simplified form to the sense one has in awakening in a strange place, such as a foreign hotel room, and gradually focusing on some object in the room as one pulls together the where and when and how of one's situation. The second aspect of emergence lies in the recognition that the baby's own activity brings about the perception. This recognition comes, of course, not from reflective awareness but from feedback information. Proprioceptive feedback tells the infant that he is moving his head, focusing her eyes, putting an object in his mouth or grasping an object. Further, the activity is innately monitored for consequence. Infants work with the coordination of their musculature, vision, and tactile and proprioceptive mechanisms to get their fingers in their mouth. Fetuses suck to soothe themselves and often suck their fingers; the experience of that sensual sensation precedes birth. After birth, the task of approximating to finger-to-mouth movement differs because air resistance is so much less than that of fluids. The arm movements, body hunching, and mouth protrusion are at first discoordinated and overly rapid and flailing. But within 10 to 11 days, babies will usually accomplish the task. To do so, they must track the contingent effect of their sensorimotor activity, learning the needed coordinations and control. Thus monitoring a contingent effect adds to infants' sense of agency. They develop awareness of their part in the exploration and assertion of an innate, preformed intent (to suck one's fingers). This relatively simple feedback contingent awareness helps to self-organize the exploratory-assertive motivational system at an elementary level. The affect that is triggered by the earliest innate and learned patterns of exploration and assertion is a mood state of interest. The linking of exploratory-assertive activity and the triggered interest is, we believe, "hard-wired" (Hadley, 1989); but, once experienced, interest becomes a target mood state to be reexperienced, each reexperience consolidating through memory the desirability of the increasingly familiar perceptual-action-affect state.

SELF-STABILIZING

Whereas self-organizing of the exploratory-assertive motivational system in the earliest weeks and months originates with the affect state of interest, self-stabilizing occurs with the development of a pattern that triggers the pleasurable affects of efficacy and competence. Self-stabilizing can be illustrated by the Papouseks' (1975) classic experiment in which four-month-old infants were exposed to five seconds of bursts of multicolored light. The infants oriented themselves toward the stimulus with interest, and then, typical of responses to unvaried stimuli, their orientation diminished after repetition. The experiment was arranged so that when in the course of their movements the infants rotated their head 30° to a predetermined side three times successively within a time interval, the light display was switched on. As soon as the infants turned on the light presentation by their own head movements, their behavior changed dramatically. Their orientation reactions increased in intensity, and they continuously made all kinds of movements to try to switch on the visual stimulation again. To this point, the experiment might have been simply a proof of classic conditioning, of stimulus–reward response. But the Papouseks then made a significant observation. They found that the infants, after a few successes, would leave their heads turned 90° even though the lights were to be seen in midline. Furthermore, the infants did not seem to be watching. Nonetheless, they continued to turn on the display and responded to their success with smiles and happy bubbling.

What was the source of the pleasure? Not in problem solving alone, for example, the discovery of a contingency between two external events; but in the infants' awareness that they themselves had produced the result. A sense of efficacy and pleasure is experienced when the infant recognizes "a contingent relationship between one's own initially spontaneous behavior and an event in the external world and the subsequent ability to produce at will the external event through repetition of the antecedent act" (Broucek, 1979, p. 312). The infants in these experiments were motivated not by exploration alone (that is, by the discovery of the connection between two external events) nor by assertion (that is, random then purposefully directed movements), but by a combination of the two. Problem solving by exploration and assertion together triggers the pleasure that comes from a sense of efficacy and competence.

In moments of disengagement from physiological need and attachment activities, "the conditions are optimal for infants to differentiate effects contingent on their own initiative. The experience of contingent effects has a profound impact on the alerting and focusing of infant attention" (Sander, 1983, pp. 98–99). Sander attributed the profound and highly personal impact of these developments to the richness of individual selectivity or option that occurs. By virtue of the self-organization of the exploratory-assertive motivational system, infants are able to initiate new behavioral organizations that have "the qualities of 'real' and of 'own' " (p. 99). The affective marker for this experience lies in competence and efficacy pleasure. Expressed in the language of later life, this might be: I can recognize it, I can match it, I make it go on or off, I have discovered it and I have altered it, exploration being closer to the "Aha!" of insight and assertion being closer to power and mastery.

A sense of competence appears to result from the infant's being able to reproduce the experience of a desired state. Innate and quickly learned patterns of response to preferred stimuli trigger affects of interest and surprise. Novelty and detection of contingent effects prolong states of attentive arousal. As the state of aroused attentive alertness consolidates, infants can be inferred to experience, along with interest and surprise, a quality of "aliveness" quite different from their affective experience during states of physiological need, crying, fussiness, drowsiness, or sleep. Looked at in this way, the exploratory and assertive activity of infants would not be to seek stimuli as such, but to experience the particular affective sense of aliveness of the aroused exploratory state. Competence would then be a measure of infants' ability to organize and regulate their activity to produce a new version of the desired state.

For the infants studied, success was twofold: (1) having a desired "reward," the preferred stimulus of the lights; and (2) having the sense of success at having produced the desire state. This concept presumes that infants have a complex capacity for matching. One matching capacity permitted the infants to recognize that the external stimulus of the flashing light coincided with an internal criterion for a preferred stimulus. An additional matching capacity employed feedback information and contingency tracking for recognizing that the light display had been activated as a consequence of the infant's own activity. But Sander (1986) proposes another matching capacity, by which infants compare an experiential state they are in with an experiential state that past experience has marked as desired. Recognizing their ability to create the match successfully conveys a sense of competence and pleasure. This conception establishes three sources of motivation: the pleasure to be derived from a preferred stimulus, the pleasure to be derived from being the source of a desired activity, and the pleasure to be derived from being the source of re-creating a previously experienced desired affective experiential state.

The exploratory-assertive motivational system can be said to have become self-stabilized when a basic schema has become established: a need or opportunity for exploration and assertion → interest and perceptual-action activity patterns → a sense of pleasure from efficiency and competence. Once stabilized, this schema forms a fundamental motivational pattern that persists throughout life and underlies the infant's and toddler's activities of practicing (Mahler, 1968) and of play; the latency child's learning; the adolescent's experimentation with ideas and careers; the adult's exploration and assertion at work and in recreation; and a host of problem-solving activities, including those in dreams.

Throughout life, competence as an outcome of a person's exploratory-assertive motivations is commonly experienced as concordant with the actual, assumed, or fantasied confirmation and approval of others. A sense of competence rapidly becomes entwined with the encouragement and values of caregivers, family, and culture. For example, research studies (Bornstein, 1985) indicate that cognitive competence is the result not only of the infant's information-processing capabilities and maternal encouragement, but also that infant and mother mutually influence one another. Infants who process information well at four months pull their mothers into encouraging them to note more and more properties, objects, and events; mothers who give encouragement stimulate more active interest and provide more opportunity to practice processing. The reciprocal stimulation of infant to mother and mother to infant at four months influences the child's later success at verbal comprehension and the acquisition of vocabulary. Self-stabilizing of the exploratory-assertive system thus involves an intrapsychic schema solidly embedded in the contextual world of relationships with others who provide opportunities for disengaged exploration, who participate in and encourage learning, and who thereby further enliven the sense of efficiency and competence.

DIALECTIC TENSION

Three sources of dialectic tension within the exploratory-assertive motivational system can be identified. Tensions arise in response to choices and preferences, the making and carrying out of plans of a purely personal nature; these are the tensions of achieving internal regulation. Tensions also arise when personal choices and preferences collide with the choices and preferences of others; these are the tensions of achieving mutual internal–external regulation. The tensions of internal (self) regulation and of internal–external (self–other) regulation of exploration and assertion may occur throughout life at any time when the exploratory-assertive system is activated. The third source of tension is most apparent when a maturational transition occurs. During periods of important maturational transitions that affect exploration and assertion, tensions arise as the person is torn between maintaining the continuity of one mode of exploratory-assertive activity and striving to utilize a new form of seeking and processing information.

When we consider the genetic programs that contribute to individuality, we can cite innate preferences for sensory modalities for exploring the world around us. Infants vary in their predilection for visual, auditory, and tactile processing – for looking at, listening to, grasping, and mouthing. The degree of internal tension stimulated by competing sensory modes is probably relatively minor, especially since the information from each source is processed intermodally. That is, the infant looking at the smooth pacifier not only records this object visually but also records it tactually. Having felt the smooth pacifier in its mouth, the infant can indicate recognition of a familiarity with it when the smooth pacifier is presented visually (Meltzoff and Borton, 1979).

The small variations commonly found in infants' preferences for stimuli and modes of processing can be appreciated when observed in their more dramatic polarities. At one pole are the creative types who process visually (Picasso) or auditorily (Mozart). At the other pole, are those whose hypersen sitivity to light, sound, or touch may render them unable to tolerate even ordinary stimuli. Infants' innate preferences also involve types of stimuli – visual patterns that contain the outline of the human face, others that are abstract but regular; sounds in the higher range, sing-song rhythms; textures that are soft and smooth. The tension of choice can be demonstrated experimentally by confronting an infant with alternatives in each of these modes and forms. Further minor tensions arise in response to the mode of presentation. If a preferred pattern is repeated at fixed intervals, interest wanes. If a new pattern is introduced, interest reawakens; but if infants have a choice between a familiar pattern and an unfamiliar pattern of equal stimulus potential, they will attend the familiar. A stimulus too unfamiliar may lead to an aversive reaction. Viewed overall, the innate and learned preferences and the rules about familiarity and novelty that trigger minor dialectic tension make infants prone to explore their own particular environments; the objects and people present become sources of continuing interests.

More dialectic tension in exploration and assertion inevitably arises when the intentions and plans of infant and caregiver must be coordinated. Often their intentions will coincide as when each can play and work separately or when they are playing together. Inevitably, infants will want to explore electric plugs, earrings, and many other items that parents will object to. Infants will not always wish to play with the toys offered or at times when parents prefer. These situations can generally be managed with only temporary antagonism.

These regulatory exchanges between parents and children employ inherent dialectic tensions for adaptive learning. Possibly the most significant is the intuitive feel by a caregiver with a particular child of the need for disengagement, to create an "open space" during which optimal self-exploratory-assertive activities can progress to competence. Winnicott's (1958) concept of the ability to be alone in the presence of the other characterizes this state – alone but not lonely, with another but free to follow one's own interest. A caregiver takes cognizance of the child's tension between needing an open space in which to explore on her own, and thus develop an increased awareness of self-agency, and needing the active participation of another. How parents interact intuitively to promote learning has been the subject of many studies (Bornstein, 1985; Stern, 1985; Papousek, 1986). These studies indicate that mothers demonstrate with gesture and facial expression, and through a verbal flow of dialectic instructions, what they want their babies to learn. Long before the words have conceptual meaning, infants and young toddlers are bathed in a gestural and verbal flow of communication that guides and limits their exploration and assertion. As babies act independently, mothers give responses of rhythmic attunement that encourage the activity and ensure its liveliness. Parents adjust their approach to the maturing child in keeping with changes in the child's potential to master tasks. Often they stay just a bit ahead of the infant or toddler to encourage the child to move forward. At the same time, they will monitor the degree of frustration, helping when necessary but not overanticipating or interfering with solutions. Many parents marvel that the solution the child comes to is one they would not have thought of. The point of these observations is that the dialectic tension inherent in choice making and match–nonmatch experiences for children and the tension between the approach and level of cognitive capacity of parents and children become the dynamic "playground" in which learning takes place through continuing episodes of exploring and asserting of individual preferences.

Hornik, Risenhoover, and Gunnar (1987) investigated the dynamic interplay between children's inclination to explore a toy and assert their preference and the influence of their mothers to instruct them. Three groups of 12-month-old children were tested with toys when their mothers displayed, by face, voice, and gestures, positive affect, negative disgust, or neutrality and silence. One toy used was a musical ferris wheel that attracts children. A second toy was a stationary robot that recited facts about outer space in a machinelike voice and elicited neither strong approach nor avoidance. The third toy was a mechanical, cymbal-clanging monkey that children tend to avoid. The mothers, training to convey negative affect, were told to imagine that the toys were crawling with horrid bugs and to talk about how "yucky" they were. The researchers found that, regardless of the infant's inclination toward the toy itself, if the mother signaled negative disgust, the child treated the toy as aversive.

The researchers asked three questions: Did the child recognize the message as specific to the toy? Were the children more sensitive to negative or to positive communications? Did the effect carry over time? Because the infants, given an opportunity for free play after the maternal instruction, did so without an alteration in mood, the researchers reasoned that the children regarded their mothers as delivering specific messages about particular objects and not about play or toys in general. Moreover, since the infants were more influenced by their mothers' registering disgust about otherwise attractive toys than by the mothers' registering positive affect (go ahead, it's fun) about the ambiguous robot or the unappealing clanging monkey, the researchers concluded that, in the test situation, infants responded more immediately to being warned off than to being encouraged. The infants were retested with the same toys after a three-minute break. The mothers were now instructed to be silent and neutral. The infants maintained their aversion to the toys that had been singled out by the mothers as "yucky."

These findings indicate that the dynamic tension for children between interest in exploring and asserting preferences or aversive responses can be influenced by maternal reactions but not evenly. Mothers telling children that a toy they might prefer to explore is bad warns them off, but telling the children that a toy they do not want to explore is good does not create interest. Interest is an internally self-stabilized affective response.

Dialectic tension becomes painfully apparent when the interactions between infant and parent are persistently misattuned, oppositional, and competitive. Viewers find it disconcerting, even painful, to watch videotapes of caregivers pushing toys at infants at rates too fast for a response or punishing toddlers for "letting" a ball roll under a couch where they have difficulty retrieving it, or insisting that a toddler play with a toy the mother prefers rather than the toy the child is engaged with. We empathically sense the conflictual tension of the child trying to respond to the stimuli and retain a positively toned affect of interest while aversive anger and an inclination to withdraw mount.

Dialectic tension at work during development is illustrated in instances in which seemingly self-stabilized interest in exploration and assertion is lost. These puzzling occurrences are of particular interest to psychoanalysts. One example is the familiar observation that infants at about nine months will suddenly become frightened in the presence of nonhousehold members in whom they previously have shown interest. A number of explanations have been offered for "stranger anxiety" (Spitz, 1957, 1959). One explanation has the child differentiating between mother, a primary libidinal object, and others, "strangers" onto whom the child projects aggressive urges. This explanation is opposed by two findings. First, infants from birth on can be shown experimentally to be able to differentiate between mother and father and others. Recognizing both the familiar and unfamiliar and exploring both constitute an important daily activity of infants. Nine-month-olds have a clear capacity to distinguish between familiar people (the household members) and others, including grandparents, to whom they may suddenly react with fear rather than interest. Second, the fear response does not occur when the nonhousehold member attempts to engage nine-month-olds in attachment activities—holding, cuddling, or loving play. The response occurs when the person appears in the distant field of vision and especially if the person approaches more rapidly than infants can seem to adjust. Previously the same or similar people were subjects for exploratory interest, regardless of whether attachment experiences did or did not follow.

Another explanation is the maturation of fear as a category of affect. The reasoning is that only at nine months can infants organize their responses to strange situations in response to fear because previously that affect was unavailable. The opposing argument is that infants have been organizing responses in the form of aversive withdrawal since birth and that many observers believe a fear response, especially to trauma, occurs much earlier than nine months.

We suggest that a major cognitive development, the imaging capacity (Lichtenberg, 1983a), begins at about eight months. Perception during the early months has a kaleidoscopic quality as motivational dominance shifts and self and object are involved in the actions and affects characteristic of one system or another. Recognition is highly developed but is action bound; that is, what is recognized is not the object per se, but the whole action sequence connected with the object—a bottle is to put in the mouth, a ring is to grab, a smiling mother is to smile back at. As the action dissolves, so presumably does the "image." The properties of the object and its independent existence have not become abstracted out of an action sequence. What the imaging capacity does is to create what Werner and Kaplan (1963) call "things-of-contemplation, that is, objects that one regards out there, rather than things upon which one merely acts" (p. 67). The properties of the image (its appearance, its attributes, and the information it conveys) are conceived as having an existence independent of the perceiver's presence: My mother is there whether I see her or not. My room is there whether I am in it or not. (The representation in word symbols involved in the language used for illustrative purposes does not apply to the initial experience of the imaging capacity.)

According to Lichtenberg (1983a),

> The most developmentally normal response to the not-mother person (often no "stranger") is one of wary exploratory interest; that is the approaching person becomes in Werner and Kaplan's (1963) phrase an object of contemplation—a problem to be puzzled through. . . . The approaching not-mother person may be the first of a group of objects that is responded to as an image that has become objectified. Put another way, the response to the stranger may be the first example of the functioning of the imaging capacity.
> What is the basis of the need to exercise this capacity? As the infant's attachment to mother intensifies, each approaching person is scanned to see if that person raises or lowers the infant's sense of security, the central pivot of which lies in the mother's presence. It is not the presence of the relatively familiar grandmother or the totally unknown visiting aunt that determines the response, but the status of the mother's security-providing support, measured ✗ against other factors such as the startle pressure exerted by the stranger. Thus infants in their own homes, with their mothers available for physical contact, will react to the not-mother person in a way that indicates that it is important that he or she is not mother. This person is lifted out of the surround and regarded as an object in his or her own right [pp. 102–104].

This explanation remains plausible but is inadequate. To say that mother represents security is to present a truism; she has represented security since the baby was born. What was not previously recognized was that infants at eight or nine months use a different means to elicit that sense of security: they read the affect state of the mother by rapidly scanning her facial expression. Mother's smile conveys the information "I am pleased" or "This person is our friend"; mother's frown indicates "I am displeased" or "This person's presence arouses annoyance"; mother's fear expression means "I am frightened" or "This person's presence arouses alarm." From this time on, infants are guided by the subjective interplay of the emotions of others and of themselves. But as yet they are practiced only at "reading" the affective facial expressions of those most familiar to them. Following this line of reasoning, we can say that the "stranger," who often is not at all an unknown person, is one whose affect state cannot be read and whose friendly intent cannot be instantly incorporated into the infant's security system. That this particular response of "stranger anxiety" involves people, not inanimate objects, suggests that a response applicable to people only—the subjective reading of an affect state—is involved. The imaging capacity is the cognitive precursor for affect referencing, not the cause of the anxiety response.

Infants at about nine months are thus between two markedly different methods of processing information. An aversive state of wary or fearful avoidance of people who previously were a source of interested exploration results from the dialectic tension between an old approach that provided security and a new maturational advance not yet absorbed adequately into the infant's repertoire. The almost universal inclination to distrust the stranger-foreigner whose "inscrutable" affect state we cannot easily assess suggests that this dialectic tension may never be fully resolved.

Between 18 and 22 months, another period of heightened dialectic tension arises from the simultaneous presence of an earlier and a later method of processing information. Toddlers of this period have long been observed to be "difficult." Many toddlers will seem to want to be close to their mothers, only to resent any attempt to be held or helped, and then demanding the very closeness or help they rejected. Their displeasure is often indicated by tantrums or other forms of antagonism or by withdrawal, shyness, or sad pensiveness. Almost all children at some moments during this period do not seem to know what to do with themselves, and parents often feel equally uncertain and helpless. Early analysts explained this phenomenon as a psychic reflection of an anal erotogenic zone conflict between retention and expulsion. Mahler et al. (1975) explain the occurrences of this period on the basis of the relationship between child and mother. In the prior months, the child is captivated by the opportunities for play with toys and practicing skills while coming to mother for occasional "refueling." Gradually the child becomes more aware of himself or herself "as a relatively helpless, small, and separate individual, unable to command relief or assistance merely by feeling the need for it, or even by giving voice to that need" (p. 78). Toddlers are thus pulled between their rapidly developing individuation and their fear of separateness (helplessness). They turn toward mother, shadowing her and involving her more in all their activities (rapprochement). But they are also confronted with their limitations and the call of their personal interests. Mahler and her colleagues concluded that the crossroads they termed the rapprochement crisis lay in the painful relinquishment of the delusion of parental omnipotence and the toddler's own grandeur. The toddler is thus vulnerable to abrupt deflation of self-esteem.

Lichtenberg (1983a) writes:

> Toddlers are under pressure from competing high-intensity sensations from the mouth, skin, bowels, bladder, perineum, and genitals. They are under pressure from the upsurge of assertiveness associated with their developing but fragile sense of themselves as directors. They show a heightened responsiveness of reactive aggressiveness and resentment to any frustration or frustrator. The strain on the parental support system from the move toward greater autonomy, body exploration, intentionality, and privacy stirs up confrontations in the foreground, and sometimes threatens the background ambience of basic support and trust as well. The total effect of the moment-to-moment swings of experience creates the pulling and tugging, dysphoric states Mahler has characterized as the rapprochement crisis [p. 143].

We now add that an unrecognized source of dialectic tension arises from the developing toddler's having to shift from one method of processing and communicating information to another—the use of symbolic representation in the dual modes of primary and secondary process. Viewed from the perspective of the exploratory-assertive motivational system, toddlers can be seen to be making the transition from a method of solving problems from which they have learned to derive efficacy and competence to another that is at first far less reliable. Younger toddlers have worked out whole areas of their life with a high degree of efficacy. They know where the items of their daily needs are placed and the timing of most events. They know the meaning of such signs as mother taking her coat alone or taking both hers and theirs— mother taking only her own coat means she is going out alone; mother taking both their coats means they are going out together. They know how to negotiate many intentions by taking their parents' hands and leading them, by pointing and vocalizing, by rapid reading of facial expressions, and most of all by what "works" with each parent in the form of the right mix of insistence and compliance.

Suddenly two things happen to them. Because of myelination of the frontal cortex and the associational pathways, processing of information in each frontal lobe comes "on line," providing greatly enhanced complexity. The toddler suddenly has verbal comprehension and a flow of communicative words that seem to spring up in bursts and a whole new way to play with toys and people, giving them symbolic meaning as expressions of wishes and fantasies previously impossible. Concurrently, a second vicissitude confronts toddlers. Parents now regard them as becoming capable of more adultlike symbolic functioning, and they intuitively pull on the children to express their often puzzling wishes and demands in words, that is, through a symbolic language as yet too uncertain for children to grasp with a feeling of efficacy and competence. Thus, sources of the dialectic tension of the rapprochement crisis arise from the cognitive transition to symbolic representation and the effects on the parent-toddler relationship.

Another transition point in cognitive development that arouses dialectic tension occurs at entry into adolescence. Wolf (1982) called attention to the impact of the transition point in cognitive development that occurs at age twelve to fourteen, when formal operations (Piaget, 1969) replace concrete operations. "This newfound capacity to combine propositions to isolate variables in order to confirm or dispose of hypotheses, and to carry out these operations with symbols rather than only with objects or concrete events has a great impact on the adolescent self" (p. 178). Adolescents can now create a more personal system of values, ideals, and ethics. Wolf noted the inevitable disappointment (deidealization) that accompanies this greatly increased cognitive capacity: "The adolescent can no longer hide from himself the inevitable discrepancies between who he has imagined his parents to be and who the parents really are" (p. 179). This transition places a burden on both early adolescent and parents. The parents must accept the loss of the earlier, more consistent idealization with relatively good grace and support their offspring's new adventures in exploration and assertion, especially the adolescent's glee at finding that his parents' feet are made of clay. The adolescent must seek affirmation and support from elsewhere, commonly by turning to peer groups, older adolescents, teachers, and fictional heroes. The interim period during which the adolescent's cognitive capacity for formal operations develops is thus often one of great dialectic tension. When the parents' and the adolescent's expectations of each other are in phase, the potential for consolidation of these advances in the exploratory-assertive motivational system is enhanced.

HIERARCHIES OF THE EXPLORATORY-ASSERTIVE MOTIVATIONAL SYSTEM

The hierarchical arrangements of developmental sequences is a fundamental conception of every psychoanalytic theory. Stages in psychosexual development (Freud, 1905), successive "positions" (M. Klein, 1952), epigenetic stages (Erikson, 1959; Spitz, 1959), stages within lines of development (A. Freud, 1965), successive models (Gedo and Goldberg, 1972), stages of separation-individuation (Mahler et al., 1975), and self-developmental stages (Stern, 1985) are well-known examples. In each of these examples some combination of drive or other general motivation and object relationship (Greenberg and Mitchell, 1983) is given precedence.

A problem that has long been recognized with hierarchical concepts of development is the nature of the relationship between early and later stages. Do later stages totally replace earlier ones, do they, for the most part transform and thereby also coexist with earlier stages? The transformational concept is illustrated by the belief that at the completion of the oedipal phase (and at adolescence) genitality transforms pregenital configurations (Arlow, 1963). We have noted the transformation that takes place in the perceptual life of infants when the properties of physical objects become subjects of contemplation and when the emotions of humans become guides for sharing and security. We have emphasized the major change that occurs in perception, cognition, and problem solving when, at 18 months, the myelinization of associational pathways and the frontal cortex ushers in symbolic representation in the dual modes of primary and secondary process. We can compare the dynamics of this momentous development to Pirandello's *Six Characters in Search of an Author.* Each character has a story to tell but needs a way to give his or her life representation in the play. Episodic memories of the events of the child's prior life, especially those in each motivational system that are given significance by strong or persisting emotion, are available for or in a sense call for the new form of representation. All emotionally significant trends that occur in the present and that activate associative memory to those of the past can now be formed into the contents of play, of fantasy, of dreams, and of increasingly organized intentions. Clearly the transformation is very widespread, but considerable evidence indicates it is not complete. Numerous clinical examples indicate the persistence of residues of early traumatic events in the form of behavior patterns (Anthi, 1983; Lichtenberg, 1983a, 1989a), character traits (Gedo, 1979), and pathogenic beliefs (Weiss and Sampson, 1986). Evidence of continuity rather than transformation can also be deduced for both adaptive and maladaptive residues of procedural memory in the manner in which parents "intuitively" respond to their infants and older children (Lichtenberg, 1989a). While most discussions of the fate of earlier hierarchical levels contrast continuities and transformations, Horowitz (1972) noted that the sequence of modes of representation from enactive to imagic to lexical suggests a more dynamic integrative formulation:

> The early forms of representation . . . do not disappear as the new lexical capacity is gained. They do not remain at primitive organizational levels. They probably continue epigenetic development because the acquisition of lexical capacities increases the availability of schemata for organization of information in any mode [p. 805].

Horowitz suggests that when lexical capacities can enhance an earlier form of representation, some degree of integration will occur. In many interactional gestural activities, words further define the situation and make it more flexible. Alternatively, in many activities guided by procedural memory (for example, many athletic skills) representation of an enactive nature may be more effective without the ambiguity or discursiveness of verbal representation.

These theoretical formulations of hierarchies are efforts to account for developments in the functioning of the individual as a whole whether construed as a tripartite structure, self, or self-organization. In contrast, Piagetian (1969) theory provides a hierarchical conception of cognitive development or, in our terms, an accounting of the significant features of the exploratory-assertive motivational system. The intricate presentation of developments leading to and from formal operations constitutes a standard against which all other presentations of exploratory-assertive motivation may be measured. A contemporary view adds the effect of cross-modal processing of early perceptual information (Stern, 1985) and the essential role of affects as sources of motivation (Lichtenberg, 1989a). The sense of efficacy and competence that motivates child and adult alike can be inferred from Piaget's schema. The subtle relationship between pleasure in intimacy and the competence pleasure that motivates play and helps to explain the emotional difference between work (efficacy and competence alone) and play (efficacy and competence plus intimacy) is less clear in the structuralist epistemological focus. Evaluated overall, the Piagetian schema serves well as the basis for a hierarchical account of stages of dominance of exploratory-assertive endeavors by denoting a level and method of information processing available at different ages.

We believe, however, that dominance is equally well conceptualized as meaning the choice among alternatives that a particular individual makes to approach exploration and problem solving at any given moment or, more commonly, repeatedly over time. We examine studies of information processing to suggest alternative possibilities of hierarchical ascendance that account for an important aspect of individuality.

In 1959, Gardner and colleagues, a group of psychologists well versed in psychoanalytic theory, reported a study of individual consistencies in cognitive control. A central finding of their study confirms their premise that individual differences in controlling perception and cognition do not imply distortion but exist as alternative ways to explore the external world.

Under conditions in which people are free to direct their attention, some will scan extensively, others relatively little. Extensive scanners will note properties of objects relevant to their intentions and fringe properties as well. They have the advantage of forming stable concepts of the objects they explore, but, because they deploy attention to relatively many aspects of external and internal fields, they are slow to make decisions and are prone to doubt.

Scanning refers to the *breadth* of attention in ordinary situations; another cognitive factor, field-articulation, refers to the ability to direct attention in situations of perceived incongruity. The ability to concentrate on relevant aspects of stimuli, focusing on certain aspects while avoiding or withholding attention from other aspects, makes it possible for one to cope well with incongruities. Those who lack this capacity organize along simpler lines and are less able to resolve an incongruity.

Another area studied was modes of organizing behavior in respect to experiences that violate normal assumptions of reality. One group, who can be spoken of as intolerant of unreality, engaged in continual efforts to make their experience conform to the actual state of affairs in the external world. Another group, those tolerant of unreality, while in equally adequate contact with external reality, were much more relaxed in their acceptance of both ideas and perceptual organizations that called for deviation from the conventional. They displayed "more direct evidence of the influence of momentary feeling states on their experiencing of the external world" (Gardner et al., 1959, p. 94).

Another dichotomy in cognitive control, leveling or sharpening, is relevant to situations involving the temporal patterning of stimuli. Levelers tend to blend together a current percept with a memory of a past percept so that the elements lose their individuality. In sharpeners, both memories and current percepts are more differentiated, less assimilated. In an investigation of dream recall of levelers and sharpeners, Lachmann, Lapkin, and Handelman (1962) found that college students who were sharpeners recalled significantly more dreams during a two week period than did a comparable group of levelers. The levelers were at either end of the dream recall frequency. Some recalled very few dreams, and some as many as the sharpeners. Gardner et al. (1959) proposed that the leveling-sharpening continuum parallels the operation of repression. Thus, a capacity for recalling dreams would be associated with a reliance on defenses other than repression. Levelers, however, may rely heavily on repression and thus not recall their dreams or may be able to apply repression selectively and permit themselves to recall dreams.

Another cognitive difference occurred in the way people make judgments about equivalences between perceptual objects. One group emphasized disparities; they responded to the inherent properties of objects rather than to their conative implications. The other group emphasized similarities; they responded not to differences in details of physical properties but to associated meanings. This group linked objects because of similarities in where they were seen or because of their relevance to a personal activity.

What are the hierarchical implications of these cognitive approaches to exploration and assertion? First, each cognitive-control tendency represents an unconscious preferential choice, the alternative being possible at another time. But the relative consistency of the same tendency indicates that a dominance or hierarchical arrangement has occurred. Second, several cognitive tendencies work in combinations that the authors call cognitive styles. For example, a person whose style is to be passive in exploration would be inclined to *leveling* (that is, easily assimilating a present percept with a memory by ignoring differentiating factors), *low field-articulation* (that is, to direct little attention to differentiating features that reveal incongruities), and *low scanning* (that is, when regarding a visual field to pay attention to a narrower field and to fewer details of properties). Such persons would be more likely to use repressive defenses in either a global or selective manner. They are less attentive to inner, imagistic contents that would be disruptive to them. People with this cognitive style are easily satisfied that they have explored a problem. They are apt to be satisfied with an understanding that might seem simplistic to someone with a different cognitive style.

Lichtenberg (1983a) described two well-defined markedly different cognitive styles of talented six-year-olds, James and David. James is a fictional version of the analyst-to-be Adrian Stephen, described by his exquisitely observant sister, Virginia Woolf (1927), in *To the Lighthouse:*

> Since he belonged, even at the age of six, to that great clan which cannot keep this feeling separate from that, but must let future prospects, with their joys and sorrows, cloud what is actually at hand, since to such people even in earliest childhood any turn in the wheel of sensation has the power to crystallize and transfix the moment upon which its gloom or radiance rests, James Ramsay, sitting on the floor cutting out pictures from the illustrated catalogue of the Army and Navy Stores, endowed the picture of a refrigerator, as his mother spoke, with heavenly bliss. It was fringed with joy. The wheelbarrow, the lawnmower, the sound of poplar trees, leaves whitening before rain, rooks cawing, brooms knocking, dresses rustling—all these were so colored and distinguished in his mind that he had already his private code, his secret language, though he appeared the image of stark and uncompromising severity [pp. 9–10].

David, on the other hand, frequently played alone with his soldiers. He constructed forts for them and had elaborate but distinct battle plans, both offensive and defensive. Although he had a number of friends with whom he played outside games, he enjoyed playing soldiers only with Jack, because Jack, alone of his friends, shared his passion for accuracy. David, who already at six read at a fourth-grade level, had his soldiers organized in units: foot soldiers, cavalry, and artillery. He knew how far the rifles and the cannons would fire; how large the squads, platoons, companies would be; how fast and how far the cavalry and horses could travel. The floor on which he played was, in his imagination, carefully scaled from inches to miles. When Jack and he argued about the validity of a plan, he would consult one of his books or, if necessary, wait for his father to supply the needed information. Although he enjoyed the fantasied charges and the battles as a whole, his real satisfaction came from the categorizing of information and the simulation of objective reality that his carefully made distinctions gave him. To add a new fact from a book or from his father to his catalogue of knowledge gave him as much joy as the whoop of victory when the walls of the fort were breached in a successful assault.

These examples of James and David illustrate the manner in which differing hierarchical arrangements of cognitive control tendencies combine to produce a wide variety of individual approaches to exploration and assertion. The creative potential of both hierarchical arrangements can be easily appreciated, James's possibly more suited for aesthetic pursuits, David's for scientific exploration, but both possibly flexible enough to do either.

HIERARCHICAL RELATIONS BETWEEN MOTIVATIONAL SYSTEMS

The form or style the exploratory-assertive system takes has innate proclivities often recognized as mixtures of family predispositions plus identifications, but all systems form in dialectic tension with the other systems. The interplay between attachment and exploratory-assertive motivations is particularly delicate. Parents who can sensitively provide children with the opportunity (time and tools) to play on their own help to establish a solid base for exploration and assertion. On the other hand, parents whose loneliness or isolation forces them to use their children for their own attachment needs will interfere with this development; and parents whose attentional focus is drawn inward or away from their children may provide "time and tools," but the children's exploration is apt to have a desultory, lonely quality. A child and mother ideally can comfortably shift between the child's fingering mother's earring while engaged with mother and the child's exploring the earring that happens to be on mother. Such moments, plus those of mutual exploration with toys and books, give play its special quality of exploration and assertion combined with intimacy, even if done alone.

The struggle for hierarchical dominance between the need for psychic regulation of physiological requirements and the desire for exploration and assertion is a daily experience. This struggle can be typified by the child who persists in building his blocks or playing ball while straining and squirming to hold back his urine or feces, or by the diver, hoping to see a bit more, who prolongs submerged snorkeling to the point of discomfort. At the same time the psychic regulatory motive inevitably uses the exploratory-assertive system to explore new approaches to eating, eliminating, sleep patterns, and exercise while asserting preferences, often against those of others. Alternatively, physiological requirement-regulation is a source of interest so that ingestion, excretion, sleep (and, by extension, death), health, illness, and injury are universal triggers for exploration from the older toddler, who forms an analogy between the mysteries of bodily functions and the toilet flushing, to the adult physician, who makes a career choice of this exploratory interest.

At first glance the relationship between the sensual-sexual motivational system and the exploratory-assertive system could seem to be simply that the mysteries of creation and gender differences are *primary* sources of curiosity. In this view, perception and cognition are low-tension, neutralized, conflict-free functions (Hartmann, 1964) unless taken over by sexual (libidinous) drive urgency. Any observation of the intensity with which infants pursue their exploratory interests and struggle against restraints to assert their preferences in nonsexual or sexual areas disproves the "neutralized" contention (Parens, 1979). Thus, exploratory-assertive motivations do not depend on sensual-sexual motives to be intense. Interest, efficacy, and competence pleasure are powerful affective motivators.

Paradoxically, sexual motivation often depends on exploratory-assertive motivations (as well as antagonism; see Stoller, 1975) for successful potency to occur. To understand this paradox, we must compare the premise of libido theory with clinical psychoanalytic observations. According to libido theory, a drive for orgastic satisfaction motivates people more or less persistently and thus requires defensive measures to prevent (socialize) coital urgency. Unlike animals, whose estrus cycles govern the rise and fall of sexual periods, the human's hormonal levels are relatively constant. However, although biologic factors are responsible for upsurges in genital sensation at certain periods, such as at 18 months and in early puberty, potency, responsiveness, and orgastic expression are essentially psychically triggered. Clinical observation confirms the dependence of sexual arousal on conscious and unconscious fantasy, exploratory-assertive activity in the form of looking and display, and illusions of mysterious discovery, novelty, and variation. Thus, a sizable segment of the film, magazine, lingerie, and swimsuit industries, and all of the pornography and topless nightclub industries, are designed to titillate curiosity and stimulate or reinforce fantasies that ensure potency. The hierarchical arrangement is that the search for sexual excitement as a dominant motive recruits the exploratory-assertive system as a subset reinforcement.

The aversive motivational system and the exploratory-assertive system are complexly interrelated and often conflated by psychoanalytic theoreticians. A child who is frustrated in an exploratory activity may become angry, exerting thereby an additional thrust enabling the assertive effort to be effective. The sequence of assertion augmented by anger then conveys a sense of power. The hierarchical arrangement would be a dominant exploratory-assertive motive commixed with or briefly supplanted by an aversive motive; but, with success, competence pleasure becomes dominant and the anger quickly recedes. Especially with toddlers, if the exploratory-assertive task is too complex or the child is prone to rapid acceleration of frustration-anger, a temper tantrum may ensue, with aversive motivation totally superseding exploration and assertion. Dominance of aversive motivation may also occur if becoming angry when frustrated is regarded as unacceptable. Then, the frustration of an exploratory-assertive effort may lead not to an instrumental augmenting by the vigor of anger, but to shame, guilt, or both. The outcome will not be competence pleasure with exploratory-assertive success and the rapid fading of anger, but a prolongation of aversion, often characterized by withdrawal, lack of interest, or even the grudge-holding associated with a narcissistic injury.

Alternatively, fear, shame, and guilt are the affects parents most commonly evoke to erect prohibitions against exploratory-assertive activities they regard as dangerous or damaging: climbing on tiltable chairs, running after a ball into a street, grabbing a toy away from another child, pulling on mother's earring or glasses to inspect them. A subtle but important interplay exists in the parent's perception of the child's motive. Parents who recognize their child's activity as exploratory, self-assertive, and playful in nature, after effectively prohibiting a dangerous pursuit, will help the child to switch to another exploratory-assertive goal, including exploring the danger when appropriate. Parents who regard their child's exploratory-assertive activity as aversive, that is, as antagonistic and rebellious because they do not like it, after prohibiting the dangerous pursuit, shame the child as foolish, malicious, and bad. Consequently, the child will confuse assertion with antagonism and the persistent carrying out of a self-conceived agenda as shameful and evil. The subsequent permutations of this confusion of assertion and aversion will be pathogenic beliefs (Weiss and Sampson, 1986) that others are hostile suppressors to whom one must be compliant, that the self is faulty and bad and that self-exploratory motives are not to be trusted.

The final relationship between the exploratory-assertive and aversive systems that we will discuss deals with the psychoanalytic discovery of the mechanisms of defense. This relationship may seem to require no comment. Each phase of psychoanalytic theorizing would place the mechanisms of defense as functional capacities responsive to aversive needs. Ideation unacceptable to the dominant mass of ideas, to the censor guarding the preconscious and conscious realms, and to the ego and superego is subject to denial, disavowal, projection, introjection, repression, isolation, reversal, identification, intellectualization, and other similar regulatory efforts.

Most discussions of defense mechanisms have tended to follow two trends. A. Freud (1936) and Lichtenberg and Slap (1971, 1972) considered the relationship between normal (adaptational) and pathologic (conflictual) aspects of defensive functions. Theoreticians as diverse as Kernberg (1975) and Gedo and Goldberg (1972) grouped mechanisms developmentally into those earlier or later in origin, the earlier being associated with more severe pathologic entities; the later, with the psychoneuroses. We emphasize that many of the so-called mechanisms of defense are identical with the means of controlling and regulating cognition used by the exploratory-assertive system. Gardner et al. (1959) stated: "It is . . . doubted that two sets of controls are involved, each invoking different mediating structures. It seems more likely that defenses and cognitive controls involve the same signal and action apparatuses" (p. 12). They assert that the crucial vantage point lies in *the motivational conditions* present, an assertion to which we shall return. First, we summarize examples they present or their findings suggest.

1) Levelers and repression: Freud (1915) described repression as the removal of a potentially dangerous idea from consciousness by assimilating the current idea to something previously repressed. Since levelers during exploratory activities emphasize similarities at the expense of distinctions and have memory organizations in which fine shadings are lost, their memory organization is congenial to the kind of easy assimilative clearing of consciousness performed in repression. The studies confirmed that subjects who relied on repression as their principal means of dealing with conflictual ideas were predominantly levelers.

2) Extreme scanners and isolation: Extreme scanners are those who deploy their attention very broadly across a perceptual field. In this broad scanning, expressive attributes and emotional reverberations are apt to be deemphasized. Extreme scanners indicated an active dislike of stimuli with sexual and emotional connotations. The defense of isolation operates by full focus on ideas from which affects are separated. By this means, isolation increases the breadth of consciously accessible ideas including perverse, murderous, and incestuous thoughts. Experimentally subjects for whom isolation was a conspicuous defense had significantly high scorings as extreme scanners.

3) Broad equivalence ranges and displacement: When asked to judge the similarity of disparate stimuli, subjects with broad equivalence ranges dismissed differences in detail and linked objects because of their associated meanings, such as visual impressions of the places in which they were seen. The defense of displacement functions by allowing a source of a troubling problem to be regarded as equivalent to another source which bears even a loose resemblance, thus disguising the real source.

4) Extensive scanners and obsessional doubt: Extensive scanning slows decision making since attention may be deflected back and forth from external and internal stimuli. Because of the emphasis of scanners on factors and properties, the affective side of preferences may be neglected so that emotion as an essential guide to choice is relatively absent. Obsessive doubting operates to slow down decision making when the emotional urgency that might underlie the decision is aversive and must be denied conscious awareness.

What can we conclude from the preceding review of the relationship of cognitive controls to the defense mechanisms of repression, isolation, displacement, and doubting? First, the development of the cognitive control capacity is a precondition for the use of the same regulatory approach for aversive (defensive) purposes. Each defense mechanism becomes operative along a time continuum of cognitive development. Since cognitive development forms in clusters, groups of defenses are arranged hierarchically. Second, the term defense mechanism is a label having historical significance and the convenience of designating a function, but it may be misleading. If we fail to recognize that neither aversive responses nor cognitive exploration is mediated by a separate group of "mechanisms," we can easily become involved in an unproductive argument about whether a response is adaptive (a cognitive control) or conflictual and maladaptive. The main point of our focus should not be the means but rather the motivation that the means has been recruited to serve. We propose giving precedence to the motivation that dominates an experience we have under consideration. Thus, motivational-system dominance and the affects that serve as the goals of that system receive precedence as hierarchical organizations.

SELF AS A HIERARCHICAL SUPERORDINATE

If an acceptable explanation for mental functioning lies in the postulate of motivational systems, each having a hierarchical arrangement within and each capable of being the dominant governor of experience at any moment, do we require a conception of capacities hierarchically superordinate to the systems? Two observable phenomena argue for such a hierarchical conception, which we call self or self-organization.

The first phenomenon is the relatively seamless manner in which most people are able to shift from the dominance of one motivational system to another without a sense of disruption. We can easily take this experiential sense of self-sameness for granted and ignore the remarkable psychological feat it represents. At all ages transitions of state—from asleep to awake, from happy to sad, from tantrumlike anger and rage to being friendly and pacified, from feeling separate to feeling as one with another, from being sexually aroused to being relaxed, from postmenstrual to premenstrual to menstrual—exert a continuous strain on a person's sense of unity. At different stages of life, one may function with remarkable variances of compliance and rebellion, of risk taking and conservatism, of sociability and reclusiveness, which presents a challenge to maintain a sense of continuity. Moreover, gaps in memory, ranging from instrumental nonretentiveness to prevent information overload to defensive repression and the distorting of denial and disavowal, inevitably occur and must be bridged. Because of this remarkable capacity for unity, we amend Kohut's (1977) definition of self as an independent center of initiative and perception to self as an independent center for initiating, organizing, and integrating experience and motivation.

The second phenomenon that compels us to recognize the organizing and integrative capacities of the self is failures in unity of experience. For many years, failures in unity were recognized primarily in the "splits" of cognitive experiencing that gave schizophrenia its name and the markedly altered affective states of manic–depressive psychosis. Increasingly, under the close scrutiny of intensive treatment, pattern disorders of "personality" and "character" have revealed clear discontinuities of experience. These include the exuberant grandiosity and fragmentation-depletion of narcissistic personality disorders; the entrenched, hostile, depreciatory, and awe-filled compliant states of borderline disorders (Lichtenberg, 1987b); the blackouts attendant to alcohol and drug addictions; and the dramatic discrepant dissociative organizations of those with multiple personality disorders. From these clinical findings we have learned that the organizing and integrating capacities of the self can be adversely affected. The factors are varied and complex. On one side are the person's experiences of subtle and gross instances of empathic failure: coldness, physical and sexual abuse, smothered individuality, unreasonable demands for success without adequate support, a hostile home environment. Severe disruptive traumata may occur at any age, as evidenced by many victims of the Holocaust and the Vietnam war and others with posttraumatic syndromes. On the other side are factors that make a child less able to respond to an ordinarily responsive nurturant environment – faulty genetic predisposition, prematurity, drug toxicity at birth, sensory deficits, severe hypo- and hyperactivity. Learning disorders such as those of E, with whose problems the chapter opened, are at risk for disruptive personal and interpersonal experiences.

As clinicians we are drawn to an investigative interest in failures of integration, but our study of hierarchies indicates that the integrative-organizing capacity itself needs to be a central focus for future research. At present the self as an independent center for initiative, organizing, and integrating is easier to define than to specify. We can recognize correlations to the integrative centers of the brain. The enormously rich associational pathways in the prefrontal and frontal cortex, the interplay of the right and left brain hemispheres, and the great redundancy and overlap of function assure the brain's overall capacities for integration and cohesion of experience once maturity has occurred. Even in the brains of infants and small children, stimulating and inhibiting centers assure complex regulation and dense feedback loops assure integration. The findings of infant research point to memory representations based on the ability to abstract core elements of experiences in each motivational system and generalize their properties (Stern's, 1985, RIGs). Thus, we begin life with the capacity to organize and integrate experiences central to the infant's regulation under conditions of empathic support. The self or self-organization develops from this core to take its eventual superordinate hierarchical position. We can recognize its functioning by the age of five in the narratives of oedipal themes that build and change through life while maintaining the remarkable sense of continuity that characterizes the uniqueness of human beings.

5

Unconscious Mentation

When the portal of entry into human motivations is shifted from the couch to the crib, major reformulations must follow. In this chapter we examine "the unconscious" in relation to both past and current theory and with respect to the metaphors that have come to reify it. We propose and illustrate a fundamental level of unconscious mentation and a symbolic, dynamic level of unconscious mentation. Whereas we maintain Freud's distinction between primary and secondary processes, we integrate these with current work on episodic and procedural memory. This chapter also provides the theoretical, developmental, and clinical basis for our proposal that self-state is on a conceptual par with the intrapsychic and intersubjective domains as salient in the shaping of unconscious mentation.

Freud's discovery of the "dynamic unconscious" marked the beginning of psychoanalysis as a depth psychology and the end of humankind's illusion that thoughts and actions are under full conscious control. Freud's theory of the unconscious appears in two major propositions: first as a topography of the mind and second as a structural theory. Originally Freud attempted to understand psychological phenomena as qualities of consciousness and systems based on those qualities. In this theory, the system unconscious contained contents unacceptable to the dominant mass of ideas as well as repressive forces (Gill, 1963).

Gill's critical study of the topographic theory led to a reevaluation of the role of the "here and now" in the transference by recognizing an interaction between what is pressing forward to the surface from the patient and what is contributed from the side of the analyst as well.

Sandler and Sandler (1984) went beyond traditional theory in postulating unconscious motivations. They proposed a division between *past unconscious* and *present unconscious*. The past unconscious contains the gamut of a person's immediate, peremptory wishes, impulses, and responses formed early in life. The present unconscious involves a repression barrier erected to prevent current experiences of shame that might arise from revealing associations made to the analyst.

Shame

We hold that shame, embarrassment, and humiliation can be evoked through thoughts, feelings, and actions arising from any of the five motivational systems. Thus, shame is an important source of aversiveness to more open awareness and communication as the Sandlers observe. We would not say that shame alone forms a barrier to a freer flow of associations, but, rather, we believe that any aversive affect (fear, anger, sadness, disgust) can lead to disjunctions in the availability of information of self-knowledge and sharing. We are in accord with the Sandlers' inclusion of early lived experience along with drive pressures as constituents of the past unconscious. Rather than supporting a dual-drive basis for motivation, we propose a fundamental level of unconscious mentation organized by five innate, intersubjectively developing, structured motivational systems. Rather than emphasizing a strict division between two forms of unconscious, we emphasize the capacity of the developing self to organize and integrate unconscious mentation in fluid interaction with experience. Motivations derived from fundamental unconscious mentation shape, and are reshaped by, the later developing unconscious (and conscious) symbolic mentation.

On the basis of their theory that all mental phenomena are constituted in an intersubjective matrix, Stolorow and his colleagues (1987) delineated three types of unconscious organization: the "prereflective unconscious," which refers to organizing principles that operate outside a person's conscious awareness; the "dynamic unconscious," which consists of defensively walled affect states that failed to evoke attuned responsiveness from the early surround; and the "unvalidated unconscious," which consists of unarticulated experiences that never evoked the requisite responsiveness from the surround (Stolorow and Atwood, 1989).

Stolorow and his coworkers approach the task of delineating unconscious organization from observations derived solely in the analytic setting. In contrast, our approach attempts to combine findings from empirical infant research with the yield of clinical experience. Having organized the research data into five motivational systems that shape unconscious mentation, we are able to specify the organizing principles or schemas that affect an individual's development across the spectrum of shifting physiological, attachment, exploratory, aversive, and sensual-sexual needs. We offer a tentative formula-

tion and integration of basic schemas formed in infancy with later development of fantasy and model scenes and suggest the significance of the role of
"states" as a dimension of unconscious mentation apart from the intrapsychic
and intersubjective.

intrapsychic
psychic, mean
Not meaning
self reg

Later in this chapter we define and illustrate "state." By "intrapsychic" we
mean the way in which one responds to one's own competing and
cooperating motivational priorities. We include one's innate and learned
preferences, one's contributions to the fantasies, beliefs, and model scenes that
participate in the shaping of one's experiences, and one's appreciation and
response to one's own thoughts, feelings, attitudes, and sensibilities. We use
the term "intersubjective" to refer to the manner in which one person
appreciates and responds to the thoughts, feelings, attitudes, sensibilities, and
affects of another's actual or "experienced" presence. The appreciation of the
subjectivity of another person is a developmental achievement that begins at
birth (and probably to an as yet unclear degree, in utero). At nine months, a
transformation occurs as infants recognize and seek guiding information
from their perception of the affective state of caregivers. Our use of the term
"intersubjective" is consonant with the work of Trevarthan (1980) and with
its usage by Stern (1985). Our usage is more restricted than that of Stolorow et
al. (1987) in that we regard intrapsychic, intersubjective, and state as
constituting differently organized domains. Stolorow and his coworkers
present as their overarching conception that invariant principles are organized
by two intersecting subjectivities.

In recommending our narrower definition of an intersubjective perspective,
we hold that a developmental or clinical event can be better explained by
having three domains of influence to consider. Developmentally, most attachment experiences call for an intersubjective focus. Exploratory-assertive solitary play and the learning of efficacy call for an intrapsychic focus. Periods of
overwhelming anger, withdrawal, or fever call for a focus on state. Alternatively, the fullest conception of any experience we wish to explicate, whether
developmentally or clinically, calls for a consideration of the saliency of all
three perspectives. Therefore, we carry our distinctions of intrapsychic, intersubjective, and state forward from early development into our understanding
of the mental life of the adult and the salient aspects of the treatment situation.

Our appreciation of the emphasis that Stolorow and his colleagues place on
the intersubjective domain is illustrated in our account of the manner in which
memories are recalled and reconstructed within the treatment's dyadic relationships. In Chapters 2 and 3, on model scenes, we offered a conceptual tool
through which analyst and patient can highlight and encapsulate experiences
representative of salient conscious and unconscious motivational themes.
Through the construction and exploration of model scenes by analyst and
patient, both unavailable or fragmentarily available aspects of past experience
and problematic aspects of the "here-and-now" analyst–patient relationship

become open to analytic inquiry. Through the interplay of contributions from patient and analyst, memories, and "lived" transference experiences, their origins, functions, and developmental transformations can be addressed in the analytic setting.

When we apply our conceptualization of model scenes to unconscious fantasies, we are able to clarify problems inherent in that concept. Unconscious fantasies, like model scenes, do not "exist." They are not stored in a deep layer of the psychic and then brought to the surface. The concepts themselves are metaphors for highly plastic constructions that take a particular form as a result of the special intersubjective conditions of analytic work. An unconscious fantasy refers to an assumption that significant experiences and motivations associated with them can be given representation in the course of analytic work through a particular form of largely sensory imagery. Recurrent behaviors, dreams, and themes, especially those which evolve in the transference, may lead the analyst to postulate that certain motivations have been given symbolic representation in the form of an unconscious fantasy. The joint participation by analyst and patient that follows accounts for the organization of an "unconscious" fantasy as it becomes experienced in consciousness. Joint participation means more than the spoken words of each. Inherent in the construction of the thoughts, feelings, and imagery of what analysand and analyst organize to present to each other is the motivation to move the other along the lines of some desire—for example, agreement, sympathy, or opposition—and optimally toward expanded exploration. In contrast, daydreams are largely a self-regulating intrapsychic phenomenon. They may bear no direct or immediate reflection of the influence of analyst or of any other person. They give imagic representation to a motive, the fulfillment of which is organized in accordance with the preferences of the self, that is, toward the goal of a self-constructed selfobject experience (see Chapter 7; Bacal's, 1990 "fantasy selfobject" is a related concept). As in model scenes, by means of the construction and exploration of unconscious fantasies by both analyst and patient, important developments occur. Frightening, depressing, painful, guilt-filled, and shame-ridden aspects of past experience and problematic aspects of the here-and-now analyst–patient relationship become shared sources of information available for further analytic inquiry.

The conceptualization of model scenes as including unconscious fantasy and having a role in analytic work has far-reaching implications. These conceptualizations of model scenes and unconscious fantasy lead us to reconsider what we mean by unconscious.

THE UNCONSCIOUS: A SPATIAL METAPHOR

Despite the effort by ego psychology to jettison the topographic systems (e.g., Arlow and Brenner, 1964) from a metapsychological point of view (Rapaport,

1960), analysts have consistently resisted dispensing with the convenience of a place ("topos") in which mental content is contained, sequestered, or hidden and from which it can be freed, surfaced, or exposed through analytic exploration or excavation.

Analysts attempting to adhere to a strictly "scientific" construction of unconsciousness as a quality of mentation frequently slip into using evocative metaphors of body, space, and archeology. Common clinical usage follows the linguistic disavowals described by Schafer (1976): "In my mind (brain, self) lives a lovable person (or a demon) that I can only let out at times." At base, this phrase draws on the body metaphors of the small child whose answer to "Where does food go?" is "In my tummy—I can't see it but I know it's there." Depicting the unconscious as a container elaborates topographic metaphors with images of walls and boundaries. The contents of this container are guarded by a censor (a sociocultural metaphor about control of information), defense (a military metaphor), repression (a physics metaphor about forces), and strangulation of affect (a metaphor referring to constriction of a body part).

What are the implications of the spatial or container metaphor? First, it adheres to a strict one-person psychology (Balint, 1968; Ghent, 1989; Lachmann and Beebe, in press; Fosshage, 1991) and does not acknowledge the effect of the contribution of the analyst to the organization of the treatment experience of the patient (Gill, 1984; Gill and Hoffman, 1982; Hoffman, 1983; Stolorow and Lachmann, 1984/85; Fosshage, 1992). Second, an observer only of what filters through the barrier, the analyst is positioned "outside" the patient's frame of reference. The analyst's goal is confined to removing the barrier of repression by interpreting both defense and drive derivative.

The main advantage of using the spatial metaphor is that it allowed the analyst to understand a great deal about the formation of symptoms, dreams, and parapraxes and thus guide in the "excavation" of buried fantasies, affects, and beliefs. To fit into the spatial metaphor, the analyzable patient had to make a therapeutic split into an experiencing and observing part. That is, to be analyzed, a patient needed to harness a consciously available messenger to dip into the unconscious contents sequestered in the container and present it to the analyst. An alliance between the observing part of the patient and analyst (Sterba, 1934; Zetzel, 1956; Greenson, 1967; Stolorow and Lachmann, 1980; Brandchaft and Stolorow, 1990) was necessary in the archeological endeavor that constituted analysis; otherwise the analyst did not have reliable access to the patient's unconscious.

The spatial or container metaphor views the patient as a closed system, therapeutic alliance notwithstanding. That is, the metaphor does not provide for an exploration of the effect of the analyst or the analyst's theory on the patient. Additionally, the spatial metaphor, by setting relatively fixed boundaries between the unconscious and conscious does not reflect the continuous fluctuations in awareness that arise from the establishment or disruption of an empathic ambience (Wolf, 1988). In the traditional, closed-system view, unconscious mentation is depicted as less accessible through the systematic use of an empathic mode of perception (Lichtenberg, 1981a; Schwaber, 1981; Ornstein and Ornstein, 1985) than we find in our clinical experience. Since sensing and exploring the analysand's inner state is, we believe, a sine qua non of analytic technique, the view of unconscious mentation should be consistent with its clinical application.

At issue for us is Freud's (1914) legacy of a theory of a dynamic unconscious whose contents are tightly bound by repression. He also left clinical examples showing how the analyst achieves a sense of conviction about the patient's inner life *before* major repressive barriers have been removed. One of Freud's attempts to resolve this apparent contradiction is found in his generally ignored papers on telepathy (Freud, 1921, 1922, 1933; see also Major and Miller, 1984; Leavy, 1984; Simon, 1984; Skinner, 1984) in which he explored unconscious to unconscious communication.

A more recent attempt to consider the markedly sensitive communication of "unconscious" contents between analysand and analyst is the Kleinian conception of projective identification (Grotstein, 1981; Ogden, 1982; Sandler, 1988). We are delineating a second approach: the exploration that arises from the systematic application of an empathic mode of perception. We believe the same phenomena explained by normal and pathological projective identification can be successfully approached without viewing parents and therapists as containers processing affects projected into them. A deep sense of normal resonance and communion between parent and child and between analyst and analysand can be understood by exploring affective attunement (Stern, 1985) and the mode of attachment present in alter ego or twinship transferences. Pathological emotional-behavioral interplay between parent and child and between analyst and analysand can be understood by the effects of role enactments based on presymbolic communication between infants and caregivers (Stern, 1985; Lichtenberg, 1989a; Beebe and Lachmann, 1992) and by the potentiality for role responsiveness that continues throughout life (Sandler, 1976). Our approach avoids an assumption of interpenetration of self "boundaries" for "the reinternalization of the projection after it has been psychologically processed by the recipient" (Goldstein, 1991, p. 153) to account for parent–child, analyst–patient mutual influence.

Despite the difference in our theoretical approach, our clinical findings coincide with those of Porder (1987), who states that projective identification

can best be understood as the chronic repetition of a childhood interaction between a parent, not necessarily the mother, and the child. This interaction may well begin early in life, although it is a highly speculative proposition to

date it to the first year of life. The repetition is a classical example of "identification with the aggressor" or "turning passive into active." Usually, the patient
consciously experiences the analyst as the powerful parent in the transference.
However, there is an *unconscious reversal* which casts the analyst in the role of the
bad child and the patient as the powerful, demanding, critical, sadistic, or
masochistic parent. . . . there is clear evidence that an affect is *induced in,* not
projected into the analyst because the patient is acting in, within the analytic hour,
in a way which provokes strong responses in the analyst. Such patients not only
speak, they enact. What is more, they continue to do so tenaciously for long
periods of time despite the analyst's interpretative efforts. As a result, they are
more likely to provoke the strong affective responses upon which all . . . authors
have commented [p. 439].

Porder objects to the narrow formulation that projective identification is
necessarily a primitive defense or a response to the earliest psychological
conflicts of infancy. Like us, Porder views the problems presumed to be dealt
with by projective identification to arise from parent–child conflicts that occur
during any phase of development. Porder notes that although many patients
identify with the aversive characteristics of their parents, not all patients create
the same unwelcome shame, guilt, helplessness, pessimism, and rage in us. To
explain the source of their pathology, Porder does not cite distortions based
on instinctual drive but rather points to the patients' actual lived experiences
with the criticalness and suffering of their disturbed parents. In their repetitive
enactments "they tell us openly and strongly, as well as in more subtle
nonverbal ways how bad and inadequate and angry and unsensitive we are.
They stir our sadism and our guilt by their endless accusations and suffering"
(p. 445). We would add that our commitment as therapists to an altruistic
approach and our own inclination toward rescue fantasies makes us particularly prone to the role responses induced by these patients' representations of
their "failure to thrive" under our approach to them.

Treating the unconscious as a space or place with walls of defense that can
be entered or sealed off reifies a barrier between unconscious and (pre)con-
scious. When this occurs, we see ourselves lifting repression like a curtain,
undoing distortion, recovering the disavowed, having contents projected into
us, and having the contents inside us identified with. While these concepts
have evocative and historical value, they easily lend themselves to a mecha-
nized view of the therapeutic process and lead away from more highly
personal questions: What experiences are being sought by the patient to
strengthen the sense of self? What experiences are aversive and why? What
part is being played at the moment by the state of the ambience between
analyst and patient?

A source of enthusiasm about the conception of the unconscious as it was
construed in the initial period of psychoanalytic discovery was the ability to
map aspects of the unconscious as they appeared in the "transference neuroses." Analysts at that time believed that the same explanations would extend

to broader aspects of the personality without modification. The hoped-for royal road to the unconscious that dreams, slips, and the symptoms promised turned out to be therapeutically disappointing. Discerning the unconscious, especially in character and personality disturbances involving severe self-dysregulation, requires a broader conceptualization of what is meant by unconscious.

FUNDAMENTAL UNCONSCIOUS MENTATION

In designating a level of unconscious mentation as fundamental, we refer to the earliness of its formation, the influence it exerts on the early (and often later) organization of motivation and experience, and its presymbolic mode of processing information. Lived experience processed by fundamental unconscious mentation may be encoded as procedural memories (the rates and rhythms and movements by which we suck, eat, walk, talk, greet people, swim, etc.), episodic memories (memories organized by events, such as being fed a bottle by mother, having a diaper changed, watching a mobile, etc.), or both. Fundamental unconscious mentation may be regarded as comprising uncoded pattern regulators. Uncoded pattern regulators are innate (constitutional) organizers that determine the features of temperament and that underlie linguistic acquisition, geographic orientation, and cognitive apparatuses including defensive operations.

By unconscious mentation, we mean the ongoing mentation that occurs outside of awareness in both waking and sleep states. A continual influence and fluctuation occurs between unconscious and conscious mentation. For example, in a waking state, data are perceived and registered either subliminally or in full awareness depending on a variety of factors, including intensity of stimulus, dominance of motivational system, selectivity in attention, and meaning.

Fundamental unconscious mentation can be distinguished from the more familiar unconscious symbolic mentation. In unconscious symbolic mentation, motives and experiences are encoded in the dual modes of symbolic representation (primary and secondary process) made possible by the maturation of the right and left hemispheres (Fosshage, 1983, 1987; Lichtenberg, 1983a; Bucci, 1985). In appraising any specific clinical entity, we may regard either fundamental mentation or the more highly plastic level of symbolic representational mentation as more important in organizing the phenomenon under consideration.

The hypotheses that bear on fundamental unconscious mentation are that 1) motivation organized as five motivational systems (Chart 1) forms the fundamental level of the unconscious; 2) the five motivational systems shape and are shaped by lived experience prior to the development of symbolic

Chart 1
Normal or Ordinary Schemas from Infancy

These schemas serve as templates of fundamental unconscious mentation for model scenes of both the presymbolic and symbolic periods.

A need for nutrient-intake → the sensation of hunger and the affect of distress (crying) → sucking and intake experience → a sense of enjoyment and a sensation of satiety.

A need for attachment → distress and pursuit behaviors → opportunities for affirmation, sharing, and idealization → a sense of intimacy pleasure and self-expansiveness.

A need for exploration and assertion → interest and functional activity → a sense of pleasure from efficiency and competence.

A need to react aversively based on pain, violation of preference, mismatch of expectancy → distress and

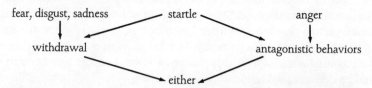

self-soothing and/or instrumentally effective use of anger → self-reliance and competence

or

relief of the source of distress and frustration, restoration of self-expansiveness and intimacy → reliance on others and trust

A need for sensual enjoyment arising as general distress and irritability and/or a specific sensation in a sensual target zone → soothing, stroking, rhythmic rubbing by self or other →

either

relief of distress and irritability and specific sensations of pleasure with reduced general tension

or

relief of distress and irritability and specific sensations of pleasure with heightened focal and general sensations of sexual excitement.

---

representational mentation; 3) the record of the early lived experience persists, for the most part shaping and being shaped by symbolic representation, but nonetheless contributing its own forms and rules of representation throughout life; 4) to realize further the goal of making as full as possible an empathic entry into the state of mind of an analysand, the analyst attends not only to the words and categoric affects that are regarded as the ordinary components of free association, but also to behaviors, gestures, and affects that often reveal links to early procedural and episodic memories; 5) by resonating empathically with these behaviors, gestures, and especially categoric and vitalizing affects that derive from early lived experience encoded in procedural and episodic memories, analysts can form model scenes that provide important links to the period of formation of each motivational system and the stability or instability of the contribution of each system to the emergent and core self; and 6) often the ability to form model scenes indicative of unconscious early lived experience results from the analyst's perusal of his own and the analysand's affect-laden role responses and enactments in the intersubjective field of an ongoing analysis.

During the neonatal period, affect states are triggered as the patterns of regulation of physiological requirements, attachment, exploration and assertion, sensual enjoyment, and aversive responses unfold. Infants gain a powerful sense of emergent agency from an internal experience of being able to re-create familiar affect states (Sander, 1983). In ordinary development, as needs are met, infants gain their sense of self as an active agency by re-creating positive, self-affirming experiences. Development goes awry when infants have no choice but to gain a sense of self agency from whatever they can wrest from the consistencies in their environment by re-creating the negative, painful, or deficient affect states from which they developed familiarity. When positive affect states and a sense of an empathic environment are the predominant sense of what infants experience themselves as re-creating, minor alterations in what is familiar are easily tolerated and even welcomed. A capacity for flexibility is established, and transitions between affect states and shifting motivations can be negotiated with ease.

When negative affect states and a sense of an unempathic environment predominate in what infants experience themselves as re-creating, the infants have no choice but to cling to the repetition of dysphoric affects. For these infants, change, even positively toned opportunities, are, at least at first, experienced as putting the infant at risk; transitions are difficult and flexibility is sacrificed. The principles described that govern infants' re-creation of familiar affect states and the different organization of the lived experience, depending on whether the affects are predominately positive or dysphoric, are uncoded regulatory organizers fundamental to unconscious mentation.

The following brief vignettes describe the perspective we hold.

Case 1

Miss D, a thin, attractive young woman came to treatment troubled about her failures in romantic relationships. She mentioned that in midadolescence she had gained weight at a time when her mother, always somewhat heavy, had been depressed by the breakup of her marriage. Miss D noted that whenever she spent time with her mother, she overate. Two months after treatment began, Miss D returned from a visit with her mother and maternal grandmother. Her whole demeanor was strikingly different than it had been. She said she was tired and had been sleeping poorly, but despite a lack of sleep, she was hyperactive in speech and manner. Her eyes were popping, her gestures overdramatic, and her movements jerky.

She related that she arrived at her mother and grandmother's house late in the evening and was offered dessert. At first she insisted on yogurt, then, with her mother's and grandmother's encouragement, began on ice cream. A large supply of candy was also available. As she ate the candy, her mother admonished her so she took the candy to bed with her and finished it. She spent the whole visit feeling charged up, eating and sleeping fitfully.

The model scene that helped analyst and patient to understand the specifics of Miss D's problem with the regulation of her physiological requirements was of a mildly overactive child whose hunger and exploratory assertiveness led her overwhelmed mother to give her the sweets she craved. Eating carbohydrates in such quantities leads to brief bursts of energy followed by tiredness and craving and often sleep disturbances. The three generations of women, craving sweets, admonishing each other, but then compliantly supplying the sweets, has been graphically described in a case of Piontelli (1987).

We have suggested that fundamental unconscious mentation organizes and is organized by lived experiences that derive from innate and learned patterns that shape and are shaped by the reactions and responses of caregivers during the period before plastic symbolic representations. Fundamental unconscious mentation, guided by innate uncoded regulators, encodes as procedural and episodic memory experiences derived from each of the five motivational systems. One uncoded regulator determines the rules that govern which experiences do or do not receive encoding as episodic memories. For example, encoding is more likely to take place when strong affects are triggered and when affective experiences are repeated. Another uncoded regulator determines the rules that underlie motivational choices, for example, the priority given to re-creating familiar affect states (Sander, 1983). The uncoded regulation is that as needs are met infants gain a sense of agency from re-creating positive, self-affirming experiences; but when needs are not met, or are met in ways that lead to dystonic experiences, infants will strive to re-create a negative or dystonic affect state in order to experience a short-term cohesive effect of consistency.

How would our proposals regarding fundamental unconscious mentation apply to the case of Miss D? Miss D's lived experience of psychic regulation of physiological requirements would be of more rapid than usual crescendos and decrescendos affecting her hunger–satiety pattern, her motor activity pattern, and her sleep pattern. Those experiences of dysregulation of physiological requirements would be recorded as procedural memory: an experience of high bodily activity, followed by an empty, hunger sensation, the intake of a sweet-tasting substance, the sensation of fullness, and a return to high bodily activity. This sequence, encoded in the form of a body procedural memory, would then provide a goal for repetitions by which the child could self-create an affect state of vitality and the pleasures of hunger satiety, sweet taste, and an almost giddy liveliness. Her experience also included eating sweets with her mother. Thus, sharing glucose intake with her mother and the reversal of their "lows" by this means would have been encoded by Miss D as a recurrent generalized episodic memory of a shared attachment experience.

Miss D attempted to override the procedural memory associated with the glucose-loading form of regulation by including proteins in a more ordered diet. In addition, she attempted to protect herself from her detrimental attachment to her mother by staying away from her and being antagonistic toward her when they were together. We can recognize a struggle resulting from the proclivities encoded by fundamental unconscious mentation, in particular lived experiences from early childhood as well as numerous later recurrences of overuse of sweets, hyperactivity, and sleep disturbance. These proclivities were motivating her toward re-creating the "hyper" affect state, while later patterns of better dietary regulation and more controlled activity encoded as symbolic representations were motivating her toward different goals.

Case 2

One of the authors (J.L.) observed Mrs. R first as an infant and then with her own daughter as a first-time mother. He noted that in her infancy she had been extremely responsive to attachment exchanges. She easily made and sought eye contact. She had a captivating smile that pleased her parents as well as strangers who observed her in her carriage or in stores. She vocalized in a friendly way and would activate responses if her mother was distracted. As a mother, Mrs. R began very early to initiate eye contact with her baby. She vocalized to her baby and initiated her into the pleasures of intimate attachment sharing. Her baby, who appeared to observers to evidence a very similar personality profile, smiled early and would remain in attachment contact for rather long periods as mother and daughter invented new and expanding repertoires.

This vignette of Mrs. R illustrates episodic and procedural memory encoding of attachment-motivated experiences. Our assumption is that the lived experience of Mrs. R as an infant with her mother during moments in which attachment activities of eye contact, smiling, and vocalizing were dominant was encoded as an episodic memory conveying to the baby (and the mother as well) an affirmation of worth. In turn, her early experience played out in her expectation of competence as a mother (Teti and Gelfand, 1991) and the positive affect she experienced in attachment activities (Stern, 1988; Izard et al., 1991). These factors have been demonstrated to predict the likelihood of secure attachment experiences (Fonagy, Steele, and Steele, 1991).

Mutual mirroring observed in videotapes of either Mrs. R as a baby with her own mother or as a mother with her baby evoked in viewers an expansive feeling of shared enjoyment of intimacy. We believe that for the viewers an episodic memory was triggered of what their own infancy had been like – or what they wished it had been like. Assuming procedural memory of these lived experiences is particularly intriguing. Considering how much we have to learn so laboriously, it is amazing that parents "intuitively" (Papousek, 1986) know to talk to babies in high-pitched voices, make eye contact and assume exaggerated facial expressions, stick out their tongue to get the baby to follow suit, and attune their rhythms automatically to the babies (Stern, 1985). Moreover parents automatically shift the patterning of these communication games to heighten interest and prevent boredom. We assume that all this results from the unfolding of procedural memories from the parents' own lived experiences – a very economical adaptive mode of learning. But what is remarkable about this assumption is that the procedural memory must be recorded in a flexible pairing of doer and done to. The flexible shifting of experiences from the receptive baby to the adult as agent is made less mysterious by the recognition that in many of the activities of communicative intimacy sharing, the infant is an initiator 50% of the time.

Case 3

Mr. U displayed two puzzling response patterns. A favorite self-image of his was of a broken field runner darting here and there, always in motion. During his three morning hours he was an animated speaker, giving lectures to the analyst about his accomplishments, his plans, his philosophies, and his worries. In marked contrast, during his late afternoon analytic hour he felt "fuzzy headed," was often silent, and often pleaded with the analyst to speak to him. However, he was then unable to hear what was said, and he frequently fell asleep before the end of the hour. At other times, he described his murderous rage at his infant son for crying and at his wife for diverting her attention from him to the baby. He would run out of the house and chop wood to keep from molesting his son and wife.

Two model scenes involving him and his mother enabled analyst and patient to understand these responses. Mr. U's mother had suffered from a manic–depressive illness and suffered frequent lengthy episodes of depression. She could manage to do the minimal activities of the household in the morning, aided by her husband, but by afternoon, her husband gone, she would bring the child to bed with her, where he learned to escape desolating loneliness by napping with her. A second memory-reconstruction involved his own crying. Often when his mother was depleted, she would put him in his crib to contain him. He would cry with the same desperation with which he would sometimes appeal to the analyst to answer his questions. His mother would withdraw, leaving him shaking the bars of his crib until he gave up in exhaustion. In his murderous feeling toward his son he created what he assumed his father had felt toward him. The reaction toward his son was mixed with a terrible sense of envy of the care his son received from his wife.

The case of Mr. U illustrates the consolidation of aversive responses triggered by his mother's apparent neglect. In comparison, Mrs. R (Case 2) as a mother responded to her baby's signals of aversiveness – whimpering if she desired contact and tiring and looking away if she had enough – by initiating or discontinuing attachment activities. Her daughter's signals thus became well defined. Mrs. R's daughter could expect that she would be responded to without prolonged aversive states of anger, fear, shame, or sadness developing. Miss D's mother (Case 1) responded to her aversive signals as well. She met the physiological need but in a fashion that built a cycle of need-signal-response on a short-term basis that provided the underlying pattern for an addiction. Mr. U's mother (Case 3) did not meet his need. She responded to his aversive signals by a full-blown aversive response of her own. His crying triggered her avoidance and left him in a state of uncontrolled mounting anger until exhaustion set in. His need for closeness and intimacy led this otherwise energetic child to being seduced into sharing his mother's withdrawal into afternoon naps. These repeated patterns were encoded as both procedural and episodic memories. He came to share with his mother the pathologic unconscious belief (Weiss and Sampson, 1986) that he could avoid all discomfort through fuzzy-headedness and sleep. Success in understanding the background to this aversive withdrawal was possible during the three morning hours but had no ameliorative effect. The analyst concluded that at this point in the analysis the influence of the procedural memory was beyond verbal interpretation (Gedo, 1979) because it had not been embedded in a context of symbolization. He acceded to Mr. U's request to replace his afternoon hour with a fourth morning hour. Only during the termination work was Mr. U's use of this withdrawal for purposes of both self-protection and obstruction to the agenda of others brought more fully into awareness.

To summarize, fundamental unconscious mentation, at its core, organizes and is organized by schemas of five motivational systems. As each system self-organizes and self-stabilizes, the needs that constitute the system's core are met or fail to be met. As a result of the experience of match or nonmatch, fit or failure, affects are triggered. It is the amplification by affects that gives each event its experiential significance. Memory organizations give permanence to the record of the lived experience. Rules governing preferences constantly tilt the lived experience in one direction or another. An underlying potential for initiating, organizing, and integrating lived experience emerges, forms its fundamental core, and becomes subjectively "known" as a sense of self. Lived experiences arise from the unfolding of five systems derived from basic motivational needs and the categoric and vitalizing affects triggered during the unfolding. Fundamental unconscious mentation refers to procedural and episodic memories that record the lived experiences, unencoded rules that govern the direction and shape that the experiences take, and the individual-ized sense of self that arises with and coordinates the five systems.

UNCONSCIOUS SYMBOLIC MENTATION

The dual modes of symbolic mentation can be appreciated through contents of a patient's associations, dreams, and the process of patient–analyst interac-tions. The approach to contents has yielded a plethora of organizing fantasies, beginning with Freud's (1905) essays in sexuality, as well as an array of defense mechanisms that regulate the path to awareness of these fantasies. We suggest that symbolic representations of motives are organized during the development of each of the five motivational systems. These representations may be conscious or unconscious. They bear the stamp of the basic schema of each system (Chart 1) and the unique and particular shaping of the individual's lived experience. We agree with those authors who describe unconscious contents variously as fantasies (Arlow, 1969a,b), beliefs (Weiss and Sampson, 1986), ambitions and ideals (Kohut, 1977) and goals and values (Gedo, 1979).

The approach to processes of conscious and unconscious symbolic menta-tion requires three perspectives: intrapsychic, intersubjective, and self-state assessment. The intrapsychic perspective has been the most studied in tradi-tional psychoanalysis through the concepts of conflict, drive-defense inter-play, and compromise formation. Our contribution to the intrapsychic per-spective is to recognize the continuous interplay between motives of each system. This interplay often takes the form of a smooth "competition" between motives for the dominance of awareness. To regard these motiva-tional shifts in attention and functional dominance as "conflict" is experien-tially and conceptually inaccurate. We see our position as in accord with Hartmann's (1964) delineation of conflict-free adaptive functioning. The extensive psychoanalytic knowledge about intrapsychic conflict (Brenner, 1976) would apply only to those situations in which the person responds aversively to potential awareness of a motive triggered in any system. We are, then, interested in an exploration of the whole experience – the aversive response, its effect, and the motive the person is aversive to.

The intersubjective perspective adds to the intrapsychic a conceptualization needed to account for the embeddedness of each individual in his or her surround. As it develops, each intrapsychic system is a motivational-*functional* system in that 1) motivation and function are constantly influenced by an informational flow from internal and external sources (see tachistoscopic studies by Silverman, Lachmann, and Milich, 1982); 2) motivation and function are constantly influenced by the affective ambience perceived to exist internally and externally (see empathy studies by Lichtenberg, Bornstein, and Silver, 1984, and studies of affect by Tomkins, 1962, 1963; Krystal, 1974; Stern, 1985; Emde, 1988a,b; Jones, 1981); and 3) the call for activation of motivation and functioning can arise internally or externally (Fairbairn's concept of an exciting object; Bacal and Newman, 1990).

From the perspective of a self-state assessment, the concept of state refers to an overall affective-cognitive-kinesthetic organization of the self (or in the neonate to an organization of the emergent self). In infant studies, state refers to the innately programmed changes that occur as the neonate passes between states of crying, alert activity, quiet activity, drowsiness, and sleep (REM and non-REM). In each state, the rules that govern motivations, cognition, affects, and behavior vary predictably.

> In each state, the elements are organized into a particular functional pattern. A change in the state of the system alters the way in which information is processed: things are perceived differently, perceptions are differently integrated, and the nature and intensity of the behaviors likely to result are altered during a state change [Hofer, 1990, p. 58].

For example, for early social relatedness and later attachment to be observed and studied, infants must be in an alert active state.

The nonconflictual or ordinary conflictual motivational and functional shifts we have referred to imply a relatively cohesive state of self characterized by the ability to maintain attention and by smooth competition among motivational systems. The state concept has a long history in psychoanalysis dating from Freud's (1893–1895) discussion of hypnoid and dissociative states. Attention to state changes in a patient focuses analytic inquiry on the degree of depersonalization, derealization, and disorientation that accompanies and affects experience.

Kohut (1984), in formulating the concept of self-state dreams, recognized the importance of states as an aspect of subjective experience that was neither

content nor process. Like Kohut, we recognize that the state of the self—
whether cohesive or fragmented, vitalized or depleted—depends on responsiveness to empathy or vulnerability to its lack. A relatively cohesive state of
self is characteristic of neuroses; a depleted state of self is characteristic of many
depressions; a fragmented state of self is characteristic of narcissistic, borderline, and multiple personality disorders.

Horowitz (1979) defined state in the clinical setting

> as a recurrent pattern of experience and of behavior that is both verbal and
> nonverbal. States are commonly recognized during a clinical interview because
> of changes in facial expression, intonation and inflection in speech, focus and
> content of verbal reports, degree of self reflective awareness, general arousal,
> shifts in degree and nature of empathy, and other communicative qualities. The
> information that tells the observer, or the subject, that this is a recurrence of a
> familiar state is not confined to any one system, but is a configuration of
> information in multiple systems. That is why an abstract definition of states
> cannot be precise. Yet the states of a particular person are as easy to recognize in
> everyday life as the change of atmosphere in a drama, from cheerful sunlight to
> thunder and lightening, the shifts of configuration in rhythm, harmony, timber,
> and tonality in music, or the mood of color, hue, texture, form, and content in
> a painting.
>
> Each person has many states. State analysis requires selection of those that
> are most relevant. It also means that the natural flow of behavior and experience
> must be somewhat artificially segmented into episodes defined by differences in
> quality [p. 31].

What occurs when the state of self is markedly altered? Contemporary
clinicians are frequently confronted by patients (victims of sexual and physical
abuse, concentration camp survivors, Viet Nam veterans) who have suffered
the kind of trauma that produces state changes that profoundly affect the
organization of their motivation. In more cohesive self-states these patients
are able to organize and reveal experiences and fantasies reflective of their
unconscious symbolic mentation and have a capacity for self-exploration. As
these patients, however, attempt to gain access to problems that lie at the heart
of their traumatic experiences, they are at risk. The fragmented state may be
revived in flashbacks, with attendant frightening and often paralyzing affective disruption. The intrapsychic and intersubjective perspectives, as ordinarily conceptualized, no longer apply. The patient may feel flooded by
strong affects and withdraw, dissociate, or relive the trauma. When a patient
is in a toxic state from drugs or from malnutrition resulting from severe
anorexia or organic disorders, the dysfunction affects the ability of the conscious and unconscious symbolic mentation to organize motivation in an
ordinary manner. We must reconsider the aligning of motivation by unconscious symbolic mentation when parents who were themselves abused as
children enter a state of blindly insensitive abuse of their children. A marked

alteration of state alerts us to the need to map out the symbolic processes that occur in severe disruption–restoration sequences, suicidal or homicidal numbness, traumatic states, toxic states, multiple personality disorders, and psychoses.

We believe that the concept of a model scene integrates knowledge of both contents and process. Contents are contained in the idea of "scene," with its analogy to the theater and its unities of time, place, and characters. These scenes are "models" in that they reflect influential repetitive motivational organizations of experience. The contents are encoded as symbolic representations of affect-laden memories, fantasies, and beliefs. The process aspect of unconscious mentation enters into model-scene construction in that the work 1) focuses on an empathic entry into the analysand's state of mind and struggles between opposing motives and calls for functioning; 2) involves the intersubjective influence of empathic ambience, shared exploratory motivation, and the recognition and struggle with aversive motives as they affect the imaginative nature of the associative flow; and 3) requires a constant sensitivity to state, in the constructions of the sources of disruptions that occur during the analysis and of those disruptions from traumas, toxic states, and psychotic episodes in the past. The work with model scenes of altered states has a different contextual shape, moving back and forth between shared understanding and unshared reliving. Constant sensitivity is needed to appreciate the danger of the fragmented or depleted self-state's recurring, not as a revenant state, but as a new traumatic state. Thus, the joint work of forming and reforming a model scene during analysis provides a remarkable mirror and analog of dynamic symbolic unconscious mentation because both evidence shifting motivation, plastic imagery, intersubjective engagement, and state-change sensitivity.

In the clinical example of unconscious symbolic mentation that follows we use a model scene to illustrate our interest specifically in the assessment of state. In a subsequent chapter we will emphasize the role of intrapsychic and intersubjective dimensions in organizing model scenes derived from the five motivational systems.

Miss K

Miss K began psychoanalytic psychotherapy at age 28 after a suicide attempt. She had tried to kill herself when her boyfriend flirted with another woman. The intensity of her reaction to what she described as a relatively minor occurrence meant to her that she was "in very bad shape." Only after several years of treatment did it become clear that the suicide attempt, which involved taking all the pills in her medicine cabinet, had proceeded as though she were "watching her actions from a bird's eye view from a corner of the room." She described observing herself take the pills with a detached, uncomprehending attitude. As her therapy progressed, both she and her analyst recognized that her state of detached uncomprehension frequently recurred both during sessions and in her life.

Central unconscious fantasies and beliefs of Miss K's inner world can be conceptualized along oedipal conflictual lines. Memories of overhearing her parents fight amid accusations of infidelity, and with her sympathies tilting toward her father, could be dynamically linked to guilt over wishes to eliminate her oedipal rival. In subsequent explorations of this theme, Miss K's fear that she would appear too powerful and rivet the attention of others to herself was understood as an important source motivating her social seclusion and avoidance of competitive situations. None of these intrapsychic and intersubjectively organized themes, however, was amenable to analytic exploration as long as her self-cohesion was severely depleted, as manifested in her depersonalized state.

Miss K suffered from severe sleep disturbances from as early as about age five. The pattern began during the nightly fights between her parents but continued after the parents' fights ceased. Her parents attempted to solve her sleep problem by putting her in her room immediately after supper so that she could try to get to sleep early. She recalled years of being confined in her room and looking out the window, watching neighborhood children play. She felt excluded and envious. Isolated and frustrated, simmering with rage, she began to draw on the walls of her room. These creative, exploratory, assertive efforts were quickly abandoned when she was punished. She was locked in her room and given a bottle of cleaning fluid to clean the walls. Later, she was presented with a paint set, but she felt too resentful toward her parents to use it. She acknowledged in her session, though, that she would have liked to use it.

Miss K's banishment and "voluntary confinement" to her room became a central issue in Miss K's treatment. In the context of discussing the memories, she dreamed of a "barren countryside." In association she recalled that when she looked out of her bedroom window, she believed that she saw cars go by without drivers. We inferred that she had felt "aimless" and that she may have wished that someone in her family would take control.

The memory of standing in her room and looking out at life through her window was used by analyst and patient as a model scene from which individually and together they were able to gather together a number of salient issues. Miss K experienced herself apart from her argumentative family, and in this isolated state she felt safe. Then and now she feared that she might overpower others and be an object of envy. She felt equally endangered by potential expressions of helplessness, frustration, and feeling out of control. She concretized these dangers in her illusion of the driverless cars.

Miss K's state of detached inaccessibility repeated her experience of being confined in her room. From it she looked out through a closed window. The feeling of being outside of experience or feeling that she was behind a glass in social situations became understandable. She recalled two neighborhood children, a boy and a girl, at play while she was confined behind her window. This memory helped clarify a current, recurring fantasy. She imagined that her boyfriend would be a more suitable partner to another girl, a friend of hers. She had to stop herself from suggesting to them that they get together. She wondered if she was trying to re-create her "street scene" and actualize her sense of being all alone and helpless.

Re-creating various forms of the remembered experience in her room provided for Miss K and her analyst the emotion-laden content for the construction of a model scene that helped in understanding and relieving her depersonalized state. The transference at this time contained two aspects of the model scene. First, the analytic dialogue gradually provided her with a sense of the analyst's presence in counteracting her sense of being in the barren room even when she felt dissociated. In turn, this extended to her rerepresented childhood room and diminished the sense of isolation, aimlessness, and lack of vitality that was associated with her experience there. Increased vitality, however, opened her to the danger of oedipal triumphs, triggering an aversive "defensive" withdrawal back to her room. Recognition of this sequence and the motives involved could now be articulated, further diminishing her experience of isolation. Second, she reacted to many of the analyst's comments as she had to the paint set her parents had given her. She spitefully refused to use them. Exploration of this theme led to an unexpected development. For the first time in her treatment, by then in its third year, she began to respond to the analyst as a trusted, helpful advisor whose opinions about aspects of her social life and other personal matters would be welcomed. Both she and her analyst experienced the change in attitude as indicating a significant diminution of her detached, depersonalized state.

The delineation of a model scene by Miss K and her analyst provided access to symbolic unconscious and conscious wishes, thoughts, and feelings associated with her confinement in the barren room. The analytic work that ensued explored the intrapsychic and intersubjective dimensions of her psychopathology and, specifically, opened the way for empathic entry into her dominant, depersonalized state. The analyst approached her unconscious mentation by remaining constantly attuned to her state of detachment, its crescendos and decrescendos, both in the construction of the sources of disruptions that occurred during the analysis and the disruptions that were residues of past states.

Our exploration of dynamic unconscious activity has prompted us to distinguish a fundamental (presymbolic) unconscious mentation and an unconscious symbolic mentation. In both fundamental and symbolic unconscious mentation, the five motivational systems compete and collaborate.

During the first 18 months, fundamental unconscious mentation comprises procedural and episodic memories of lived experience that are encoded in accordance with innate uncoded pattern regulators (that is, rules by which patterns of experience and choice are organized). Unconscious symbolic mentation organizes motivation and experience in the complex forms of dual modes of primary- and secondary-process representation. After myelinization of the frontal hemispheres, lived experience is both shaped by and encoded by the plastic forms that language and other symbol systems (music, mathematics) permit. This change is evidenced by imaginative symbolic play, fantasies, dream contents, and successive phases of preoperational and operational thought.

6 ————————

The Path to Awareness

In this chapter, we focus on the internal dialogue–monologue of analysand and analyst during the analytic exchange. The path to awareness is understood against a background that recognizes the fluidity between conscious and unconscious mentation and the preeminence of exploratory-assertive motivations for both participants. To the extent that either analysand and analyst are averse to expressions of problems in any motivational system of the analysand, the path to awareness is obstructed for both participants.

What governs the path to awareness in infant, child, and adult? We believe that two factors interdigitate to determine the path to awareness: first, the gradient of awareness possible due to maturation; and, second, shifting dominance among motivational systems. A gradient of awareness (Lichtenberg, 1983a, 1989a) is hypothesized for the neonate that begins with perception of distant stimuli and internal sensation. At this stage, perception probably has a kaleidoscopic quality punctuated by moments of more defined focus. These moments build toward an emerging sense of self (Stern, 1985). With each month of life, especially at two and six months, the sensorium becomes clearer, alertness to both external and internal stimuli increases, and focal awareness predominates over a kaleidoscopic turn on-turn off. The infant directs attention on the basis of need and preferences. Guided by an appreciation of consequences, the core self as agent consolidates.

A second gradient of awareness occurs at nine months, when the more mobile infant looks to mother's facial expression to gain reliable information about approval–disapproval, safety–danger, shared agenda–opposing agenda. From this time on, a priority in awareness is given to matching the direction of change of emotional states between infant and caregiver (Beebe and Stern, 1977). At this point, the way an infant experiences an empathic fit probably undergoes change. Before nine months, the awareness of empathic fit would have been based on the caregiver's providing concrete responses appropriate to the infant's needs as these reflected dominant motivations (for example, feeding, "conversation," disengagement, soothing). After nine months, the infant scans the caregiver's face for an indication of emotional concurrence as well as concurrence of the response to the baby's need. With each gradient of awareness, infants and toddlers develop increasingly subtle skills in negotiations with others as the patterns in each motivational system become more complex.

A third gradient of awareness occurs at 18 months with the maturation of right and left frontal cortices and higher associational pathways. The toddler's awareness opens to processing information through the modes of symbolic representation that Freud discovered in dream analysis – primary and secondary process. The two-, three-, and four-year-old's capacity for symbolic internal and external communication through words and symbolic action in play is further enriched by a fourth gradient: self-reflective awareness. Children of five and six coordinate their experiences by an awareness of self through a narrative of who they are, who they were, and something of their expectations (when I grow up, I will marry you, mommy). Self-reflectiveness, and with it an awareness of wishfulness, pride, and guilt, are all enhanced by the consolidation of narrative creation. A further gradient of awareness arises progressively as the oedipal and latency child, adolescent, and adult check self-identification against desire on one side and actuality on the other in self-reflective thought. This process is best observed in the inner monologue–dialogue of waking thoughts.

In a view that takes a brain-centered informational approach to the gradients of awareness we propose, Olds (1992) correlates a hierarchical series of planes of consciousness with neurobiological levels. First, the brain stem contains two activating systems: one, mediated by norepinephrine, triggers basic states of arousal and organizes states of attention through the reticular activating system; the other, the cholinergic system, activates the brain, as in REM sleep, without generating alertness. At a higher level, the hypothalamus, thalamus, and basal ganglia serve as a general awareness system. Olds writes, "The brain centers at this level are necessary for an integrated but unfocused sense of being in the world, along with a general affective sense of one's condition" (p. 430). The most advanced capability of consciousness involves a sense of self and requires maturation of the cerebral cortex. The self "exists on conscious and unconscious levels, integrating proprioception sensation and affects, most of which is unconscious . . . into a central entity which becomes a center of *significance* and mediates the importance of all experiences" (p. 432). Olds adds that "consciousness involves re-representing percepts and memories selected from the brain's vast store house" (p. 432). A sense of self "involves re-representing those signs which refer to the individual as an object and as a center of significance" (p. 432).

THE SHIFTING OF DOMINANCE

A relatively clear dominance of one or another motivational system based on need can be observed in infants. Needs for nutrition, sleep, elimination, temperature regulation and proprioceptive stimulation may dominate infants' awareness and call the caregiver to assist in regulating physiological requirements. Infants respond to a caregiver's face by making eye contact, widening the mouth and eyes, moving arms and feet, and vocalizing, all indications of the need for attachment responses. Infants' visual and auditory focusing on an object and their efforts to manipulate it tactually and orally indicate the need for exploration and assertion. Similarly, crying, distress, anger, and withdrawal indicate aversive signaling; sensually enjoyable pleasure-sucking, rocking, and stroking indicate the need for sensual enjoyment. Our assumption is that motivational systems become organized from memory encoding of these experiences of distinct dominance of need amplified by affects that register bodily comforts; intimacy pleasure; interest, efficacy and competence pleasure; anger, distress, sadness and fear; or sensual enjoyment. When dominance of the basic need of each system recurs, the encoded episodic memories of the subsequent events are generalized with the salient features abstracted (see Stern's, 1985, RIGs). A recurrence of the need and the pattern of response will be experienced as familiarity. Slight variation of the pattern will arouse interest, whereas marked variance can be a breach of what the child expects and consequently arouse aversion.

These basic features of motivational systems and the experience of dominance of need amplified by affect continue throughout life, but with each gradient experiences become more complex. For example, once awareness of the caregiver's affective expression becomes a focus for awareness, the shadow of the "other" hangs over all experience in each system, not only attachment. The experience becomes one of intersubjectivity rather than interaction, although, throughout, a dynamic tension exists between these two modes. With intersubjectivity as a major factor governing the path to awareness, the significance of experiences of affirmation, like-mindedness, and idealization become solidly established as dominant during attachment experiences and a persistent if latent subset experience when other motivations predominate.

The greatest gradient for complexity occurs with the dual modes of symbolic representation (Holt, 1967, 1976; McLaughlin, 1978; McKinnon, 1979; Noy, 1979; Fosshage, 1983; Lichtenberg, 1983a; Dorpat, 1990; Bucci, 1992). The plasticity of the dual modes promotes the blurring of distinctions. Now, for example, a cigar can be a cigar, that is, a wrapped plant smoked by adults for stimulus regulation derived from the smoking effluence and chemical substance it emits. But sometimes a cigar may be experienced as though it were an attractive or repellent fecal mass implicated in conflicts about bowel regulation or as though it were a penis being sucked for sexual excitement. Analogy and metaphor, collapsing of the unities of time, space, and person make it possible to enrich or complicate the awareness of dominance of any one system by conflating its motivation with the wishes and desires of another.

AWARENESS DURING THE ANALYTIC EXCHANGE

For both analysand and analyst, complex factors govern what it is that has the experiential quality of awareness at any moment during the analytic exchange. A factor commonly described is the cognitive-affective state of the analysand referred to as regression. We feel the term is confusing because of its many meanings (Stolorow and Lachmann, 1980) and is inaccurate when used as a synonym for a childlike state. Rather than slipping back to the cognitive-affective state characteristic of a child, the optimal state of an analysand is a particular mode of attentiveness available to an adult only after practice. This optimal state of attentiveness is difficult to induce in a child more than momentarily and requires the activity of play as a means of expression.

We recognize three characteristics of the cognitive-affective state of the adult. First, analysands are more apt to be both in touch with a broad array of needs, wishes, and desires and more tolerant of that recognition than they are ordinarily during their active daily life. This cognitive-affective state coincides in important respects with Bucci's (1992) description of the patient's turning inward to delve within his private representations to capture nonverbal material that has been incubating. This includes imagery in all sensory modalities and representations of motor activity and autonomic, visceral, and somatic experience. Especially sought in this state are representations of affects. The speech patterns include pauses, repetitions, and searching "ers."

Second, analysands are more apt to monitor their internal monologue–dialogue that accompanies and supplies much of the contents of "freer" associations. This cognitive-affective state coincides with Bucci's description of a referential process in which more diffuse bits and fragments of private nonverbal and partially verbal experience are linked with the communicative verbal code. The patient embeds his or her generalized emotions in the specific details of a narrative. The patient establishes the time-and-place setting and introduces rich detail about events. Bucci notes that bringing together verbal and nonverbal experience through the specific details of an event replayed in the patient's mind or an event in the session facilitates surprise and new connections.

Third, analysands in the course of analysis become exquisitely sensitive to the context of the analysis itself, so that they are continuously blending the cognitive and affective actuality of the situation, including the analyst's verbal and nonverbal contributions, with their inner constructions (Gill and Hoffman, 1982). Because the needs, wishes, and desires are being experienced now, the internal monologue–dialogue is immediate, and the context is current, the analysand's past comes to us embedded in the present, not "regressed to." As we have indicated, we use the technique of constructing model scenes to bring those controlling and regulating experiences of the past out of their shadowy figure-ground embeddedness into the present.

What is the analyst's state of mind that potentiates the ability to listen empathically and participate in the construction of model scenes? Again, we reject the definition of regression as a return to childhood and emphasize the important parallels between the cognitive-affective states of analysand and analyst. First, analysts must be sensitive to their own needs, wishes, and desires if they are to sense fully into those emerging in the analysand; at the same time, analysts must maintain as a dominant motive their need for exploration and assertion. Second, an analyst monitors his or her own monologue–dialogue, which is filled with contents related to the experiences the patient is describing, the analyst's linkages of these experiences to knowledge of the past, and the analyst's reflections on his or her own responses and the meanings ascribed to what the patient is conveying. Third, an analyst must share with the analysand an alertness to the context, both situational and affective, in which the analysis takes place; or many transference experiences and role enactments will be unrecognized. Three characteristics of the analysand's and analyst's optimal state of mind–attentiveness to need, attention to the inner monologue–dialogue, and sensitivity to context–unfold in an ongoing analysis to affect the path to awareness.

If either analyst or patient is experiencing a strong basic need, the motivational system built around that need will be dominant. A patient who has recently suffered a loss may have a need for an attachment experience of confirmation of his sense of loss and desire for sympathy and comfort. An analytic colleague who had recently undergone a second life-threatening illness and reparative surgery chose not to return to work until completely certain of his recovery. He realized from prior experience that his illness and absence triggered associations from his patients ranging from fearful concerns of abandonment to intense antagonism and death wishes. These, in turn, pulled him from the usual dominance of exploratory motives to self-preoccupations and aversive withdrawal or anger.

At any moment, wishes and desires, values, beliefs, and ideals characteristic of the patient's immediate motivational focus press for expression. When considering the fate of these thoughts, fantasies, and affects with respect to awareness, we mean many things. For example, in the inner monologue–dialogue of a patient who has been rejected in love, his awareness may be limited to a nameless, formless sense of discontent and restlessness, or he may be fully aware of being puzzled and confused about how to handle the rejection. The determining feature might be the patient's past. His experiences with a lover's rejection at any previous time (adolescence, oedipal period) or a more general problem with nonromantically felt rejection may have led him to deal with the aversiveness of rejection by an aversiveness to its recognition (repression, isolation, disavowal).

The determining feature may be the patient's sense of the analyst's response. If he assumes that the analyst will blame him for the rejection, or be disappointed with him for once again failing, or be patronizing about his foibles, he may block his own awareness or, if fully aware, block expressiveness. The Sandlers (1984) called attention to the patient's concern about the analyst's response in their 3-box theory, based on Freud's concept of a censorship between the preconscious and the conscious as well as one between the unconscious and the preconscious: "The censorship which represses the present unconscious has as . . . its fundamental orientation . . . the avoidance of shame, embarrassment and humiliation" (p. 379). We agree with the Sandlers' emphasis on the fear or expectation of shame, embarrassment, and humiliation as the response of the analyst. This conforms with self psychology's focus on the patient's wish for affirmation and confirmation and fear of the opposite. A broader view of motivation would include the feared triggering of undesired affects in any motivational system.

Blocking the expression of verbalized associations, whether total suppression or a selective deceptive rendering, in itself has an impact on both patient and analyst. By limiting their expression, patients also limit the scope of awareness since framing a communication organizes more amorphous psychic contents into secondary process and opens the verbalized material to reflective awareness. The reflective awareness, whether spontaneous or at the encouragement of the analyst, provides the optimal psychic state for the fullest recognition of meaning.

Before turning to the analyst, we will complete this survey of the patient's path to awareness. We have said patients' awareness can be recognized in their inner monologues, their expressiveness, and their self-reflections. But patients express more than they are aware of (McLaughlin, 1982). Their expressions, as they affect both patient and analyst, include behavioral elements determined by procedural memory. For example, a patient's greeting may convey warmth and ease, or coldness and tension, or hauteur and standoffishness; the patient's posture on the couch, settling in or readiness to bolt; his speech pattern, hesitance, confiding, or filling every moment with chatter. All of this may be outside the patient's awareness. A patient who thought of herself as friendly and open to people could not understand the uncomfortable reaction of others. While her manner and intention were understood by her analyst as friendly, he came to understand that her lack of eye contact when she greeted people and her characteristic style of holding her arms at her sides with fingers clenched contained the unconscious procedural memory of her early struggle with her mother.

Analysts, too, express in behavior aspects of procedural memory – slow thoughtfulness, cautious shyness, open warmth, youthful enthusiasm, the tiredness of age or illness, austerity of expression, humor, sarcasm, or avuncular protectiveness. Moreover, analysts vary considerably in the fullness of their awareness of their postural and gestural communication, especially when these contain kernels of early identifications consolidated during training analyses with analysts who themselves never brought either their own or their candidates' procedural proclivities into the flow of associations. Furthermore, an analyst has his own inner monologue–dialogue through which he attempts to open himself to the patient's communications by focusing his attention on the patient's inner experience. Following the patient's associative flow, the analyst becomes aware of how he is being experienced by the patient. Viewing themselves through their patients' eyes, analysts often have the opportunity to expand their awareness of their own contributions to the analytic exchange. In Chapter 10, we offer a technique for utilizing patient's attributions of the analyst's attitudes and values. At times, an analyst may be averse to this expansion of self-awareness. He may attribute the patient's reflection on him as transference, projection, or both rather than a combination (compromise formation) of varying proportions of multiple determinants, including the actuality of the analyst's being.

Another stream of associations competes for the analyst's awareness during the therapeutic exchange. The source of this competing stream arises from motivations that pull at the analyst from sources of a personal nature. For example, an analyst attempting to sense into a patient's expression of how much she loves and wants to be with her children may be distracted by his desire to get the patient to question her inclination to control the children as she herself had been controlled. The potential for the analyst to be distracted by his wish to have the patient work on what he perceives to be her problematic attachment to her children is particularly likely to occur if the analyst finds himself identifying with the children on the basis of his own mother's controlling behavior toward him. While trying to maintain an empathic focus, the analyst may be affected by a physiological pull of hunger or sleep, a sexual fantasy, or the sudden awareness of a phone call he forgot to make. A flicker of recognition of the distracted state is often sufficient to reorient the analyst to an optimal listening stance. An analyst unable to restore empathic listening will benefit from a consideration of the meaning of his associations. Although we usually regard an interference with optimal attentiveness as a countertransference failing, the timing and nature of the lapse and the specific associational flow after an examination can reveal significant information that the analyst is processing (often in a primary-process mode) about the exchange with the patient (Jacobs, 1971). Such reflective awareness may open in the analyst a channel of awareness to a model scene, frequently one that explains a difficult to recognize role engagement in which he was an unconscious partner (see Chapter 2 for an example).

Much of what we have said about the analyst's and analysand's path to awareness in the analytic exchange restates long-familiar conceptions. Self psychology makes specific contributions to the understanding of blocks to the path of awareness of each partner. Kohut (1971, 1977, 1984) recognized what has come to be known as the disruption–restoration sequence (Wolf, 1988). Our understanding of this sequence is based on the observation that patients are able to associate more or less freely with a self-assertive vitality when they experience themselves to be listened to in a supportive, empathic ambience. When they experience an empathic failure, this openness to their inner world and to its free expression alters as their self-cohesion is threatened, depleted, or fragmented. The perceived empathic failure may or may not be the result of a technical error or a countertransference disturbance. All transferences of empathic failures of the past can emerge as a current experience of failed responsiveness in the analytic exchange when triggered by minor, even insignificant, cues (Lichtenberg, 1990).

Self psychology regards the occurrence of many disruptive episodes during an ongoing analysis not as undesirable regressions or unwelcome defensive postures, but as positive indications that the path to awareness of long-held needs and longings is becoming open to analytic work. The patient has established the degree of trust necessary to reopen old psychic wounds. Thus, the analyst, unlike prior or present contributors to empathic failure, must be sensitive to a full appreciation of the patient's experience and acknowledge verbally the altered affective and cognitive state. Gradually, the recognition of the disturbed state of being, as seen from the patient's point of view, encourages self-righting, that is, a return of a sense of cohesive intactness and openness to an exploratory motivation. The key concept in this type of restoration based on analytic work rather than nonspecific recovery factors such as the passage of time or a distracting event, is acknowledgment of *the patient's point of view* of the source of the disruption.

Generally, because of the sensitivity of both analyst and analysand to events and affects occurring in the analytic exchange, the analyst may recognize his contribution to the disruption as experienced by the patient. The analysts' acknowledgment of his contribution often exerts a powerful thrust toward self-righting that suggests more motivational power than solely exploratory enrichment. Wolf (personal communication) suggests that analysands experience a sense of effectiveness and competence in being able to influence their analysts to recognize responsibility. This sense of being influential may have been lacking when disruptions occurred with their caregivers. When analysands feel that they have contributed to having their analysts see an experience "their way," they may be more open to expansion of their perspective. Sensing this increased openness, analysts feel themselves and their analysands moving back together and able to share an imaginary "observational platform" (Lichtenberg, 1981b, 1983a) from which both can exchange their awarenesses. Bucci (1992) describes this as a time for collaborative work through the use of logical processes of differentiating, generalizing, forming categories, and tracing implications. This actual "analyzing" facilitates the reorganization necessary for change in the patient's emotional makeup. Collaborative work on the imaginary observational platform often permits the construction of an organizing unconscious fantasy, an unconscious belief, or, on a broader scale, a model scene that provides an integrative explanation for the experience of the disruption. Now, with the analyst's encouragement, insight into the source of the disturbance not only will complete the restoration of self vitality but also will further understanding of the patient's vulnerability. The path to awareness in the form of freer associations has not only been restored but expanded.

A disruption–restoration sequence, restricted in intensity, may occur to the analyst as well. Bacal (1985) has noted that in their overall case management, analysts aim for optimal responsiveness rather than optimal frustration, as Kohut advocated, or optimal gratification, as self psychologists are often accused of attempting to achieve. In the clinical exchange itself, each analyst develops a sense of his or her own optimal "counterresponsiveness"; that is, the analyst develops an optimal mode of applying the empathic mode of perception by *following* the lead of the patient so as to see things from the patient's point of view. By "counter" we mean parallel, not opposing, responses. Once analysts recognize their optimal parallel responsiveness, they are able to monitor a disruption in their listening stance. We speak of optimal parallel responsiveness as centered on the patient's state of mind but recognize that analysts also attend to both their inner state and their reactions to their patients' communications. Their reactions are highly individualistic–some largely sensory imagery, some more verbally organized thoughts such as "He is getting at his problem with his attachment to his wife"; "She is protesting the lack of opportunity to be creative at her work"; "He is illustrating aversive withdrawal rather than talking about it."

Just as patients experience disruptions in their sense of being empathically understood, analysts experience disruptions in their sense of being optimally counterresponsive. The two situations are often similar in their disruptiveness, but analysts may sometimes be able to use the experience to open awareness to previously unrecognized forms of intersubjective relatedness. When analysts become aware of a disruption in their analysand-centered optimal listening stance and then return to a state of alertness, their introspective reflection may reveal the triggering source. Especially when the source is found to be a change of affect state that has occurred imperceptibly in the patient—for example, one that may take the form of the patient's voice and content becoming monotonous—the analyst's identification of the source will itself serve to restore his sense of understanding. With his return to an optimal listening stance, the analyst is now prepared to help open the patient's path to awareness of the patient's altered state, which unrecognized, triggered the analyst's disruption.

In summary, free access to awareness in analysis depends on a shared purpose derived from exploratory-assertive motivation, a sense of some urgency on the part of the patient to express a problem in any motivational system, and the extent of aversiveness to that expression on the part of either partner.

THE EVER-SHIFTING SURFACE

In his papers on technique, Freud completed his spatial metaphor about the deep unconscious by defining a "surface": "the analyst should always be aware of the surface of the patient's mind at any given moment. . . . he should know what complexes and resistances are active in him at the time and what conscious reaction to them will govern his behavior" (Freud, 1911, p. 92). And the analyst "contents himself with studying whatever is present for the time being on the surface of the patient's mind, and he employs the art of interpretation mainly for the purpose of recognizing the resistances which appear there, and making them conscious to the patient" (Freud, 1914, p. 147). We believe that Freud's advice has often been disregarded. In conferences and reports of supervision, analysts admonish one another by saying, "But you aren't interpreting the unconscious" or "That's not analysis; that's psychotherapy. You are merely addressing the patient's conscious."

In our view, addressing the patient's conscious is appropriate for both analysis and exploratory psychotherapy. Our position is based on our understanding of the nature of the surface. When patients' associations bring up an area for exploration, such associations constitute the extent of safe-to-express information available to them at that moment. The goal is to expand the extent of that information. We aim especially to bring into awareness the fullest affective experience possible so that these experiences will be exposed to reflective consideration with interpretative help. This goal commits analysts to stay with their patients wherever they are at the moment and follow them where they go, especially noting the consequences of their interpretative efforts (Chapter 7). Our hypothesis is that as the path to awareness opens in the moment-to-moment exchange and the range of thoughts and feelings experienced expands, the previously "deeper" psychic contents become the surface. Three possibilities may occur. Awareness continues to expand, bringing more "depth" to the surface. The range of safe-to-express narrows; an aversive motive dominates; a disruption may or may not occur. But in any event a new task faces both analyst and patient. The motivational area previously under consideration ceases to be dominant; the work with it ceases for the moment; and a new motivation begins to occupy the surface, hopefully to expand (it is hoped) and bring new information from depth to surface.

What, then, does "depth" mean? In practical terms, depth means distance from actual or potential awareness. Under this definition, psychic phenomena coded in symbolic representations are actually or potentially near to awareness, depending on the strength of the motivational pressure for expression and the relative sense of safeness-to-express. Psychic phenomena that have been encoded only as procedural memory, unless recoded as symbolic representations, are remote from awareness but influence expression. Psychic phenomena based on lived experience that occurred prior to encoding by the dual modes of symbolic representation but that were encoded as episodic memories are generally remote from awareness but potentially open to conceptualization usually as bodily or sensory experience. Finally, psychic phenomena that characterize rules governing the unfolding of experience in each motivational system are essentially unavailable to experience.

Confusion arises when "depth" is equated with either primary-process encoding or with childhood as the time of origination. When an analyst, referring to associations buttressed by dream imagery, interprets "You want to suck your father's [or my] penis," the interpretation is not intrinsically any deeper than the analyst's suggesting, "You want to get something from your father (or me) by whatever means it takes." The patient may be equally close to or far from opening the path to his awareness of a wish articulated in either phrasing. In conventional conversation, the first is more shocking; but if analyst and patient have become accustomed to speaking in terms more expressive of primary process, one phrasing can communicate by analogy or metaphor what the other, more secondary-process phrasing communicates less graphically. If the wish is to experience sexual excitement in a particular way, the first phrasing is precise, the second discursive. If the patient's wish is to have an intimate relationship with his father regardless of the indignity he believes is involved, either phrasing may be equally telling. If the wish is to obtain from his father strength or masculinity, believed not to be forthcoming willingly but available only by taking it, either phrasing might alert the patient to be more expressive of his desire.

The misconception that a primary-process organization of psychic contents is early or deeper is based on the false surmise that before secondary process is possible infants must experience life along the lines of wish-fulfillment distortions. Studies of neonates and infants indicate that whereas before symbolic representation infants have marked cognitive limitations, they are faithful encoders of their lived experience (Lichtenberg, 1983a, 1989a; Stern, 1985). Moreover, once symbolic representation occurs in both modes at 18 months, all experience is processed in both modes continuously. The motivations in some systems are more readily expressed in gestural, affective, action modes; the motivations in other systems, more in lexically coherent verbal modes. We might assume that an expression of bodily functioning or of a desire for sexual excitement would be more readily brought to the surface by expressing the nature of the desire in gesture, movement, or language closer to primary process; but the brain will process it in both modes automatically (that is in both right and left frontal cortices and across associational paths). Thus we may question the premise that fantasies are "deeper" than thoughts expressed in more logical form. We suggest instead that fantasies are simply another mode of organizing psychic contents. If the contents expressed in primary-process modes are more threatening, they will be less available to awareness, but at other times fantasies, particularly daydreams, will be more richly expressive and thus readily available to awareness.

The assumption that earlier experiences—either oedipal or earlier—are "deeper" (i.e., less accessible to awareness) is based on the reasonable assumption that, especially in early life, memory is less well organized in narrative continuities. But another factor must be considered: most early experiences of considerable affective intensity recur in new form in each later period and are transformed into the modalities of that later epoch. Often the earlier and later experiences become telescoped (Chapter 2) so that for the purpose of openness to awareness it is not significant whether an event being remembered or reconstructed occurred during childhood, latency, adolescence, or later. An early experience may be more relevant to the immediate context of the analysis, and it may furnish more sense of causative conviction, but it is not deeper.

All that we have described about continuities, transformation, and the telescoping of experiences providing information that patients can slowly shift toward the surface applies to experiences that over time tax and some-times overtax the organizing and integrating capacities of the self. Either for sudden trauma, such as a car accident, the shocking, unexpected death of a parent or child, or physical or sexual abuse or for prolonged trauma, such as the terror of feeling unprotected for months in a battle zone or the horrors suffered by hostages and victims of the Holocaust, depth has little or nothing to do with early or late occurrence. The problems caused by trauma are the result of the organizing and integrating capacities of the self becoming para-lyzed (Dowling, 1982). Coding, in the form of symbolic representation, is fragmented and incomplete; affective experience may be either frozen or overwhelming and is generally dissociated from the fragments of thoughts. The path to awareness is determined not only by the usual sense of safeness-to-express based on the assumed level of receptivity of the analyst but also by safeness-to-experience. Safeness-to-experience is grounded in an existential fear that bringing any aspect of the traumatic state into awareness will lead to an irretrievable fragmentation of self-cohesion. Analysts' usual encouragement to patients to expand their awareness must be tempered with a commitment to assist in sharing or containing (Bion, 1959) the threatening affect state and helping to integrate the fragments into organized sequences.

Finally, to return to Freud's recommendations about the surface, we want to consider his advice to recognize the resistances and make them conscious through interpretation. We believe that a tendency has developed to presume resistance almost regardless of patients' efforts to express their associations. If patients speak of the present, we say they are defending against a "deeper" issue in the past; if they speak of the past, we say they are defending against the present. If patients speak of their boss, they are defending against a "deeper" issue in the transference; if they speak of the analyst, they are defending against a parent. This preoccupation with interpreting a presumed resistance based on displacement all too often leads not to opening the path to awareness of a deeper, defended-against content, but to obstructing the broadening and deepening of awareness of the subject matter that was introduced by the patient for exploration. Our approach is to encourage patients to expand the venue of time, place, and person they have selected. Repeated confirming clinical experience leads us to conclude that with expansion the changing surface will come to include the relevant links to other times, settings, and people. We regard resistance in a different light than Freud did. We consider resistance to be a manifestation of an aversive motivational system. Viewed in this way, an indication that patients are antagonistic or withdrawing, suppressing or repressing, using isolation, denial, or disavowal, or projecting attributions is not regarded as an obstacle to be surmounted in order to get to something deeper, but as an expression of aversive motives that require extensive exploration.

Therapeutic Implications

The shifting surface of consciousness is impinged upon by three types of affectively significant information:

1. Presymbolic procedural patterns that have not been symbolically encoded and affective expressive patterns that are poorly encoded. These appear

in awareness or potential awareness as repetitive behavior patterns, enactments, facial expressions, and autonomic nervous system responses.

2. Mood states in which the principal or only possible motive is expressive. Examples are a child having a tantrum, an adult in a narcissistic rage, a person in mourning or excited by a success.

3. Communicative states where affect and thought can be given verbal expression in mixtures of primary and secondary process and where *self-reflectiveness (introspection) is possible.*

The approach to each form of information must be responsive to the form of encoding. Unencoded information requires the analyst to go outside the empathic mode and help to identify the nature of the experience (as in Gedo's, 1979, *Beyond Interpretation*)–only then can self-righting occur.

Mood states where affect expression is intense require the analyst to provide a steady, responsive (uninterpretative) "container" (Bion, 1959), a holding environment (Winnicott, 1956), or empathic mirroring (Kohut, 1971). This kind of environment promotes self-righting as the analyst's concerned, attuned, but well-regulated affect provides a calming selfobject experience. Drive theorists and self psychologists differ most about the approach and meaning of this mode. Drive theorists value intense affective experiences as indicative of penetrating to deep, regressive, primitive fantasies expressive of murderous rage or infantile sexuality. Self psychologists, on the other hand, regard states of intense rage, panic, excitement, and depression as best understood in relation to an experience of a failure of empathic support. Self psychology does not regard such intense affects as the result of a correct interpretation's "liberating" drive energy either expressed as affect or vigorously defended against as in a so-called negative therapeutic reaction. But in labeling the affects, associations, and behaviors that occur during these disruptive states as "fragmentation products," self psychology may be failing to recognize that the mood state and disruptive contents are attempts to achieve vitalization through a selfobject experience that temporarily restores cohesion, but frequently at the cost of further disorganization. The patterns of these briefly vitalizing affect states and behaviors have their own history and development (see Chapter 8). The path to awareness of these short-term efforts at self-restoration has become opened to our sharing but cannot be trod until self-righting has occurred.

Communicative states where self-reflectiveness is possible require the analyst to promote detailed exploration of the meaning of the patient's experience in whatever motivation system is dominant. Interventions build a sense of being understood from within the patient's point of view until analyst and analysand can share the common vantage point we have described as an observation platform. Following the patient's lead, the analyst stays as close as possible to the area, issues, and affects the patient spontaneously brings forward. Model scenes are used to organize and integrate broader patterns of experience. Reflective awareness of any pathogenic belief sensed in depth invites awareness of alternative, less problematic views or plans. Awareness expands especially as contradictory views of the analyst are experienced side by side as transference configurations. This opened path to awareness facilitates symbolic reorganization.

7

The Interpretative Sequence

The exploration and understanding of the analysand's subjectivity gives primary attention to his or her associations as the fundamental source of information. Following the conceptual framework laid down in Freud's (1911–15) initial recommendations on technique, the usual way to study clinical material is to track the associations leading to comprehension by the analyst, who, in turn, intervenes, using his or her understanding to facilitate the exploration of further meaning through interpretation of the process or content.

The position that the analyst's interventions are responses to the analysand's communications, however, understates the complex mutual interactive process that occurs between analysand and analyst. What of the obverse of the traditional position, namely, *to what degree are the analysand's associations responses to the analyst's interventions?* The analyst's spoken words, silences, and other forms of nonverbal communication constitute a *sequence of interventions* that affect the patient. To shift the focus onto the analyst's activity rounds out the two-person nature of the analytic scene and heuristically enables us to consider a number of broad questions: What impact does a sequence have on the flow of the analysand's associations, the buildup or resolution of self-protective measures (resistances), the deepening of affective experience, the gaining of insight, the process of working through, the cohesion of the self, and the analysand–analyst relationship? Is the sequence of interpretations in good resonance with the analysand's affect and associations? Do the interventions within a sequence relate to one another? Are the interventions optimal (Bacal, 1985; Bacal and Newman, 1990) in facilitating self-righting, expansion of awareness, and symbolic reorganization?

Our focus shifts not to single interpretations that are studied for evidence of the analyst's understanding, or style, or theoretical stance, but to a *sequence* of interpretations. By sequence of interpretations we mean the employment in a unit of time (for example, a session or a week of sessions) of a wide range of interventions, whether investigative, confirming, affirming, reflective of understanding, self-revelatory, or explaining, that facilitate the ongoing process of understanding and explaining the patient's experience. We retain the use of the term *interpretation* because of its invaluable historical linkage in psychoanalysis, but we use it as a *general rubric for the inclusion of all the various facilitative interventions that occur in the psychoanalytic arena.* We believe that a wide range of interventions variably occurs in every psychoanalysis (for example, see Wallerstein, 1986), although many of the analyst's responses are not recognized or spoken about and are not reflected in our theory of technique. We are expanding the theory of technique to represent more accurately the psychoanalytic process as practiced. Clearly we are broadening the concept of interpretation and, in this way, use the term equivalently with "intervention sequence."[1] Ideally, through the sequence of interventions, the analyst conveys a coherent sense of purpose enabling the successive interventions to have a cumulative effect. The analyst senses from the analysand's communications and responses to the analyst's prior interventions a further interpretive sequence that will deepen the understanding and change that takes place in a successful analysis.

We do not mean to suggest that the analyst has an overarching trajectory that he or she imposes on the patient. We do assert that, as he or she carefully listens to the patient, the analyst organizes the data, intervenes with specific goals in mind, and, depending on the patient's responses, tailors the ensuing interventions. In this sense, a mutually regulating interaction occurs.

Both patient and analyst variably contribute to an evolving psychoanalytic process, one unique to each analytic pair. No two analysts, regardless of similarity in theoretical convictions and personalities, would consistently respond in the same way. With such a vast array of differences, how can we assess the analytic process? The final criterion for the assessment of interventions – and here we concur with Ornstein (1990) – is the patient's response, or

---

[1] A serious limitation of this method of study is that the written word omits the analyst's important nonverbal communications. Moreover, many of the analyst's nonverbal responses may not be intended as interventions, but very well may be experienced as such from the patient's vantage point. For example, the positive affective mood expressed in the analyst's face may be the mirroring "gleam in mother's eye" for the patient.

sequence of responses. Assessment of the patient's response also generates disagreements, but it is the only valid point of entry for understanding the impact of the analyst's interventions.

These issues will serve as our guide in focusing on and assessing the interpretive sequences in the following clinical illustration. The illustration includes process notes, followed by the analyst's description and assessment of the interventions.

CLINICAL ILLUSTRATION[2]

At the beginning of treatment, P was 28 years old, had been married for several years, and was the mother of a young son. She had just terminated a psychoanalysis of three years' duration with a different analyst. This treatment had helped her to curtail the use of drugs and alcohol and promiscuous behavior and had brought about greater order in her life. During the last year of that analysis, however, P had become increasingly depressed. During her initial consultation, she recounted that in her first analysis depressive episodes had been precipitated by the sessions themselves, had dissipated between sessions, but then extended in duration until finally depression became a chronic state. Most problematic in regard to her former analysis was that P needed desperately, and apparently frequently demanded, to know that her analyst "cared" about her. The first analyst was described as stalwartly not responding. In response to P's relentless insistence, the analyst reportedly had resorted to the interpretation that an open expression of caring on her part would be of no help to P, intimating that P would not believe her. Experiencing this interpretation as yet another evasive maneuver, P angrily had retorted that the analyst was a "walking corpse." This characterization appears to epitomize the therapeutic impasse that led to the termination of treatment.

During the initial consultation, P complained of prolonged periods of intense depression, hopelessness, and despair. Despite her depression and considerable wariness of undertaking another analysis, she appeared to be emotionally available and desperately searching for help.

P had been raised in a large family with a very successful, powerful and yet vulnerable, fragile, and explosively tyrannical father and a religiously intense mother who developed a severe paranoid disturbance during the middle part of P's childhood. Attention to P's physical needs was sporadic. For example, although P was athletic and encouraged to be so by her father, her mother sent her to several sports events inappropriately dressed. Attachment patterns with

---

[2]This clinical protocol, previously published, served as the focus of discussion, in *Psychoanalytic Inquiry* (Fosshage, 1990). A dream of this patient can be found in Fosshage (1989).

her mother included intense feelings of emotional abandonment epitomized by a memory from the age of three when P was hospitalized for an unknown physical illness. Her mother did not visit for three days, which engendered P's deep distrust. Furthermore, her mother's neediness and self-absorption resulted in P's feeling "obliterated"–wary and actually repulsed by physical contact with her mother. Yet P and her mother were able to connect more successfully through periodic "intense" psychological and religious discussions.

Because of the many difficulties in the relationship with her mother, P had turned to her father for the connection and recognition she needed. This attachment was heavily laden with sexual-romantic overtones, and her father reportedly selected her as "his special one." The promise of romantic specialness, however, was poignantly dashed on a number of occasions when her father publicly denied the existence of the special connection and required it to remain an unspoken secret between the two of them. For example, on one occasion, when she was nine, P asked her father to show to family friends the "attractive, adultlike" picture of her that she had seen innumerable times in her father's billfold. Her father's denial of ever possessing such a picture crushed and humiliated her. Her father's public denials of a special connection between them undermined P's trust of her own perceptions and colored the romantic feelings as wrong and shameful. Gradually P realized that her father, recapitulating an aspect of her relationship with her mother, had turned to her for responsiveness to *his* particular needs in what she now termed a "self-interested love."

In response to these profound disappointments and frustrations, P often turned to God, not unexpectedly in view of her deeply religious background. During stressful times, including painful ruptures that arose during the first year of the current analysis, she envisioned an idealized figure to whom she could turn for uplifting guidance. In her most despondent moments, however, she experienced even God as failing to protect and care for her.

With increased self-assuredness (for example, she felt more consistently "likable"), P, just prior to the following case material, began to experience both the "intensity" in the analytic dialogue and the "romantic" involvement to be used exclusively in maintaining the necessary connection with her analyst. The "intensity" in the analytic dialogue corresponded with a primary attachment pattern developed with her mother. To the extent that this pattern developed partially out of a feeling of accommodation, it triggered an aversive response for purposes of self-demarcation. The "romantic" involvement with her analyst corresponded with a primary pattern developed, partially out of a feeling of accommodation, with her father. This, too, led to an aversive reaction. These two attachment patterns provided ways of connecting to the analyst but were also inevitably experienced as partial accommodations because of their developmental origins. P began to feel constricted and limited by these two dominant ways of relating and sensed that there was a possibility for a "deeper connection." In response to these internal and relational shifts, P recently had added a fourth session per week to facilitate the "deeper connection."

Additional Contextual Notes

The following process material was originally collected as part of a "project" for *Psychoanalytic Inquiry* (Fosshage, 1990a). The project involved the presentation of clinical process notes from an ongoing psychoanalysis to eight discussants of varying psychoanalytic persuasions and a reply from the presenting analyst.

As the analyst contemplated this project, he experienced considerable ambivalence. His concern and hesitation were related primarily to the potentially problematic impact that such a project could have on the analysis itself, affecting both the analysand and the analyst. Such extensive, detailed reporting required him to discuss it with his patient and to seek her permission to tape and use the clinical material. During their initial discussions, his ambivalence about the project, his interjection of a personal request into the analysis, and his selection of this particular patient and its subjective meaning and ramifications for both participants had a forceful impact on the analytic situation. The analyst chose to present the sessions that followed shortly after their initial discussion of the project because of their potency. Although these sessions demonstrate the impact of the project itself on the analysis, they also show how the project was assimilated into the ongoing analytic process.

In an attempt to minimize the impact of taping, the analysand and analyst agreed that the analyst would place the recorder outside the field of vision and tape intermittently over the following month. Unfortunately, two sessions were not taped (although detailed notes were available) because at one point the analyst decided to abandon the project when he felt the impact on both participants in the analysis was too problematic. Only as these issues were sufficiently understood and managed through their subsequent work was his conviction restored that they could analytically deal with as well as make use of this experience.

Process Notes

First Session: Wednesday

P: [in a dejected mood] I don't like the additional session.
A: No?

THE SEQUENCE BEGINS WITH AN INTERVENTION THAT ACKNOWLEDGES THE COMPLAINT, UNDERSCORES A REFLECTIVE INTEREST, AND ATTEMPTS TO ENGAGE THE PATIENT IN A SHARED EXPLORATION OF HER AVERSIVENESS.

P: I'm not sure. Well, it causes all kinds of problems at home.

A: With E. [her son].

THE ANALYST IS TOO EAGER TO ENGAGE P AND GUESSES INCORRECTLY, BUT HIS INQUIRY SERVES BOTH TO REFLECT KNOWLEDGE AND INTEREST IN P AND TO FURTHER EXPLORATION.

P: No, well, that's not what I meant. My mother . . . that's not why I don't like to come. You asked me last week why I felt ambivalent about it, and I wasn't sure why, but I think it's just too hard to generate material. I get very annoyed and resentful about such things. I don't think I can generate enough, so that's part of the problem.

A: So you feel that you have to generate material here that interferes with your freedom just to *be* here.

THE BRIEF PRIOR INTERVENTIONS MAY HAVE ENABLED P TO SHIFT HER AMBIVALENCE FROM HOME TO THE ANALYTIC SITUATION. SHE RELATES HER AMBIVALENCE ABOUT THE ADDITIONAL SESSION SPECIFICALLY TO FEELING A BURDENSOME PRESSURE TO GENERATE MATERIAL. THE ANALYST REFLECTS THIS AMPLIFICATION, CONNECTS IT TO A PRIOR THEME, "FREEDOM TO BE HERSELF," AND SPELLS OUT THAT THIS INTERFERES WITH HER INCREASED EXPANSIVENESS AND ASSERTIVE MOTIVATION.

P: Yeah, I know there are days when I did and I benefited from that, but it's just very difficult. The reason that it's difficult, and I don't want to put this on anybody, but [P then explained complicated and frustrating financial pressures involving her husband and parents]. . . . I think there is a real difference with the additional session, and my own experience tells me that. I think that it wears me down enough that I have to be really here in a way that I can otherwise avoid. I think the problem is . . . I've said this before . . . I don't think that it will come out that I won't be enough, or you will see too much of me, or, if I don't have enough material, you won't like me – that's not the problem . . .

A: That's not the problem. What is the problem?

P AGREES WITH THE ANALYST AND SEQUENTIALLY CONNECTS HER APPARENT ACCOMMODATION IN HER HOME, FINANCIAL PRESSURES INVOLVING HER HUSBAND AND PARENTS, AND THE ANALYTIC SITUATION. BOTH THE ANALYST'S REMARKS AND P'S FURTHER REFLECTION CRYSTALIZE, THAT TO GENERATE MATERIAL IN ORDER TO BE LIKED VERSUS THE "FREEDOM TO BE HERSELF" IS NOT THE MAIN

PROBLEM. THE ANALYST ACKNOWLEDGES HER CONCLUSION AND CONTINUES THE
INQUIRY TO UNDERSTAND THE MEANING OF HER AVERSION TO THE SESSIONS.

P: That *I won't like you.*
A: I see. If you see me too much?

P HAS RAISED A NEW ASPECT OF HER "ACCOMMODATION" DILEMMA. THE ANALYST
ACKNOWLEDGES HER NEW STATEMENT OF THE PROBLEM AND LINKS IT, AS P HAD
PREVIOUSLY INDICATED, WITH THE ADDITIONAL SESSION FOR FURTHER EXPLORA-
TION.

P: Uh-huh. I don't know . . . it seems that . . . I know I've been aware of
     negative feelings about you. I haven't thought it out that much, but the
     more I feel the need to come, the more critical I become of you.
A: Uh-huh.
P: And my feeling about coming today was that I didn't want to come to see
     you.
A: Uh-huh.

THE ANALYST ACKNOWLEDGES P'S NEW FOCUS ON NEGATIVE FEELINGS TOWARD
HIM, AS WELL AS P'S CONNECTION, "THE MORE I FEEL THE NEED TO COME, THE MORE
CRITICAL I BECOME OF YOU."

P: It's not that I didn't want to see you and you didn't want to see me. I feel
     very negative and critical that I don't want to see you. I think that I have
     a stake in preserving you in a certain elevated, exciting . . . position. I
     think all I'm saying right now is that the feeling is not that I won't be
     enough. . . . I think you have convinced me during the last few years that
     I'm likable, and I feel that, and I often feel that. It may sound like an awful
     thing to say, and I'm feeling it right now, but I could care less that I'm
     likable. I think why I can say that is because *I feel likable* [with increased
     animation]. I'm acknowledging that you have brought me to a place
     where I could care less. I'm just underscoring that that is not what I'm
     wanting.
A: So at the moment, my liking you doesn't have priority.

P BEGINS TO BACK AWAY FROM THE EXPRESSION OF "NEGATIVE FEELINGS" FOR FEAR
THAT IT WILL ENDANGER THE IDEALIZATION. THE ANALYST'S INTERVENTION SUM-
MARIZES THE CONCLUSION IN ORDER TO ACKNOWLEDGE IT AND IMPLICITLY TO
ADVANCE THE INQUIRY.

P: But I think you do.

A: Because you feel that I do like you, you do not have to be worried about it or concerned about it, which must be freeing for you?

P REPEATED HER POINT EITHER BECAUSE SHE FELT THAT THE ANALYST DID NOT UNDERSTAND OR BECAUSE SHE WANTED TO ENJOY WITH THE ANALYST THESE POSITIVE FEELINGS BEFORE RELUCTANTLY MOVING ON TO THE NOW MORE TROUBLESOME NEGATIVE FEELINGS. TO ACKNOWLEDGE HIS UNDERSTANDING AND TO ENABLE P TO RETURN TO THE EXPLORATION OF THE NEGATIVE FEELINGS, THE ANALYST REITERATES THAT P'S FEELING UNLIKABLE, WITH ITS ATTENDANT CONSTRICTIONS, WAS NOT THE ISSUE AT HAND.

P: Yes, it is.
A: You said that you had a stake in elevating me. How would you understand that stake?

TO OVERCOME THIS MOMENTARY DERAILMENT, THE ANALYST PICKS UP P'S FEELINGS, WHICH APPEARED TO BE BLOCKING EXPRESSION OF THE NEGATIVE FEELINGS. P THEN REENGAGES IN THE EXPLORATION.

P: I'm not sure. . . . I know when I said to you on Friday that I was feeling a very relaxed way of feeling about you and I didn't find that I had to go into intense, highly emotionally charged fantasies about you. But I said to you that I didn't know what to do with this very relaxed good feeling . . . [pause].
A: So, apparently when you are feeling relaxed and liked, which feels a bit new and unfamiliar, there is no need to elevate me in highly charged fantasies.

THE ANALYST REFLECTS P'S CONNECTION THAT FEELING "RELAXED AND LIKED," WHICH IS RELATIVELY NEW AND UNSTABLE, DIMINISHES HER NEED FOR IDEALIZED ROMANTIC FANTASIES. THE THEME OF ACCOMMODATION TO RETAIN AN ESSENTIAL ROMANTIC, IDEALIZED ATTACHMENT IS STILL IN FOCUS. THE INTERPRETIVE SEQUENCE ADDRESSES ITS SELF-PROTECTIVE (DEFENSIVE) ASPECTS AND ITS MATURATION.

P: Yeah.
A: But you also said you are feeling critical of me. In what way?

WITH THE RECOGNITION OF THE SELF-PROTECTIVE USE OF THE IDEALIZATION, THE ANALYST RETURNS TO THE EXPLORATION OF THE CRITICAL FEELINGS.

P: Right at this moment?
A: Yes.

P: Right at this moment, I'm not. I was feeling critical of you on Friday.

A: Okay, how were you feeling critical of me on Friday?

P INDICATES THAT SHE IS NOT NOW FEELING CRITICAL, BUT WAS FEELING CRITICAL ON FRIDAY–PERHAPS A SAFER DISTANCE FROM THESE FEELINGS. THE ANALYST CONTINUES THE INQUIRY.

P: I don't want to hurt your feelings.

A: I see.

P: But I did feel critical about things I don't like . . . [pause].

A: You're feeling concerned that you will hurt my feelings.

P: Uh-huh.

A: And what would happen?

P: I care about you. I don't want to hurt you.

A: Uh-huh, but how do you think I would react to it?

P: I think you would be hurt.

A: I see. You're really not wanting to hurt me.

P'S CONCERN ABOUT HER CRITICAL FEELINGS HURTING THE ANALYST IMPEDES THEIR EXPRESSION. THE ANALYST ATTEMPTS TO ILLUMINATE MORE SPECIFICALLY P'S CONCERN.

P: No, because it's very personal. I've done it with B [her husband]. Right after we got married, I just couldn't stand him. I began to pick him apart. I don't think I've ever put him back together.

A: And you told him directly?

P: No.

A: But thought it?

P NOTES THAT SHE WAS EXTREMELY CRITICAL OF HER HUSBAND, AND THROUGH INQUIRY THE ANALYST ESTABLISHES THAT SHE HAD THE SAME DIFFICULTY IN TELLING HIM. P IS AFRAID OF SERIOUSLY HURTING THE OTHER PERSON, DAMAGING THE RELATIONSHIP, AND THE CONSEQUENT GUILT ("I WOULD FEEL TERRIBLE"). ASKING P WHETHER SHE TOLD HER HUSBAND IS AN ATTEMPT TO ILLUMINATE HER STRUGGLE WITH CRITICAL FEELINGS.

P: Yes. And I still . . . I think part of our problem with our sexual life is that I never put him back together again and there are certain things I just despise about him. . . . No, I haven't told him directly because it would be hurtful and I would feel terrible.

A: Do you have some thoughts as to why you shift into a negative or critical mode?

P: With you or . . .

A: Let's stay with me . . . or with B, either one.

P: I'll stay with you. . . . Well, I think it comes along with knowing that you care about me and I think that ushers it in.

A: Negative feelings about me . . .

P: Yeah, I think so.

A: How do these two get linked together?

THE SEQUENCE OF FEELING CARED FOR FOLLOWED BY NEGATIVE FEELINGS, WHICH P PREVIOUSLY NOTED, EMERGES WITH BOTH HER HUSBAND AND THE ANALYST.

P: Well, this sort of has to do with my need to idealize you. I think that, as long as I didn't know that you cared, I had to . . . I think I had to put a lot of energy into imagining that you did. And it used to be that you secretly did. But . . . I think that before I believed that you cared I felt that I was carrying almost the full weight of the relationship. And I think that . . . I don't know . . . that is very hard for me to talk about; I'm trying . . . but I've been trying to talk about it for a while, because I do think that . . . the investment I have in keeping you idealized. . . . As long as I'm doing all the work, you've talked about the two avenues of relating, as long as I'm very busy on those two avenues . . . I don't know . . . I'm not going anywhere . . . [feeling confused].

A: Apparently as long as you know that I care about you, it frees you from having to be so concerned about it and from having to keep me idealized, but subsequently you become critical.

P SPELLED OUT THE SEQUENCE, WAS CONFLICTED, AND ENDED UP CONFUSED. THE ANALYST, RATHER THAN FOCUSING ON HER CONFUSED STATE, REFOCUSES ON THE SEQUENCE OF FEELING CARED FOR THAT DIMINISHES THE NEED FOR IDEALIZATION AND SUBSEQUENTLY USHERS IN THE CRITICISM.

P: Yeah, I think these things about you that are . . . [hesitates]

A: I understand that you don't want to hurt me, but we'll have to take that risk.

P RESPONDS TO THE ANALYST'S PREVIOUS INTERVENTION BY ONCE AGAIN AP-PROACHING HER CRITICAL FEELINGS, BUT THIS TIME WITH HESITATION, WHICH FELT FAR LESS INTRACTABLE. FOR THIS REASON, THE ANALYST REITERATES THE UNDER-STANDING ARRIVED AT THAT P WAS FEARFUL OF HURTING HIM AND THEN DIRECTLY ENCOURAGES HER TO TAKE THAT RISK BOTH TO UNDERSTAND AS WELL AS TO EXPERIENCE HER CRITICAL FEELINGS AS LESS DANGEROUS THAN SHE WAS EXPECTING. IF THE HESITATION HAD BEEN UNBENDING, FURTHER ANALYSIS OF THE AVER-SIVENESS (WITHDRAWAL) WOULD HAVE BEEN NECESSARY.

P: [now without hesitation] I didn't like the car in your driveway. I was driving over on Friday and feeling so good about you, but as soon as I parked I saw a Cadillac in your driveway. [with high-pitched intensity] I hate Cadillacs, I *hate* them.

A: Why?

P: I like your other car, but I hate Cadillacs. Is it your car [intensely worried and questioning with an increasing pitch]? It's not your secretary's. Maybe it's your accountant's car. It's your car, isn't it? I can't stand it. It's probably a new car and I've never seen it before. I hate it.

A: So what does a Cadillac mean?

P: It's an older person's car. It's the kind of car to me that someone drives who's very inactive; it's too luxurious. I like your other car I saw. When it was snowing you drove up and it's great. You belong in that car. It's an expensive car, but I don't have a problem with that car.

A: So, you felt that I sold the other car and bought the Cadillac?

P: No, that you bought another car. It was too much.

A: And your vision of me was . . .

AFTER THE NOTE OF ENCOURAGEMENT, P WAS ABLE TO PROCEED AND IMMEDI-ATELY BEGAN TO DECRY THE PRESENCE OF A CADILLAC IN THE ANALYST'S DRIVE-WAY. THE ANALYST'S QUESTIONS ARE AIMED AT ILLUMINATING THE MEANING OF THE "HATED" CADILLAC. P NOTED THAT THE CADILLAC INDICATED THAT THE ANALYST WAS "GETTING OLD," "CONVENTIONAL," AND "MATERIALISTIC." THE IN-QUIRY CONCERNING THE SALE OF THE OTHER ("GREAT") CAR WAS TO ASSESS FUR-THER THE DEGREE TO WHICH THE ANALYST, IN P'S EYES, HAD BECOME NEGATIVELY TRANSFORMED. FOLLOWING THIS INITIAL ILLUMINATION OF THE MEANING OF THE CADILLAC, P THEN BEGAN TO BECOME EXASPERATED THAT THE ANALYST WAS NOT DISCLOSING IF IT WAS HIS CAR.

P: That you were just getting old, that you had too much money and you didn't know what to do with it, and . . . you were just heading into this conventional, American, materialistic way. Is it your car? Tell me. [with a heightened pitch quickly escalating to exasperation] You're not going to tell me?

A: It wasn't my car.

THE PRIMARY TRANSFERENTIAL CONFIGURATION UNDER EXPLORATION WAS P'S CRITICISM AND THE MEANING OF THE CADILLAC, WHICH WAS BECOMING CLEARER. A SECOND TRANSFERENTIAL CONFIGURATION THEN BEGAN TO BE TRIGGERED WHEN THE ANALYST DID NOT DISCLOSE WHETHER OR NOT THE CADILLAC WAS HIS. HIS NOT ANSWERING PROVOKED THIS SECOND TRANSFERENTIAL THEME OF THE "OTHER" DENYING "REALITY" (RELATED, FOR EXAMPLE, TO HER FATHER'S DENIAL BOTH OF THE PICTURE IN HIS BILLFOLD AND OF HIS FREQUENT SADISTICALLY PRO-

VOCATIVE BEHAVIOR TOWARD HER MOTHER) AND, RELATEDLY, NOT TREATING
HER AS A PERSON (A THEME THAT HAD RECEIVED CONSIDERABLE ANALYTIC FOCUS,
BUT WAS STILL AN AREA OF VULNERABILITY FOR P). THE ANALYST FELT THAT HIS
REFUSAL TO ANSWER WOULD HAVE, AT LEAST MOMENTARILY, SIDETRACKED THEM
BOTH FROM PURSUING THE "HOTTER" ISSUE OF THE CRITICISM AND RAGE RELATED
TO THE CADILLAC. INDEED, P MAY HAVE RAISED THIS SECOND ISSUE TO MOVE AWAY
FROM DEALING WITH HER CRITICISM. QUICKLY WEIGHING THESE ISSUES, THE ANA-
LYST ANSWERED THE QUESTION DIRECTLY. IN THIS INSTANCE, HE WOULD HAVE
DIRECTLY ANSWERED THE QUESTION EVEN IF THE CADILLAC HAD BEEN HIS, SO AS
NOT TO PROVOKE WHAT AT THAT MOMENT HE CONSIDERED TO BE A SECONDARY
ISSUE. (ALTERNATIVE INTERVENTIONS ARE ALWAYS POSSIBLE, EACH AFFECTING THE
ENSUING ANALYTIC SCENARIO DIFFERENTLY. FOR EXAMPLE, THE ANALYST COULD
HAVE VOICED THE SILENT WEIGHING OF THE ISSUES SPELLED OUT IN THE DISCUSSION
AS AN AVENUE OF INTERPRETING THE MEANING AND IMPLICATIONS OF THE QUES-
TION. THIS APPROACH MIGHT HAVE ENGAGED P REFLECTIVELY, OR IT MIGHT HAVE
FURTHER ACTIVATED THE SECOND TRANSFERENTIAL EXPERIENCE AND DETRACTED
FROM THE EXPLORATION OF THE FIRST.)

P: It wasn't? I'm *very glad.* [greatly relieved] I'm glad you told me.
A: A momentary reprieve [mutual laughter].

THE ANALYST REFLECTS P'S FEELING RELIEVED *BOTH* AT BEING TOLD AND AT THE
NEWS THAT IT WAS NOT HIS CADILLAC. THE ANALYST DESCRIBES THE REPRIEVE AS
"MOMENTARY" TO CONVEY THAT THESE ISSUES WERE CRUCIALLY IMPORTANT AND
WOULD NOT BE RESOLVED BY AN ANSWER ALONE. THE MUTUAL LAUGHTER AND
HUMOR WAS A WAY OF SHARING, SOMEWHAT WISTFULLY, THE REALIZATION THAT
TO HIDE BEHIND THE ANSWER AND RETURN TO THE REALM OF IDEALIZATION
WOULD *SURELY* MAKE LIFE EASIER FOR BOTH.

P: I'm glad.
A: But more important, you have very strong feelings about Cadillacs, and
you seemed to be greatly disappointed in me.
P: Yes.
A: The disappointment was a sharp one as your view of me changed.

THE ANALYST RETURNS TO THE EXPLORATION OF THE MEANING OF HER INTENSELY
AVERSIVE REACTION TO THE CADILLAC. THESE INTERVENTIONS FACILITATE P'S
FURTHER EXPRESSION AND EXPLORATION OF THE MEANING OF HER CRITICAL FEEL-
INGS. THESE INTERVENTIONS FORM A SEQUENCE THAT FIRST FOCUSES ON P'S SUP-
PRESSION OF HER CRITICISM, EXPERIENCED AS A NECESSARY ACCOMMODATION IN
ORDER TO RETAIN A NEEDED RELATIONSHIP. HER EXPRESSION OF CRITICISM TO-
WARD THE ANALYST CAN LEAD TO THE "FREEDOM TO BE HERSELF" WHILE RE-
TAINING AN IMPORTANT CONNECTION.

P: I don't know you very well. I really don't. Part of what's happening here
     . . . because of the set up I can't get to know you very well, but . . . I think
     as you become less idealized, you are more accessible or I'm more willing
     to see certain things about you, including some things I can't stand. . . .
     And you wore a sweater.

A: A sweater?

P: [hesitantly] I'm not telling . . . [animatedly] you wore a sweater I hate. I
     love your sweaters. [laughing] I always look forward to winter time so I
     can see your sweaters. That's an exaggeration.

A: So which sweater was it?

P: I'm a horrible person. All of your sweaters are pullovers, and this was a
     vest type.

A: What does that mean?

P: It made you look old. It make you look as if you belong in a Cadillac.

A: I see.

THROUGH EXPLORATION OF ITS MEANING, P AND THE ANALYST ESTABLISH THAT
THE SWEATER MAKES THE ANALYST LOOK "OLD" THE WAY THE CADILLAC HAD.

P: And I have a stake in keeping you young.

A: How come?

P: I haven't the slightest idea [said facetiously and with laughter]. Well . . . I
     think that I get a lot of . . . I have, and this is all shifting, but I think I have
     been able to get a lot of energy from liking you and from thinking about
     you and having fantasies about marrying you. And, if it suddenly turns
     out that it's an old man who drives a Cadillac, that energy is gone. Now,
     I know we'll be friends and that you will care about me and all of that; but
     I'm losing something.

A: And the loss sounds sharp. The disappointment involves seeing me all of
     a sudden as old and unavailable to you, which potentially drains you of
     energy.

WITH DIMINISHED SELF-PROTECTIVE IDEALIZATION, THE ANALYST SUMMARIZES
AND REFLECTS THAT A PARTICULAR VIEW HAS EMERGED WHEREIN HE BECOMES
SUDDENLY AN "OLD MAN WHO DRIVES A CADILLAC." HE THEREBY BECOMES UN-
AVAILABLE FOR THE SELF-SUSTAINING IDEALIZED FANTASIES.

P: Yes.

A: And it sounds similar to some of your disappointments with B.

THE ANALYST BROADENS THE THEME BY INCLUDING HER HUSBAND, AS P HAD
PREVIOUSLY NOTED, ALL OF WHICH IS TO BE EXPLORED.

P: Definitely.

A: I also have the feeling you may have had some other thoughts as well.

P: Yeah, but I got some good ones out there.

A: I'll see you Friday.

ENDING THE SESSION, THE ANALYST RETURNS TO P'S TRANSFERENCE STRUGGLE OVER CRITICAL THOUGHTS THAT MAY NOT YET HAVE GAINED EXPRESSION.

P: Okay.

Second Session: Friday

P: [with intense affect] I had a very upsetting dream last night.

There was a general call to the family, a crisis. B's dead father–people had to come and stay with B's dead father–that was the crisis. I traveled a great distance to come to his crypt. I walked into the doorway of the crypt; inside was the body of B's father. On the stone next to it was S [P's younger sister] in a deathlike sleep. She was performing the duty of staying with him. She was cold, gray, "rigid mortis," but alive. She was in a deep sleep for three days. She had gotten there first. On the other side was D, a friend of S's and mine, lying also in this deathlike sleep. I walked over and saw that B's father was dead, but animated in terrible pain, writhing in pain, clearly dead. He was saying, "Death is so painful, full of pain and suffering." I picked him up, tried to cradle him, tried to soothe him . . . but he was unconsolable. I realized that this was going to be eternal. He wasn't going to die and I couldn't do anything about this pain–horrifying to me. This was absolutely hopeless and I could not do this. I gave up–an impossible situation. I laid his head back down on the stone. I knew I had to leave.

I have an investment to keep you idealized. When you spoke to me about the project [taping the sessions for *Psychoanalytic Inquiry*], you were in need. There was emotion in your voice. You asked me for something. You seemed vulnerable, human. . . . I need to keep you idealized, because human pain is so overwhelming to deal with. . . . Old, lifeless people drive Cadillacs. The last Cadillac I rode in was to B's father's funeral. B's father died of cancer. It was extremely painful. In fact B's father at one point in the dream, when I put his head back down on the stone, seemed like you, very vulnerable–the way you were the other day [when we discussed the project]. When I came out of that session, I had a string of hostile feelings toward you. It started two weeks ago [prior to our discussion of the project]. As I shift into a more human relationship, I'm becoming more critical and negative–that's why I keep you idealized. I don't see you as exploitative [as in the past], but needy; it's different. I found myself reaching back for the more idealized and the more romantic. I'm afraid there's a dead space . . . In the attic dream,[3] the price I pay for this perfect lofty place, the flip side, is unmanageable messiness that I can't do anything with . . . something hopeless, so much disorder, a lot of dead space.

A: The dead space seems to be originally connected to your father, since it's his room in the dream.

P ARTICULATED HER DILEMMA IN THE DREAM REGARDING THE ETERNALLY DYING, SUFFERING MAN WHOM SHE ASSOCIATES TO THE ANALYST. HER IDEALIZATION IS A WAY OF PROTECTING HERSELF FROM THE "NEEDY," DYING OTHER. P THEN REFERS TO A DREAM DISCUSSED FOUR MONTHS EARLIER, AND THE ANALYST CONNECTS THE "DEAD SPACE" MOTIF TO THE FATHER, TO AMPLIFY FURTHER THE ORIGINS OF THIS TRANSFERENTIAL MOTIF.

P: He was tyrannical, but he's given us the message he's terribly vulnerable. And we can't tell him what we think because he's so fragile. The feeling [he conveys] is no one will do anything right. Everyone protects my father. He's demanding that things are perfect, but we can't please him. No one says "fuck you" or "what's the big deal?" He is so disappointed and throws such a tantrum and makes us feel guilty.

A: So as you idealize me less and as I become more human and show vulnerability, as I did when I discussed the project, you are prone to experience me as *terribly* vulnerable and fragile and in this dead space.

P ELABORATES THAT HER ACCOMMODATION TO HER FATHER'S TYRANNY WAS UNDER DURESS. SHE FURTHER DESCRIBES HER FATHER'S VULNERABILITY AND HIS REACTIONS TO IT. THE ANALYST NOTES HER DEIDEALIZATION, ACKNOWLEDGES HIS VULNERABILITY, WHICH TRIGGERED HER REACTION, AND EXPLAINS HOW, IN THE LIGHT OF HER HISTORY, SHE UNDERSTANDABLY TENDS TO VIEW AND REACT TO HIS VULNERABILITY AS TERRIFYING "DEAD SPACE."

P: Yes, it's horrendous and frightening.

A: And if you are critical of me, you apparently become afraid that I will not

---

[3]The "attic dream," which occurred four months earlier, involved P's packing up in her college dormitory room to leave at the end of the semester. Her room in the attic of the building was spacious, but impossibly dusty, moldy, and messy. It had been her father's room in college and was "bigger, secluded and supposed to be a romantic, sentimental room." As she entered the room, she felt tired and depressed. She hated the room. The women below were lively and energetic and happily packing. She was leaving the attic room and wanting to join these women.

Both patient and analyst came to understand that, although this sense of elevated specialness was spacious and momentarily enhancing (as she experienced it in relation to both her father and her analyst), it was messy, isolating, and overall undermining.

be able to withstand it, that I will fall apart or throw a tantrum and that you will lose me in this suffering dead space.

P CONFIRMS THE UNDERSTANDING AND FURTHER EXPRESSES HER FEAR AND HOR-ROR. THE ANALYST FURTHER INTERPRETS THAT THIS SCENARIO, AT LEAST PAR-TIALLY, ACCOUNTS FOR P'S EXPERIENCE OF HER CRITICISM AS *SO* DESTRUCTIVE. HE THEN NOTES HOW P EXPECTS TO LOSE HER CONNECTION WITH HIM.

P: *Yes.* And there are two ways of meeting it. S goes to sleep. I first *try* to console her. But then I decide that I *must* leave [said with determination and resolution] and I was in the process of leaving at the end of the dream.
A: If a person is in an eternal suffering deathlike space, you would have to leave to preserve yourself. No wonder it is important for you to keep me young, idealized, invulnerable, and without human pain in order to protect me from becoming old and beset by overwhelming neediness and deathlike suffering.

FOLLOWING P'S FOCUS ON THE RESOLUTION IN THE DREAM, THE ANALYST REFLECTS AND EXPLAINS THE SELF-PRESERVATIVE FUNCTION OF HER LEAVING IN THE DREAM. HE THEN REITERATES WHY IT IS CURRENTLY IMPORTANT FOR P TO KEEP HIM YOUNG, NAMELY, TO STAVE OFF OR PROTECT HERSELF FROM BEING DRAINED BY HIS OVERWHELMING NEEDINESS AND DEATHLIKE SUFFERING (IDEALIZATION SERVING A PROTECTIVE FUNCTION). THE OTHER FUNCTION OF IDEALIZATION AS A SOURCE OF VITALIZATION IS NOT IMMEDIATELY SALIENT AND IS NOT ADDRESSED.

Third Session: Monday

NOTES OF THE ANALYST'S INTERVENTIONS WERE NOT TAKEN AND, THEREFORE, CANNOT BE CLOSELY FOLLOWED.

THE SESSION BEGAN WITH P BEING VERY ANGRY AND DISTRESSED THAT HER MOTHER HAD CALLED THE DAY BEFORE. HER MOTHER WAS FEELING "OUT OF SORTS," "NOT ALIVE," AND NEEDING HER DAUGHTER JUST TO "TALK ABOUT ANYTHING" TO HER.

P: I tried to find out what had happened to her to make her feel this way. I resisted giving in to what she really wanted me to do, to talk about myself as a distraction for her. She wanted to use me and the things that were important to me for her own purposes, not because she was interested really in me, but in what I could do for her—a distraction from her suffering [said emphatically]. I avoided doing this for most of the conversation and then I gave in. I started telling her about my problems in my relationship with E [her son] and I sensed her relief. This made me angry. I felt used up. . . . This was sapping me like the crypt dream.

THE CRYPT DREAM WAS MORE LIKE HER EXPERIENCE WITH HER MOTHER. SHE WAS INTENSELY ANGRY ABOUT HER MOTHER'S OVERWHELMING NEEDINESS, WHICH "OBLITERATED" HER. P RECALLED THAT, WHEN HER MOTHER WAS GOING THROUGH HER BREAKDOWN (WHEN P WAS EIGHT AND NINE YEARS OLD), HER MOTHER WOULD NOT GET OUT OF BED AND WOULD CALL HER CHILDREN "TO HER ROOM TO MAKE HER FEEL ALIVE." SHE WOULD NOT CALL THE CHILDREN IN "TO SEE US." HER MOTHER MADE HER SISTER WALK ON HER SO THAT SHE (HER MOTHER) COULD "FEEL HER OWN BODY AND FEEL ALIVE." THIS WAS THE ETERNAL SUFFERING, DEATHLIKE SPACE OF WHICH THE DREAM PROVIDED PATIENT AND ANALYST WITH A FULLER UNDERSTANDING.

P: I feel so physically repelled by my mother. It's the same feeling of horror that I feel in the dream. I used to think that this was a feeling of sexual repulsion, that there was something indecent about being touched by her, something horrifying and unnatural. But it's more the feeling in the dream as if she, particularly her body, was a dead corpse [all said emphatically]. I can't touch it. There is all the same horror of its suffering, its living deadness. She seems decaying and *in need of something alive–my life!* I have to leave the crypt in the end, because otherwise I would spend my whole life there.

P NOTED THAT SHE AND THE ANALYST HAD FOCUSED A GREAT DEAL IN THE ANALYSIS ON THE RELATIONSHIP WITH HER FATHER AND HER EXPERIENCE OF HIM AS EXPLOITATIVE, BUT THEY WERE NOW ENTERING THE WORLD OF HER MOTHER AND THAT WAS THE ARENA OF THE "DEEPER CONNECTION." PREVIOUSLY SHE HAD EXPERIENCED THE ANALYST PERIODICALLY AS EXPLOITATIVE. NOW, THEY DISCUSSED HOW, AS SHE IDEALIZED THE ANALYST LESS, P BECAME TERRIFIED THAT THE ANALYST WOULD BE THE SUFFERING, DEATHLIKE, NEEDY PERSON, EMERGENT IN THE CRYPT DREAM, WHO WAS BOTH DRAINING AND UNAVAILABLE FOR HER–THUS, THE AMBIVALENCE ABOUT BECOMING MORE DEEPLY INVOLVED WITH THE ANALYST. P'S EXPERIENCE OF THE ANALYST AS "NEEDY" WHEN THEY WERE INITIALLY DISCUSSING THE PROJECT WAS A CATALYST FOR THIS TERRIFYING IMAGE.

Fourth Session: Tuesday

P: After yesterday's session I feel very hopeless. I think I'm feeling that I can't be in a relationship, not just a love relationship, because I feel so threatened by anybody's needs. And lots of human beings are around me – my son, my friends, my family . . .

A: Your analyst.

P: My analyst . . .

A: And your reaction when we feel needy.

P WAS DESPAIRING ABOUT BEING IN A RELATIONSHIP BECAUSE SHE FELT THREATENED BY THE OTHER'S NEEDS. SHE NOTED THAT THIS AFFECTED HER IN RELATIONSHIP TO HER SON, FRIENDS, AND FAMILY. THE ANALYST INCLUDES HIMSELF TO MOVE PAST P'S POSSIBLE MOMENTARY HESITATION TO INCLUDE THE ANALYST IN THIS PRIMARY RELATIONAL CONFIGURATION.

P: [with a tone of disparagement] It's so extreme.

A: You experienced intense neediness and suffering around you as you were growing up and understandably you become fearful and intensely reactive when you sense vulnerability and neediness in others today.

P RESPONDED WITH A SENSE OF DISPARAGEMENT THAT HER REACTION TO NEEDINESS WAS SO "EXTREME." THE ANALYST DOES NOT ADDRESS HER "EXTREME DISPARAGEMENT" BUT EXPLAINS THE GENESIS OF P'S REACTIVITY AS EMERGING OUT OF A FAMILIAL RELATIONAL SCENARIO.

P: [reflectively]. I know that. But how am I going to change that? [with a sense of despair and some skittishness about asking so directly for a solution]

A: As you continue to become aware of your reactions and to understand and fully appreciate how it came about that you tend to experience others' pain and neediness as so extreme and anticipate being overwhelmed and drained by their feelings, you will be able gradually to experience others' neediness and pain as not *so* frightening and as manageable. You are also learning that in extreme situations you can take care of yourself by actively choosing not to take care of the other, as you did in the crypt dream.

P: You really think so? [daring to hope and ask directly for reassurance]

A: Yes, I really do.

P ACKNOWLEDGED KNOWING ABOUT THE ORIGINS OF HER REACTIVITY BUT THEN INQUIRED, STILL WITH A SENSE OF DESPAIR AND NOT KNOWING, "HOW AM I GOING TO CHANGE THAT?" BY UNDERSTANDING P AS GROPINGLY EXPLORATORY AND NOT AS RESISTIVE IN TRYING TO FIND A WAY OUT OF HER SEEMINGLY INSURMOUNTABLE IMPEDIMENT IN HER RELATIONSHIPS, THE ANALYST RECAPITULATES THEIR PREVIOUSLY ACQUIRED UNDERSTANDING OF HER STRUGGLE AND DIRECTLY DESCRIBES HOW THE ANALYTIC PROCESS OF CHANGE TAKES PLACE. HIS DESCRIPTION WAS

AIMED AT SPECIFYING AND DEMARCATING FURTHER AN ANALYTIC AVENUE OF
CHANGE FOR P AND THEREBY FACILITATING THE CHANGE PROCESS.

P: [pause] It was very helpful for me [with a more energetic tone] to be able
to tell you, to feel that I could tell you the things I despise about you. That
I felt you were strong enough. You see [emphatically] I don't tell B; I don't
tell my father. I don't tell people. I give a very strong message, but I'm
very quiet about it. But I think it's very helpful to tell you that and know
that you wouldn't fall apart. I was afraid that I hurt you, but . . . that was
a new thing for me actually to be able to tell you. And you're still here and
[with laughter] not dead. These are the kind of problems . . . now we are
getting into the "deeper connection."
   I also wanted to follow up on what I talked about yesterday about my
mother's neediness and I told you she was very depressed and at times felt
very alone. I sensed it [speaking with increasingly intense affect]. I
wanted to bring up the hospital incident again – seeing my mother so
self-absorbed. What I saw was something much bigger, overwhelming,
that blocked me out and just wasn't fair. She looked so absorbed. And I
remember . . . I don't remember thinking at the time that there was
something I could do about that; but I do remember thinking that I had
caused it, that it was *my* responsibility, that it had something to do with
me. And I think that feeling of being up against something that was
overwhelming, that it was much too big for me to deal with. That crypt
dream, the dead man who was suffering was too much, it was *too much* for
me to deal with.

A: Yes.

FEELING AFFIRMED AND VITALIZED, P COULD PROCEED ENERGETICALLY.

P: I was *trying* to deal with it. The mistake I made with it . . . two things are
going on. Well, I'm sure as a three-year-old *that is overwhelming*. I don't
think that as an adult B's depression is *that* overwhelming, is *that* big, *that*
hopeless or impossible. But I believe that what I was up against was real,
much bigger than what I could deal with, that obliterated me. I was just
not . . . I wasn't in the room. It's kind of ironic, because the whole first
part of that experience, *she* was not in the room.[4] When she came in and
I didn't see her, I don't remember any of this, but she was not in the room

---

[4]As previously noted, P had been hospitalized at the age of three for an undiagnosed illness. P
was told that when her mother arrived at the hospital for her first visit three days later, her mother
stood by the bed but P did not "see" her for over a half hour. Apparently her mother then became
overwhelmed with remorse and guilt because her daughter did not recognize her. She sat down,
forlorn and self-absorbed. Shortly thereafter, P "saw" her mother in this self-absorbed state and
experienced her as "not in the room for me."

for me. My memory was that she was feeling something so big and so terrible and was so focused on herself that there was just no room for me at all. So I just wanted to bring that back up . . . And I can see that my despising the other person, hating him, not caring about him, hating his neediness, hating his suffering, hating his vulnerability, is a way of remaining intact.

A: Uh-huh.

P: And that's what it's all about; that's what it feels like to me. And that's what it felt like. And *here,* it felt like a life-and-death situation [said with intensity and certitude].

A: Uh-huh.

P CONTINUED TO REWORK AND TO REWEAVE THE CURRENT SITUATION WITH HER HUSBAND'S DEPRESSION AND NEEDINESS AND WITH THE HOSPITAL INCIDENT AND HER MOTHER'S DEPRESSION AND SELF-ABSORPTION. SHE RECOGNIZED THAT TO AN ADULT HER HUSBAND'S DEPRESSION WAS NOT *"THAT* OVERWHELMING," BUT TO A THREE-YEAR-OLD HER MOTHER'S DEPRESSION WAS UNDERSTANDABLY OVER-WHELMING AND "OBLITERATED ME." SHE ALSO NOTED THAT HER "DESPISING" AND "HATING" THE NEEDINESS AND VULNERABILITY IN THE OTHER PERSON "IS A WAY OF REMAINING INTACT." AVERSIVENESS PROVIDES A SELF-PROTECTIVE FUNCTION FOR HER. THE ANALYST CONFIRMS HIS UNDERSTANDING OF P'S REMARKS.

P: But what feels a little hopeless to me is that I've chosen not to relate . . . I know why. That happened in the attic dream – I'm choosing to be up there in an isolated place, but it's a little sad really. And I think that I wanted to talk about the avenues or a way of trying to relate, a way of trying to elevate everything to such a perfect level that I can relate. I mean when you're perfect, when you're the perfect person for me to marry or when, you know, when we're sort of soaring in the realm of ideas, when we're both idealized, we can relate in some ways.

A: Uh-huh.

P: I wonder why I didn't stay with that . . . with those two ways of relating to you. *Why* [with a note of irony] did I want to get into this extra stuff? [mutual laughter]

A: So you're wondering?

P NOTED THAT THE IDEALIZATION OF THE ANALYST AND HERSELF IN A WORLD OF SPECIALNESS PROTECTED HER FROM THIS TRAUMATIC CONFIGURATION AS DE-SCRIBED IN RELATION TO BOTH HER PARENTS. SHE WONDERED, WITH A NOTE OF IRONY, WHY SHE HAD GIVEN UP THIS IDEAL WORLD "TO GET INTO THIS EXTRA STUFF." WITH FURTHER EXPLORATION A MUTUAL PLAYFULNESS WAS EMERGING AROUND THE NOTION THAT IT CERTAINLY WAS UNDERSTANDABLE TO WANT TO

RETURN TO THE IDEALIZED WORLD IN THE FACE OF THE POTENCY OF THIS "EXTRA
STUFF."

P: Yeah, I'm wondering why I chose to push for that.
A: That's a thought.

THE ANALYST REITERATED AGAIN TO FURTHER P'S REFLECTION, AND BY HIS TONE
IMPLICITLY CONTINUED THE PLAYFULNESS THAT NOW SURROUNDED HER CON-
SCIOUS RELUCTANCE TO EXPLORE.

P: I think probably that I trust you more, that it's a possibility to relate to you
     at this deeper level. Before I did not want to take that risk. It was a safe
     place, but not that great. [pause]
A: Well, you must *want* a deeper connection [mutual chuckles].

BY POINTING OUT HER DESIRES FOR A DEEPER CONNECTION THAT MOTIVATED HER
SUFFICIENTLY TO FACE THIS "EXTRA STUFF," THE ANALYST NOTES THE DEVELOP-
MENTAL STRIVING AND MOVEMENT TO FACILITATE BOTH.

P: Yeah, [emphatically, yet ambivalently] I must. [a reflective pause] I'm
     feeling I don't know where things are going to go from here. I came in
     feeling that they were not going to go anywhere. Now, I'm just feeling
     that I don't know and that's sort of all right. I'm calm about that . . .

ADDITIONAL NOTES

The analyst came to understand that P used idealization within the analytic
relationship both developmentally and self-protectively (defensively). Developmentally, idealization provided the necessary safety and caretaking experiences that enhanced her sense of self and resulted in greater "energy" and
vitality. Self-protectively, idealization provided protection against the expected repetitious traumatogenic relational experience of a "fragile and vulnerable" father and of an "overwhelmingly deathlike needy" mother, who would
"obliterate" P as well as be unavailable for her requisite developmental needs.
Additionally, the idealization protected against the reactive rage to this childhood scenario. As P's developmental need to idealize the analyst diminished
(e.g., P saw the analyst as more "human"), the idealization also became less
available self-protectively. These changes, in combination with the analyst's
contribution vis-à-vis the project, precipitated the particular powerful transference configuration and a profound selfobject rupture.

DISCUSSION

Rather than conceptualizing interpretation as a singular and discrete event, we view interpretation as a sequence of interventions that cumulatively facilitate deepening the analytic experience. The sustained application of the empathic mode of inquiry maintains a focus on the illumination of the patient's subjective world. The patient's associative trend, shaped by his or her shifting needs, motivational systems, schemas, and life's stresses, demarcates the direction of the analytic process and the corresponding collaborative search to understand and explain the patient's experience. In addition to the patient's setting the direction, the analyst approaches the analytic task with his or her particular subjectivity and analytic intentions, which shape the sequence of interventions and, in turn, the patient's responses.[5] All these create the particular encounter unique to each analytic pair. Tracking the analyst's sequence of interventions highlights the particular contribution of the analyst as we focus our attention on the affective and cognitive resonance between two unique individuals.

The frequency of interventions clearly differs within a session, between sessions, and with each patient–analyst pair. The rhythms of exchanges in any analysis are, among many factors, influenced by unconscious communicative procedural inclinations of each person and the fit they establish with each other. The analyst's interventions in the illustration ranged from 44 to 4 per session. P's analyst observed that the analysand and he had developed a variable rhythm. The analyst was highly active in the first session during a time when P was at first confused and then reluctant to express critical thoughts. In the remaining sessions, P was more actively engaged in exploring and expressing her innermost thoughts and required less input from the analyst. What is crucial is not the frequency of interventions, but that the interaction is facilitative of the patient's expression and associative flow.

Ideally the analyst's sequence of interventions has a purposeful, cumulative effect in illuminating the patient's subjective experience and in facilitating developmental processes. Overall, we feel that the sequence of interventions in the clinical illustration evidenced a coherent sense of purpose designed to enable successive interventions to have a cumulative effect. This coherence is summarized as follows:

> The sequence of interventions over the four sessions begins with a period of sustained inquiry about P's aversion to the sessions, which emerged when a fourth session was added. With clarification that P was harboring critical feelings toward the analyst that she was reluctant to express, interventions

---

[5]Atwood and Stolorow (1984) have conceptualized and delineated this "intersubjective context" of the psychoanalytic situation.

focused on this reluctance. The conflict emanated primarily from her fear of "hurting" the analyst and of destroying the idealized relationship (both of which she felt had occurred with her husband). The understanding of these expectancies, together with the analyst's mild encouragement, enabled P to express her critical thoughts and feelings. The criticisms involved seeing the analyst as "old," "needy," and unavailable to her as the idealized energy-giver.

The ensuing sessions clarified that the analyst's vulnerability, when he was describing the "project" and his "need" for P to participate in the project, precipitated in her a terrifying image of the analyst as beset by overwhelming neediness and deathlike suffering. This intense experience of the analyst was initially connected to her father, but then more specifically to her mother, P's associative work and the analyst's interventions resonantly focused back and forth on the transference and its historical antecedents.

Additionally, P came to see that her hatred was a reaction to, and was used protectively against, being overwhelmed by a painfully needy other. The experience of expressing her criticism and anger without destroying her analyst, along with a growing self-reflective awareness of the meaning of her aversive motivation, began to ameliorate her feelings of destructiveness and her fear of being overwhelmed by the vulnerability and neediness of others.

In focusing on the major rupture and schema that had been triggered, the sequences of interventions, apart from a momentary disruption in the first session, facilitated the flow of the analysand's associations. The disruption was related to the analyst's momentary impatience (P might have reacted to the analyst's desire to move on to what had priority, possibly manifest in his tonality [page 102]. The analyst's impatience applied pressure that P met with momentary aversiveness (in this instance, brief withdrawal from exploration). The analyst was able to return rather quickly to the analysand's agenda and associative flow. During these sessions, self-protective measures were worked through, resulting in a deepening of affect, a gain in insight, and an increase of self-cohesion.

TECHNICAL GUIDELINES FOR INTERVENTIONS

We note the following guidelines for interventions that were evident in the clinical material.

1) Our overarching principle is to listen with hovering attentiveness, to focus on and understand as much as possible the affective and cognitive inner state of the analysand; that is, we are guided by the use of sustained empathic mode of perception (Kohut, 1959, 1982; Lichtenberg, 1984). We attempt to understand from *within* the perspective of the analysand and thereby mitigate (clearly not eliminate) the imposition of our perception of reality onto the analysand.

2) In addition to our investigative and exploratory remarks, we acknowledge (if only with an "uhuh") when we feel we have an understanding of what the patient is attempting to convey to us. If patients feel they are being understood, whether in their attempts to reveal themselves or in their attempts to convey their aversiveness to self-revelation, they will be more motivated to express fully their experience with emotional depth. Offering an appreciative awareness of where analysands stand at any moment in their thoughts and feelings first implicitly validates their self-experience and then facilitates the development of a shared "observational platform" from which greater insight can be gained, alternative perspectives conceived of, and symbolic reorganization can occur.

3) Our interventions, although based on empathically gathered data, range widely with regard to the introduction of the analyst's perspective. For example, acknowledgment that we understand the patient remains close to the patient's experience. Such acknowledgments are often introduced by phrases like: "So what you are telling me is . . ." or "What you're feeling is . . ." or even "Uh-huh." An explanation, on the other hand, introduces more of the analyst's perspective in the organization of the data. Explanations are often phrased as "The way I understand what you are experiencing is. . . ." And finally, using implicitly or explicitly the discrepancy in the subjective experiences of analysand and analyst for further illumination of the patient's schemas introduces most directly an alternative perspective as, for example, when the analyst delineated P's expectation that her criticism would cause the analyst to throw a tantrum and become lost in the suffering dead space. The analyst's interpretive response, in contrast to a tantrum, implicitly juxtaposed his response and subjectivity with P's schema, which further illuminated the latter.

A patient's needs vary. At times a patient requires the analyst's closest attention and response to his or her experience without the slightest deviation to enable the patient to feel validated and cohesive. On other occasions, the patient will desire to experience the analyst and the analyst's perspective for self-delineation (Stolorow and Atwood, 1992), expansion of awareness, or both.

4) We pay careful attention to the patient's reactions to our interventions and investigate problematic reactions. We focus on what the patient experiences as empathic failures, note the extent of any disruption in his or her self-cohesion, and attempt to repair the disruption by understanding the precipitants from the patient's vantage point. Once self-righting is achieved and restoration takes place, the nature of the disruptive experience and what triggered it may become the focus of further inquiry to expand awareness and broaden perspective.

5) By listening carefully to the patient's associative flow, we hone in on

thematic experiences that reflect unconscious organizing principles or schemas.[6] The illumination of the problematic schemas as they are activated within the analytic experience is enhanced by the "here-and-now" analyst–patient exchanges and their exploration. For example, P feared the overwhelming neediness and pain of others.

6) In our interventions, we remain close to what is readily available to the patient's immediate awareness. We speak in language closely allied to the patient's mode of speech and metaphoric inclinations. Through the mixture of a mode of inquiry and a conveyed sense of understanding, we aim to encourage an investigatory attitude and a sense of safety. Our goal is not to present as finished products our more global formulations, but to facilitate as much as possible the patients' recognition and assertion of the fruits of their own exploration.

7) As we listen to the patient's feelings and thoughts, we attempt to identify the motivation that is dominating a patient's experience and the patient's attitude toward the particular motivation. We pick up on changes in motivation or conflicting motivations of which the patient is often unaware. For example, the analyst focused in on the aversiveness that P experienced as destructive and in conflict with her attachment needs. We remain especially attuned to and supportive of patients' exploratory-assertive motivation in their attempts to master and problem solve. Here our focus corresponds to Kohut's "developmental strivings" that create the "leading edge" of the material (Miller, 1985). For example, P's decision to leave the dying corpse in the dream was understood as one way of mastering the painful situation.

8) In an attempt to expand the patient's awareness of the associative links between present and past events, analyst and analysand construct model scenes to organize and illuminate previously puzzling transference experiences, integrate previous understanding, and initiate further exploration of the analysand's experience and motivations (see Chapters 1 and 2). For example, P's hospital experience, at the age of three, of emotional abandonment first through her mother's physical absence and then through her mother's forlorn self-absorption was a model scene usefully reexamined in these sessions.

9) We do not actively apply the concept of optimal frustration (Kohut, 1971, 1984) but, rather, are guided by an attempt to be optimally responsive (Bacal, 1985; Bacal and Newman, 1990) in facilitating the analytic process, the patient's developmental needs, and the patient's exploratory-assertive motivation.

10) Finally, if self-righting occurs, if emotional intensity mounts without a

---

[6]A number of authors have contributed to the reconceptualization of transference as unconscious organizing principles or schemes, including Wachtel (1980), Gill (1982), Hoffman (1983), Atwood and Stolorow (1984), Stolorow and Lachmann (1984/85), Lichtenberg (1990), Fosshage (1990b), and Lachmann and Beebe (in press).

fragmenting change in state, if associations expand, if perspective about the matter under inquiry widens, if symbolic reorganization is occurring, analyst and analysand can draw confidence in the interventions each is making with the other.

We believe that the analytic process can be studied productively from the vantage point of an interpretive sequence. The sequence of interpretations is the point where the theories that shape technique (Pulver, 1987; Stolorow, Brandchaft and Atwood, 1989; Miller and Post, 1990) intersect the individuality of analyst and analysand. Rather than lifting the particular to a generality that an author wishes to propose or affirm through a case summary or vignette, tracking the interpretive sequence focuses attention on the particular features of affective and cognitive resonance between two unique individuals. Special emphasis is placed on how the qualities of the analyst allow him or her to listen empathically and respond optimally. Regardless of theoretical goal, listening and responding are universal features of the analyst at work, and by tracking an interpretative sequence, we are able to develop and enrich our understanding of the analyst's contribution.

8

The Selfobject
Experience

Reevaluation of the "selfobject" concept is pivotal to our attempt to provide a theory of technique. Conceived by Kohut (1971) at a time when considerations of psychic structure and function, drive, internalization, and cathexis dominated psychoanalytic theory, the selfobject concept requires redefinition to conform with the current emphasis of self psychology on experience and our introduction of motivational systems. First, this valuable term, which has caught the imagination of a broad spectrum of mental health professionals, has tended to lose the precision given to it by its originator. In popular usage, selfobject has come to mean anyone who does something good for someone else. While this meaning carries some of the import of Kohut's original usage, it becomes simply a value assessment about a person or situation. Thus, a reconsideration is necessary to rekindle Kohut's far-reaching serious scientific intent.

Second, that selfobject refers to those affective experiences that are sought by the self to build and maintain, or restore, cohesion. Selfobject *experiences* are central to motivations in each of the five systems. Thus, central to our theory of technique is the thesis that empathic perception must be directed to the patient's search for the effective vitalization of selfobject experiences, which are triggered when needs in any motivational system are met and signals of distress are responded to.

Third, we consider the selfobject experiences of mirroring, twinship, and idealization to be particular aspects of the attachment motivational system and, from a more generalized perspective, as fundamental sources for the maintenance of self-cohesion. We apply a figure-ground or foreground-background dimension to the shifting dominance of particular motivational needs and desires and those of a more general supportive-restorative nature.

Fourth, we attribute deficits of adaptive selfobject experiences to empathic failures. In the development of pathological states, especially those involving addictions, we are able to recognize the desperate search for temporary selfobject experiences to shore up disruptions and depletions of self. This recognition is critical to our ability to sense into the motivations involved in many maladaptive choices.

Let us explore five assumptions derived from Kohut's clinical descriptions of the "selfobject."

THE SELFOBJECT FROM THE INTRAPSYCHIC PERSPECTIVE OF FUNCTION BUILDING

Assumption 1

Observing patients with narcissistic pathology, Kohut (1971) found that a patient's self-cohesion was disrupted when the patient experienced an empathic rupture in relation to the analyst. When analyst and patient addressed, acknowledged, and understood the meaning of the occurrence that had ruptured the tie, the cohesion and vitality of the self were restored. The patient was assumed to have experienced the analyst as a component part of the patient's self, necessary for the maintenance of vital functions. It was assumed that in the absence of certain developmentally necessary experiences, the patient was left vulnerable to the experience of disruptions in self-cohesion, self-continuity, affect regulation, and the like when another person fails to provide those functions. In this usage, *selfobject is defined concretely—as a person supplying a necessary but absent function.*

Kohut (1971) wrote

> Some of the most intense narcissistic experiences relate to objects; objects, that is, which are either used in the service of the self and of the maintenance of its instinctual investment, or objects which are themselves experienced as part of the self. I shall refer to the latter as *self-objects* [p. xiv].

"Self-objects" are a special category of objects that are, in this conventional definition, depersonalized people; thus the sentence reads "objects which," not "objects who."

But we also know that psychoanalytic references to "objects" involves a form of speech in which object refers to people, the opposite of subject. In the sentence, "John loves Mary," John is the subject, Mary the object, the target for his action (loving) and his emotion (affection). But in Kohut's definition, some objects are different from the Mary in our sentence – rather than being the target for an action of the subject, they do something that influences (services) the state of the subject either by aiding the subject to maintain an investment in himself, or by being experienced as a necessary part of the self. The sentence would now read either "John is enabled to maintain his love for himself by Mary," or "John experiences himself as expanded and strengthened by inclusion of Mary in his sense of self." In both sentences, John is still subject and Mary an object. Kohut carefully avoids describing the connection from an interpersonal perspective, as for example a loving relationship. Kohut retained for self psychology an intrapsychic perspective in which Mary is perceived by John in terms of the function she serves for him. She affects John's self.

Thus, we begin with an unambiguous answer to our query – a selfobject is an object that, or a person who, is used by a subject in the service of the subject's self. Let us now consider whether defining a selfobject as a person servicing or supplying functions is optimal or whether selfobject should be considered a quality of affective experience with associated symbolic representations. We pose this question so as to be able to place the "selfobject" into a developmental context that includes what the infant and the later adult are motivated to seek and how the experience is represented and symbolically elaborated. To try to resolve the question of selfobject as person and function or experience and representation, we follow the path Kohut traversed to arrive at his formulation, a path that explored clinical findings with a group of patients suffering from narcissistic personality disorders.

Analysts have long been familiar with patients' protests, depressions, and regressions at times of extended separation. The traditional explanation for these complaints seemed straightforward to several generations of analysts. Patients in analysis activate their childlike, largely oedipal selves. They experience a dependency on their analyst/parent. The rage, despondency, and dysfunctions are thus considered throwbacks to preoedipal holdovers. Patients, according to this explanation, regarded their analysts as a parent (separate object) onto whom they project their "infantile" dependent needs. Kohut (1971) observed that one group of patients seemed particularly susceptible not only to reactions of rage, despondency, and emotional withdrawal when facing extended vacations but "to such apparently trivial external events as minor irregularities in the appointment schedule, weekend separations, and slight tardiness of the therapist" (p. 91).

Some analysts (Kernberg, 1976; Masterson, 1987) consider narcissistic patients to be characterized by predominantly preoedipal pathology especially as manifested in their dependency and rage. Few of the patients Kohut described, however, resembled a clinical group of infantile, clingy, dependent people. In fact, when not in the throes of such transference responses, these narcissistic patients appeared to be cold, aloof, and relatively independent, high-level accomplishers. Another finding did distinguish these patients from the conventional clinical picture of the psychoneurotic. The narcissistic patients not only reacted with rage, despondency, and retreat to slight irregularities of scheduling, but also "to small signs of coolness from . . . the therapist, or to the analyst's lack of immediate and complete empathic understanding" (Kohut, 1971, p. 91). Kohut considered these reactions not as an indicator of dependency, but as an indication of marked sensitivity and vulnerability to minute lapses in experiencing intimacy and being understood. In pursuing the question of what this sensitivity and vulnerability should be attributed to, Kohut concluded that his observations pointed in two directions: 1) the particular ways by which the analyst was being perceived by the patient, and 2) the particular circumstances in which the patient was most apt to perceive the analyst in this way.

(1) *The perception of the analyst by the patient.* What is the particular way in which the analyst is perceived by the patient who is vulnerable to experiencing coolness, and lack of understanding? Kohut (1971) inferred that the patient's response to the analyst indicated that the analyst was perceived as "archaic, narcissistically cathected, and prestructural" (p. 21). The analyst was not experienced by his vulnerable patients as a separate person, like, for example, a father threatening castration, but as a component part of the patient's self, necessary for the self to maintain integrity of vital functions. Archaic meant that the analyst was perceived in the way a very young child might perceive a parent. Kohut's view of infancy was based on assumptions that analysts held about infancy prior to the extensive empirical research that followed in the next decade (see Lichtenberg, 1983). Kohut assumed that neonates experience their world primarily narcissistically, that is, in a general state of bliss and omnipotence with no differentiation between self and other.

Prestructural refers to Kohut's belief that enduring, stable, self-regulating functions are only gradually acquired by a process of internalization similar to the identifications that occur during mourning postulated by Freud (1917). These transmuting internalizations (that is, something done for one is changed to something that one does for oneself) are assumed to follow when, in the course of successful caretaking, inevitable lapses in attunement occur. When these minute failures are phase appropriate and nontraumatic, the infant, using prior experience as a guide, identifies with the previously supplied function and builds up capacities for self-regulation (Tolpin, 1971). Examples of the acquisition of such functions include being able to self-soothe, self-amuse, and self-feed. Kohut's (1984) statement that "the baby is strong" (pp. 212–213) refers to his seeing the baby as ideally "designed" to fit with caretakers into a niche. This fit facilitates the baby's developing psychic structure by transmuting internalizations of functions previously performed for the baby by the caretaker.

To restate this in the context of an analysis, the narcissistically vulnerable patient's self is "prestructural," that is, presumed to lack those internalized functions by which others are able to sustain their feelings of self-steem and self-worth. The analyst is called upon not to interfere with the patient's use of him. The analyst is perceived to be supplying certain functions, for example, mirroring, through which the patient experiences self-worth, a change in self. When a disruption occurs in this sustaining state and the analyst is experienced as fulfilling selfobject needs by addressing this rupture, the patient is enabled to develop an increased internal capacity to restore self-cohesion. Whether referring to baby or adult, Kohut assumed that structures or functions were built as a result of processes of internalization, through minute, phase-appropriate ruptures and their repair.

(2) *The circumstances in which the patient perceives the analyst as selfobject.* What are the circumstances in which the patient is most apt to perceive the analyst as a selfobject whose affirmation or shared idealization is necessary for the restoration of self-esteem? Kohut found that in response to the analyst's perceived coolness, lack of understanding, or unavailability, the narcissistically vulnerable patient would experience a state of disruption of self-cohesion. Kohut (1971) recognized this state of disruption by the fragmentation of the patient's normal modes of functioning and by the depletion of the patient's normal stores of energy. In the most far-reaching of these disruptive dysregulations, the patient's entire mind-body-self seemed in danger of fragmentation, of being outside the realm of control.

> It is significant that the patient uses negative terms when he tries to describe the experience of the fragments of the mind-body-self or of the self-object. His lips feel "strange," for example; his body has become "foreign" to him; his thinking is now "odd," etc. – all terms which are expressive of the fact that the regressive changes are, in essence, outside the patient's psychological organization [p. 30n].

In less extensive fragmentations, the patient will complain of not feeling himself or will report reenacting some pattern such as drinking, seeking stimulation from food or drugs, Don Juan-like behavior, going to porno flicks, or resorting to excessive sleep and other withdrawals.

Investigation of these changing states led Kohut to conclude that loss of functioning occurred when patients experienced a failure in a responsiveness they assumed to be as necessary as the air they breathed. The metaphor of air carries further – we are aware of air only when deprived of it; then we become gaspingly aware of the function it serves in maintaining our mind-body-self equilibrium. Kohut believed that, in treatment, before self-reflective awareness and verbal reference, patients look to selfobjects on whom they can rely to fill gaps in their sense of self. Therapists learn of their significance to patients as selfobjects when their patients respond to a disruption of that supportive functioning. Then something outside the patient – the empathically responsive therapist – and something inside – a function such as initiative or integration or organization – are both recognized to be missing.

In his last statement on the subject in an answer to critics of the term, Kohut (1984) wrote:

> Throughout his life a person will experience himself as a cohesive harmonious firm unit in time and space, connected with his past and pointing meaningfully into a creative-productive future, (but) only as long as, at each stage in his life, he experiences certain representatives of his human surroundings as joyfully responding to him, as available to him as sources of idealized strength and calmness, as being silently present but in essence like him and, at any rate, able to grasp his inner life more or less accurately so that their responses are attuned to his needs and allow him to grasp their inner life when his is in need of assistance [p. 52].

During successful analysis, the self, or rather self-selfobject ties, become more structurally firm. "But this increased firmness does not make the self independent of selfobjects. Instead, it increases the self's ability to use selfobjects for its own sustenance, including an increased freedom in choosing selfobjects" (p. 77).

The historical development of the term selfobject leads us to the following conclusions: First, the term gives primary emphasis to a person's serving a function. Second, the term was embedded in the metapsychology of ego psychology, the dominant theory of the time, as evidenced by its references to narcissistic libido, functions and structures, and undifferentiated (archaic) stages of self and object. Although Kohut later dropped the references to archaic (it is lifelong) and to narcissistic libido, the term continues to carry some of its origins. Third, the term has given rise to conceptual confusion about its placement with respect to concreteness – is it a term for a parent seen in a particular light? This view is reflected by Kohut (1977) and is contained in subsequent self psychology literature, for example:

> Selfobjects refer to aspects of caregivers – mother, father, teachers, etc. – who are experienced as providing something necessary for the maintenance of a stable, positively toned sense of self. The mother of an 18-month-old, who, at about the same time as the child, recognizes his hunger, functions as a selfobject (close to self as an empathic perceiver of his needs, close to an object in her providing of the food) [Lichtenberg, 1983b, p. 166].

That the term continues to engender confusion can be demonstrated by the variation in definitions by recent authors. Goldberg (1988) retains the link to person while broadening the functions from those that involve only affirmation giving experiences to those that also include experiences that involve restraining. Goldberg states

> the term selfobject, which usually connotes another person who is experienced as performing a necessary psychic function for the self, would include the range of functions that have to do with impulse control, limit setting, and others dealing with the containment of action and behavior. However, for the most part, the illustrative clinical material in self psychology treats selfobjects as primarily gratifying or enhancing, using terms such as mirroring or consolidating and avoiding those that are suggestive of prohibition or injunction [p. 204].

In contrast, Stolorow (1986) states, "The term *selfobject* does not refer to environmental entities or caregiving agents–that is, to people. Rather it designates a class of psychological *functions* pertaining to the maintenance, restoration, and transformation of self-experience" (1986, p. 389; see also Stolorow et al., 1987). Stolorow's emphasis is on a particular dimension of the *subjective experiencing* of an object based on the function the object serves. Wolf (1988), like Stolorow, defines selfobject in terms of subjective experience. He states:

> Precisely defined, a selfobject is neither self nor object, but the *subjective* aspect of a self-sustaining function performed by a relationship of self to objects who by their presence or activity evoke and maintain the self and the experience of selfhood. As such, the selfobject relationship refers to an intrapsychic experience and does not describe the interpersonal relationship between the self and other objects [p. 184].

The range of functions served by the selfobject by mirroring, twinship, and idealizing has been expanded to include adversarial responses (Wolf, 1980, 1988; Lachmann, 1986) to provide opportunities for oppositional self-assertiveness. In addition, Wolf (1988) describes the necessity of "efficacy experiences" (1988, pp. 60–62). Self psychologists (for example, Bacal, 1990) have also spoken of a negative selfobject or a negative selfobject experience to refer to occasions "when the selfobject is experienced as responding faultily with corresponding loss of the patient's self cohesion and feeling of well being" (Wolf, personal communication). In this usage, positive and negative selfobjects both personify the analyst as either succeeding or failing to serve the functional needs of the patient. A selfobject that is negative would be consistent with Kohut's (1984) reference to a "pathogenic selfobject" (p. 6) from whom a child needs to detach in order to thrive. The pathogenic selfobject refers to a parent whom the child counts on for functional help but whose "help," like that of Schreber's father, has a devastatingly pathologic effect. While "negative selfobject" is consistent with the personification of the term, negative selfobject *experience* seems to be an oxymoron if selfobject experience refers to a vitalizing or cohesion-producing affective state.

We argue against the use of such terms as "negative selfobject" or "pathogenic selfobject" because they conflate two dimensions of experience: the necessary vitalizing selfobject dimension and a pathological (object) relationship that may, for example, be characterized by exploitation, sadism, or masochism.

We argue for inclusion of protective prohibitory and adversarial experiences as manifestations of needs of the aversive system and for inclusion of efficacy experiences as manifestations of needs of the exploratory system (Lichtenberg, 1989a).

THE SELFOBJECT FROM THE PERSPECTIVE OF DEVELOPMENT

Assumption 2

A contemporary theory of infant development redefines the term selfobject as referring primarily to *a vitalizing affective experience, the selfobject experience.* The part-self/part-object aspect of the definition becomes more definitively metaphoric, a reference to a *fantasy* about a relationship.

The psychoanalytic conception of development (Lichtenberg, 1983a, 1989a; Stern, 1985) has changed markedly since Kohut proposed that self-objects are archaic, narcissistically cathected, and prestructural. The findings of researchers, as summarized in Lichtenberg (1983a, 1989a), strongly suggest that infants do more than react superficially to their surroundings. Experiments demonstrate that infants both experience a world with affective meaning and record that affective meaning in memory. They develop expectations of intimacy pleasure from attachment activities and efficacy and competence pleasure from exploratory-assertive activities. When their expectations are frustrated, when the patterns are interrupted externally, infants are aware of the disruption and react aversively. We need no extensive research to be convinced that similar effects occur if violations of expectancies occur in feeding, sleep, ranges of stimulus intensity, or the infants' patterns of sensual enjoyment.

Stern (1985) conducted observations and experiments that bear directly on our thesis about the "selfobject." Stern observed that when infants engaged in activities such as shaking a rattle, crawling, or pushing a block back and forth, mothers made a body movement, vocalization, or facial expression that matched their infants in rhythm, intensity, and duration. During play interactions, these concrete evidences of attunement occurred every 65 seconds.

The mothers' responses were intuitive; until demonstrated on videotapes, the mothers were unaware that they were responding to their baby in this attuned way.

Stern asked, does this sharing have an impact on the infant? In comparison with activities of the mothers during which the impact could be observed, attunement responses appeared to have no demonstrable effect. The infants continued to shake their rattles, crawl, or push their blocks. Stern had the mothers deliberately go out of phase, pretending to jiggle more slowly or more rapidly. The infants noticed the discrepancy and stopped their activity. When the mother resumed, the infant resumed. Stern's experiment establishes that frequent unnoticed intuitive attunements convey the information to infants that their internal feeling states are shared and responded to by the person or people closest to them.

Obviously this attunement promotes attachment, but what other effect does it have? Stern reasoned that the caregiver's attunement responses influence the infant's affective state. The infant, shaking a rattle, crawling, or pushing a block, experiences affects of interest and enjoyment; the mother's responses amplify the interest and joy. The "vitality" of the affect state is increased. Stern theorized that affect states cannot be adequately appreciated merely by recognizing the categorical emotion present – enjoyment, interest, anger, fear, sadness, shame, guilt and so on – but that affect states must include descriptors that take into account qualities of feeling such as surging, fading away, fleeting, explosive, crescendo, decrescendo, bursting, and drawn out. These he called "vitality" affects.

Like Stern, we believe that the vitality dimension of affects, crescendos, and decrescendos is inextricably involved with all the essential processes of life – those of mounting hunger and getting fed, falling asleep and waking up, as well as feeling the coming and going of all categorical emotions. From infancy on, all through life we experience qualities of rise and fall, surge and fade both from our own activity and from the activities of others. How a mother picks up her baby, folds the diapers, runs her fingers through the baby's hair, and moves toward or away contributes to the quality of vitality present in the affective exchange. From the mother's facial and vocal expression and from a multitude of activities, a small infant will abstract general affective qualities such as liveliness, or the slowing down that occurs during depression, or the jerky tension of bursts of anger, or the soothing effect of comforting, or the persistent modulation of a calm unruffledness. Similarly, therapists convey more than cognitive understanding to the quality of the therapeutic exchange. Through our lively interest, tempered concern, or apathetic indifference, ritualized correctness, or restrained irritability, we influence the vitality present in any categoric affect – pleasurable or dystonic – as well as the therapeutic ambience as a whole.

Stern's observations of the vitalizing effect of attunement between mother and infant can be used to support Kohut's conception of a selfobject as neither self nor separate, whose positive effect on cohesion arises from the selfobject's availability for merger. Stern believes, as we do, that the overwhelming evidence from other studies points to the conclusion that self-with-other involves intimacy but not merger. Stern posits that since the observational and experimental research indicates that infants experience agency and volition, body coherence as locus, affective coherence as a source of awareness, and continuity of experience in the form of memory buildup, infants must be considered as capable of differentiation of self and other. Thus, infants do not begin life as fused or merged with their mothers in a state of undifferentiation from which they only gradually emerge over the first year or more. The differentiation of self in infancy differs from the differentiation evident in later experiences of subtle identifications and the formation of *fantasies* of entering and leaving merger states (Lachmann and Beebe, 1989).

To appreciate the differentiation of self during infancy, let us reconsider the impact of the mother's attunement responses on the infant who is shaking a rattle, crawling, or pushing a block. First, the infant is experiencing agency and volition. The crescendo or decrescendo, surge or fade, of his own activity will influence his vitality. Second, the mother's attunement will add to that vitality, thus enhancing the sense of agency and volition, without creating a loss of boundaries or of differentiation of self. Further, in each attunement experience during direct attachment play, infants initiate fully half of the responses and exercise considerable control over the patterning. Differentiation is enhanced, not lost. Not merger, but a combination of having needs met and being vitalized by attunement responses triggers selfobject experiences that strengthen the core self.

The point of this review of infant studies is that, while Kohut's clinical discovery remains poignantly compelling, the theory of development on which it is based, and the terms he used to describe it, require reconsideration.

INTERNALIZED FUNCTION OR VITALIZING EXPERIENCE? SELFOBJECT OR SELFOBJECT EXPERIENCE?

Assumption 3

Shifting emphasis to "a selfobject experience" raises new questions about the nature of that experience. Viewed clinically, the core feature of the experience lies in the restoration of cohesion and *vitality* of the self. Viewed developmentally, the core feature of the experience lies in the attunement of caregivers to the infant's motivational needs and the vitality of the intimacy this affords.

Intimacy and the affects that arise from attunement to needs and wishes in any of the motivational systems are "instrumental in bringing about the wonderfully blissful experience of BEING, of experiencing oneself as a person, a self, in other words, the bliss of a self being evoked via a selfobject experience" (Wolf, personal communication). Restoration in the clinical setting is dramatic; attunement in normal development occurs with little notice—the vitalizing occurring as an accompaniment to ordinary responses to needs.

We have now considered evidence from two sources: clinical psychoanalysis and infant research. From the clinical findings we conclude that when patients experience a threat to self-cohesion, they require understanding of the source of their altered state of self in that a sustaining experience of being affirmed or included in an alterego or idealized sharing has been disrupted. When the understanding occurs, the sustaining experience is reconstituted, self-cohesion is restored, and a minute advance in self-solidity will have occurred. From the infant studies, we conclude that infants gain self-functional capacity through the exercise of motives in the five systems. The experiential meaning of the exercise of innate and learned patterns derives from affects triggered by the perceptual-action patterns. The affects of infants and caregivers are both categoric and something more—there is the presence or absence of a vitalizing quality. Each affectively meaningful lived experience is remembered as a generalized version of repeated episodes of self interacting with others. Small variations in each subsequent lived experience lead to adjustments in the responses and the memories, hopefully potentially adding to both the functional range and the vitality of the self.

The common thread between these two sources is the significance of affective experience. With this in mind, let us reconsider Kohut's (1971) definition:

> Some of the most intense narcissistic experiences relate to objects; objects, that is, which are either used in the service of the self and of the maintenance of its instinctual investment, or objects which are themselves experienced as part of the self. I shall refer to the latter as *self-objects* [p. xiv].

On the basis of our critical explorations, we restate the definition: "Some of the most intense experiences involving one's sense of self are triggered in the context of empathic responsiveness of others. When empathic responsiveness ensures an experience of cohesion and vitality of the self, we designate it as a *selfobject experience.*"

The shift to experience has two virtues to recommend it for a theory of technique. First, the core of the self-psychological approach to therapy lies in its emphasis on an empathic mode of perception, and selfobject experiences are appreciated empathically. Second, selfobject experiences fit into the theoretical perspective of self psychology's recognition of the intersubjective world

of the therapeutic exchange (Stolorow et al., 1987) and away from conceptions of archaic merger states, archaic fantasies of omnipotence, and qualities
of energy such as narcissistic libido.

Still problems remain. How do we recognize empathically and introspectively a selfobject experience? What is the source of the experience? A patient
enters analysis in a state of distress. Gradually he feels intact, more himself. He
feels understood, his good intentions appreciated, his failures sympathized
with, his accomplishments affirmed and admired. He is having a selfobject
experience. But from whose point of view? His! His view may well be shared
empathically by his analyst, although introspectively the analyst probably has
some degree of divergence–less confidence in his own understanding, less
sympathy for the patient's failures, maybe even a touch of envy for his
accomplishments. Now, at some point, the analyst speaks when the patient
wants only to be heard. Or the analyst does not respond as needed by offering
reassurance, advice, admiration, disagreement, or explanation. Or the analyst
fails to indicate affective attunement when the patient feels he needs that
response. The patient's state of mind undergoes a radical shift. He feels
depleted, irritable, wounded, humiliated, spiteful, withdrawn, apathetic. He
has experienced an empathic failure from the analyst. From whose point of
view? His! The analyst (or an external observer) may recognize no disturbance in the analyst's attentiveness and resonance.

Technically the analyst's task is then to investigate the patient's experience
of the empathic rupture; for example, how the patient heard the analyst move
in her chair "disgustedly." The analyst will or will not be sensitive to the
disgust. If she is, she must own up to it privately and understand it personally.
She may or may not acknowledge her contribution as she perceives it; but, for
the immediate therapeutic exploration, her view, acknowledged or not is
often beside the point. The nature, form, context, and intensity of the patient's
experience of disgust needs to be investigated from within the patient's
perspective. Since it triggered the loss of a selfobject experience of being
approved of, this exchange must bring about a sense of shared understanding
about the loss and its trigger to provide an optimal opportunity for the
restoration of a selfobject experience.

For contrast, let us now consider another clinical situation. A patient is
experiencing herself approved of, the analyst moves in his chair, and she
exclaims, "I hate it when I hear you move. It makes me worried that you are
having a bad thought about me. It reminds me of my father at the dinner table
getting restless if I took too long telling him something that happened to me."
No depletion, humiliation, or the like at the hands of the analyst–only a
person with an intact sense of self talking about a concern recognized as based
on a lived experience of a past empathic failure. Or the analyst offers an
interpretation that turns out, from both the patient's and the analyst's perspective, to be faulty. No vulnerability of the self is triggered by the misunder-

standing. It is an empathic failure, but, to use the phrase of Stolorow et al. (1987), *not* a selfobject failure.

We are ready to draw our first conclusion: In the clinical situation, a selfobject experience implies the existence of mental contents forming an intact or restored, affectively invigorated sense of self; an affirming, like-minded, or idealized other (or any combination of those); and whatever else a dominant motivation calls for. A selfobject experience is thus not a reference to actual interpersonal relations or to the internalization of functions, but to an affect-laden enhanced self-state. And the specific relationship between self and affirming, like-minded, or idealized other – that of part self, part other – gains symbolic representation in the form of such fantasies and metaphoric expressions as being merged, twined, or in an inspiring relationship with another. Consequently, when we, as therapists, consider our contribution to helping the patient create or restore a selfobject experience, we must think of ourselves not as the individuals we are but as the metaphor (symbolic representation) the patient forms of us in his or her psyche.

Does this depreciate the importance of what we do? Not at all. Just the opposite. As Stolorow et al. (1987) state, "Once an analyst has grasped the idea that his responsiveness can be experienced subjectively as a vital, functional component of a patient's self-organization, he will never listen to analytic material in quite the same way" (p. 17). As was true of good analytic practice before self psychology, the analyst will listen empathically to all the patient's associations to understand their meaning from the patient's perspective. But, because of the contribution of self psychology, *in addition,* the analyst will listen empathically to all the patient's associations to sense the presence or absence, waxing or waning of himself as contributor to the patient's self-cohesion from the patient's perspective. Thus, we are relieved of trying to be selfobjects. We can only be therapists. But our skill is crucial to whether or not the patient can create, from our shared exchanges, selfobject experiences.

We must utilize our skills in three ways. First, by establishing the framework of the treatment through our consistency, reliability, caring, concern, and essential friendliness, we establish a therapeutic ambience; second, through our persistence in attempting to understand the full range of the patient's motivations, we institute an empathic immersion into the patient's world of wishes, aims, beliefs, values, conflicts, and torments; third, through our persistent effort to track the patient's sense of self, we immerse ourselves empathically in the patient's world of resilience to or vulnerability to loss of self-cohesion and depletion of self. Thus, in the clinical situation, by doing the ordinary work that promotes restoration of the self (self-righting), expanding awareness, and the reorganization of symbolic representations, the optimally responsive (Bacal, 1985) therapist triggers *pari passu* selfobject experiences.

In infancy, the definition of a selfobject experience as a fantasy or metaphoric expression in which the self is experienced as being completed by another cannot be applied because symbolic representations of this type in all probability do not occur before 18 months. Self engaged with other in attachment activities, self disengaged from other in exploratory activities, self engaged with other in numerous activities of physiological regulation, self aversive to other, and self engaged with other and with self in seeking sensual enjoyment, all are lived experiences. In these lived experiences the self, as represented in perception during an event and in memory afterward, is commonly separate and distinct, the representations of self and others being generalized from prior lived experiences (Stern, 1985; Lichtenberg, 1989a). Rather than a sense of the self being completed by a caregiver, affect is triggered in the course of these activities that is crucial to their psychological meaning. Later, after the child is 18 months old, symbolic alteration provides an associative molding to events and the people in them as well as a lively world of fantasy and imagination. Then we can properly speak of a selfobject as a metaphor or fantasy for part self/part object. Still, the affective experience provides a major link assuring continuity between motivation in the pre- and postsymbolic periods.

Each infant, together with the matrix of caregivers with whom he or she develops a sense of self and systems of motivation, presents a unique challenge to create a fit that not only triggers a full range of categoric affects but also the particular "value-added" experiences of affect crescendo and decrescendo that give vitality to the exchanges. Thus, caregivers cannot be selfobjects to children; they can only be mothers and fathers taking part in the complex exchanges of lived experiences. But their capacity for

> affect attunement leads to a shared world . . . if affect attunement is not present or is ineffective during [the] early years, the lack of shared experience may well create a sense of isolation and a belief that one's affective needs generally are somehow unacceptable and shameful [Basch, 1984, p. 35].

Attunement must not be thought of as limited to a few types of attachment experiences; it involves a wide variety of responsiveness to the different needs of each motivational system for selfobject experiences to be triggered. The recurrent nature of the need for caregivers to restore comfort and satisfaction after the physiological distress of hunger and the like, to engage in intimacy pleasure, to facilitate the enjoyment of competence in exploration and assertion, to recognize accurately signals of aversion, and to participate in and affirm the infant's seeking of sensual enjoyment provides ample opportunities for selfobject experiences to be enjoyed by both infant and caregivers. The triggering "selfobject" may be a satisfying feeding, a shared look, a hand that plays pat-a-cake, a mobile that captures attention, a burst of anger that makes a frustrated effort at assertion work, or a blanket that soothes, depending on whether included in the experience is a vitality of affect that heightens and enriches its meaning. Thus a wide range of activities of self with others constitute the selfobject triggers and the selfobject experience of normal development in the presymbolic period.

MIRRORING, TWINSHIP, AND IDEALIZATION VIEWED THROUGH A FIGURE-GROUND PERSPECTIVE

Assumption 4

Kohut's view of the self led him to emphasize the particular selfobject experiences of mirroring, twinship, and idealization. As his theory altered, his accounts of mirroring, twinship, and idealization experiences changed somewhat, but these experiences remain paramount to the formation and cohesion of the self. The problem that arose is how to juxtapose these experiences with the many other affect-laden experiences of daily life. Are selfobject experiences a separate category of experience central to the self while the other experiences are central to object relations (Bacal and Newman, 1990)? Clinical experience pointed to another solution based on the analogy between the awareness of psychic experience and the experiencing of visual perspective—a changing, flexible foreground-background, or figure-ground, relationship (Lichtenberg, 1983b, 1989a; Stolorow and Lachmann, 1984/85). Our concept of motivational systems adds depth and texture to the foreground-background relationship by suggesting that 1) mirroring, twinship, and idealization are central to the development of the attachment motivational system; 2) other selfobject experiences are central to the development of the other four motivational systems; 3) while mirroring, twinship, and idealization are of lifelong significance, other selfobject experiences, such as mentoring and sponsoring, rivalry and competition, and dependent/altruistic and romantic love, convey significant vitalization to attachment; 4) when any of the five motivational systems is dominant, those selfobject experiences crucial to the affective life of that system can be recognized empathically as foreground motives; 5) at these times the acquisition of mirroring, twinship, or idealization from prior successful experiences can provide a sustaining background as delay and even failures are endured in the foreground; and 6) when, in the foreground, an empathic failure is experienced for whatever reason (overlong delay, intolerable aversive arousal, perceived insensitivity) and a disruption in self-cohesion occurs, the need and demand for a restorative mirroring, twinship, or idealization experience propels these particular selfobject experiences into the foreground.

Kohut (1971) described a child's replacing lost perfection by establishing a grandiose self and by giving over the previous perfection to an admired omnipotent selfobject: the idealized parent imago. Reactivation of the grandiose self takes three forms of mirror transferences:

> In the most archaic form – the merger through extension of the grandiose self – the patient experiences the analyst as a part of himself and expects unquestioning dominance over him. In the less archaic alter-ego transference, the patient experiences the analyst as a twin form of the patient's self. In the most mature form, the analyst is experienced as a separate person, but one who is to serve as a mirror, responding with pleasure to the patient's exhibitionistic display and confirming the value and importance of it [p. 61].

Reactivation of the idealized parent imago may involve archaic states of ecstatic, trancelike, religious feelings or hypomanic excitement; intermediate states of hero worship; and mature states of respect and admiration. At this early period in self psychology, Kohut achieved a measure of theoretical clarity by dichotomizing along lines of economic and structural concepts. *"Narcissism . . . is defined . . . by the nature or quality of the instinctual charge,"* Kohut wrote (p. 26). Narcissistic libido cathects (invests) narcissistic self or selfobject imagos and strivings while object libido cathects object imagos and strivings.

In the decade that followed, Kohut (1984) made significant revisions that pointed away from the dualism of 1971 to a unified theory of a self-selfobject unit.

> In view of the fact that we now conceive of the self as consisting of three major constituents (the pole of ambitions, the pole of ideals, and the intermediate area of talents and skills), . . . we subdivide the selfobject transferences into three groups: (1) those in which the damaged pole of ambitions attempts to elicit the confirming-approving responses of the selfobject (mirror transference); (2) those in which the damaged pole of ideals searches for a selfobject that will accept its idealization (idealizing transference); and (3) those in which the damaged intermediate area of talents and skills seeks a selfobject that will make itself available for the reassuring experience of essential alikeness (twinship or alter ego transference) [pp. 192–193].

Kohut no longer was speaking of "narcissistic transferences" but of "selfobject transferences" because "the need for, and the experience of, imagoes used for the creation and sustenance of the self undergoes a lifelong maturation, development and change" (p. 193). Since the experiences used for sustenance of the self are mirroring, twinship, and idealization, the place of other experiences remained a problem. Kohut now spoke of two separate frames of reference: one in which a person is experienced as a selfobject supporting the cohesion, strength, and harmony of the self, one in which a person is either the target of desire and love or the target of anger and aggression if he blocks the way to the desired object. But, Kohut added, such divisions as self and object, internal response and external response are concessions to entrenched thought patterns and conventional language. In fact – in *psycho-logical* fact, that is – the two experiences are two facets of the same central constellation inasmuch as the indivisible self-selfobject unit, while undergoing many changes from infancy to old age, continues to exist as the essence of psychological life from birth to death [p. 213].

Clinical experience suggests that foreground-background shifts offer a relation between experiences that center on mirroring, twinship, and ideali-zation and those that center on the multitude of other relationships and situations (Lichtenberg, 1983a; Stolorow and Lachmann, 1984/85). Fore-ground meant the immediate content and meaning of the associations the patient was relating, either well-organized feelings directed to a separate, distinct, outside person or to "a selfobject needed to serve some suspended, unavailable, or underdeveloped function" (Lichtenberg, 1983b, p. 167). Back-ground referred to the supportive aspects of selfobjects that invariably form in any successful analysis. These background supports for the patient's self-cohesion, basic trust, and hopeful expectation have been characterized as the unobjectionable positive transference, the basic dyadic relationship, the ther-apeutic relationship, the working alliance, and by self psychology as the empathic ambience.

The shift to an emphasis on selfobject experiences and an understanding of motivational systems changes dramatically the perception of foreground–background relationships. Selfobject experiences triggered by needs and de-sires being met in any motivational system may dominate the foreground of experience at any moment. Kohut (1984) foreshadowed the vitalizing effect of a need being met in any motivational system when he stated that "object love strengthens the self, just as any other intense experience, even that provided by vigorous physical exercise" (p. 53). The self is strengthened or vitalized by experiences of appropriate responses to the need for sleep, nutrient, elimina-tion, and exercise, by involvement in and successful accomplishment of exploration and assertion in play and work, by aversive responses removing obstacles or assuring safety, and by sensual soothing and sexual orgastic excitement. Any of these motivations may dominate the foreground of an analytic exchange.

Let us consider a situation when the attachment motivational system dominates the foreground. The need being sought may be for mirroring, twinship, or idealization in response to some specific matter under consider-ation. Or the need or desire may be for sponsoring, mentoring, or romantic love or rivalry responses. In ordinary daily life, the responses to these attach-ment needs and desires would be direct – an affirmative statement, a loving gesture, competitive challenge. In an exploratory treatment, the responses to these attachment needs and desires would be less direct – an empathic recog-nition and acknowledgment of the importance of an affirmative statement or a loving gesture. In either daily life or an analysis, there is apt to be more overlap than these guidepost statements convey. However, as long as the person (in ordinary life or analysis) experiences the necessary response, the cohesive, sustaining response of a vitalizing intimacy will be triggered. In analysis, this will permit the further expansion of awareness of attachment wishes, or, if these needs become quenched, the needs and desires of another motivational system may become dominant.

Alternatively, if attachment (or other) needs in the foreground are not met and aversive responses of anger, fear, depression, shame, humiliation, or guilt occupy the foreground in any marked degree, a disruption of the attachment bond, of the communicative capacity, and of the cohesive functioning of the self may occur. As noted, Kohut (1971) gave as examples of disruptions patients' descriptions of body parts feeling strange and foreign, thinking becoming odd, and skin feeling excessively cold. Then, issues that center on fundamental aspects of mirroring, twinship, and idealization may of necessity move to the foreground. For instance, a patient had placed in the foreground of his associations a desire to have his courage in defending the analyst against his parents' criticism acknowledged. The empathic failure – the analyst's not affirming his act – created a shift to a need-demand for affirmation of the patient's worth in general and even of the value of his existence. In another instance, a young woman indicated a desire to have the twinship experience of perceiving the analyst as sharing her opinion about the value of her closeness with her feminist friends, a closeness that disturbed her husband. Following the analyst's empathic failure – not confirming a mutual opinion – her foreground motivation shifted to a need-demand for confirmation that the analyst understood and shared anything at all about her. Another analysand indicated a desire to have the analyst consistently and patiently understand her righteously indignant rages against her daughter because the idealized analyst's patience and goodwill toward her served as a model. When she perceived the analyst as irritated by her criticism of him, the prior foreground selfobject experience of a pleasant, lighthearted idealization was replaced by accusations that he was a charlatan, a "technician" whom she would be better off leaving. The restoration of her cohesiveness, trust, and positive expectation required a foreground exploration of the precariousness of her past and present experiences of idealization and the devastating effect on her ability to retain an affirmative intimacy experience in the face of an ever-present danger of dominance by aversive antagonism and withdrawal.

ABNORMAL DEVELOPMENT AND SELFOBJECT EXPERIENCES

Assumption 5

In ordinary development, a reservoir of selfobject experiences forms as a consequence of needs being met and signals of distress being responded to.

Affects during these recurrent moments range from the quiet satisfactions of intimacy, efficacy, sensual enjoyment, and the sense of security as distress is relieved, to the more lively, exuberant moments of active social play, stimulating new experiences, and sexual excitement. Inevitably every child will experience heightened dystonic moments of physical distress, minor injury, interactive anger and fear, task frustration, and sexual confusion and overstimulation. In ordinary development, the child will respond to these dystonic moments by searching for someone or something that will trigger selfobject experiences that affirm self-cohesion and vitality.

If one's consistent lived experience, however, is that needs have not been met in one or more motivational system, one will seek satisfaction, joy, a sense of security, relief of distress, self-cohesion, and vitality through alternative experiences. The many patterns of activities that constitute the functioning of each motivational system provide ample opportunity for intense lived experiences in which the affects may be pleasurable but the consequences maladaptive. A bored lonely listless child may restore vitality by excitedly crayoning all over a newly painted wall and producing more arousal through a spanking that follows. The combination of an exciting forbidden act and the further excitement of punishment may establish a pattern for future relief of a depleted self-state. Or the affects may be unpleasurable, such as a younger brother's having his arm twisted in a wrestling match. The result may be that he learns to wrestle effectively. On the other hand, being lonely, he may be seeking the excitement of pain from his older brother (and, later, others) as the basis for an attachment experience. When needs are generally met, lived experiences such as the crayoning or arm twisting may have relatively few negative consequences. When these experiences form a persistent recurrent pattern, however, and when needs are not met, then intense alternative experiences can come to be desired. The person will then create and re-create comparable situations, thus gaining affect-intense experiences and an immediate, reassuring sense of familiarity and control despite long-range maladaptive results.

The assumption that the effect of abnormal or variant development is to seek selfobject experiences through means other than ordinary responses to ordinary needs is consonant with self psychology views of the genesis of psychopathology. This view holds that although pathology often results from what has been done to the developing child in the form of neglect, abuse, and traumatic events, the *experience* of these happenings centers on (1) what was not done in the form of empathic responsiveness to the child's needs, and (2) the child's symbolic elaboration of his experience of what was and was not done in the context of the child's hard-wired, unique organization. Where self psychology has spoken of caregiver failure in empathic responsiveness as producing deficits in the development of self-structures, we speak of the failure creating an expectation of nonresponsivity that leads to aversion to attachments. Such aversiveness is a consequence of interferences in vitalizing selfobject experiences sought from ordinary sources: the pleasure of satiety by oral intake, of relief by elimination, and of restoration through sleep; the multiple satisfactions of intimacy; the sense of efficacy and competence pleasure gained from exploration and assertion; the effective use of antagonism and avoidance; and the enjoyment of sensuality and sexual excitement.

When the lack of affective vitalization from ordinary sources consistently leaves one with a sense of depletion, one may seek vitality and cohesion from maladaptive, perverse, or pathogenic sources: First, the repetition of experiences of a traumatic or abusive nature may have a strong organizing effect because of the intensity of the experience. Where physical pain has been a recurrent experience it may create a more cohesive experience than comfort would. Where humiliation or guilt have been recurrent experiences (Weiss and Sampson, 1986), these negatively toned affects may convey more intensity of an intimate relationship than would respect or an uncomplicated assumption of responsibility. Similarly, the numbing confusion and bad self-feeling of repeated failures in exploration and assertion, especially those that may accompany learning disabilities, may become more familiar cohesive states than those created by occasional bursts of competence pleasure. Anger, especially tantrumlike, destructive rages, may be sought for temporary vitalization; extended states of hatred and of the pursuit of vengeance may be resorted to for their long-term contributions to self-cohesion. Sexual excitement states, often divorced from intimacy, may be sought, with or without accompanying states of degradation, for the temporary exuberance of the experience.

A second instance of seeking selfobject experiences from pathological sources may arise from those objects or substances that can provide comfort or relief from a wide range of discomforts and dystonic experiences. The mother's hand to hold, the finger to suck, the "pacifier," and the "transitional object" are the normal prototypes for later, more problematic activities, objects, or substances. These activities, objects, or substances do not deal directly with the specific source of the discomfort, as would food with hunger or a lively toy with boredom or a playmate with loneliness. These substances, activities, and objects have a hedonic and regulatory effect in their own right because of their inherent triggering of affects. One group of activities triggers affects through either the calming or stimulation of sensual pleasure, as when a child in a state of loneliness, boredom, uncertainty, hyperactivity, or generalized excitement will reach for his or her genital. Other activities that become available as inherent triggers of affect are risk taking such as gambling, the multiple stimulating and calming effects of smoking, and the whole range of effects of drugs, drinking, and toxic substance usage (Ulman and Paul, 1990).

The great significance of these activities, objects, or substances lies in their providing relief not for one specific need but for a panoply of current or potential distresses and discomforts. Threats that the multipurpose relief or security will become unavailable are a major source of distress, sometimes far greater than would be the distress of the primary source of discomfort. Once a child has come to rely on a cuddly for comfort, regardless of the source of distress, for example, the expectation of a period of hunger, mother's absence, the unavailability of toys, or being punished, will often not evoke the kind of alarm that the loss of the cuddly triggers. Similarly, a habitual smoker may be able to bear a sleepless night without snack, spouse, or book, but having run out of cigarettes, be driven to find an open convenience store (Tomkins, 1988, personal communication). Like a toddler's use of his security blanket, using and relying on any age-appropriate means to obtain a selfobject experience that relieves a multitude of possible discomforts is not pathologic in itself. It becomes pathologic when obtaining and preserving the activities, objects, or substance become a central focus of the person's motivation. The *sources* of discomfort are not then pursued, nor is a search for a solution. The goal has become to assure the availability of the means to obtain the relief–the addictive demand is for the activity (being repeatedly reassured, gambling), the object (the person of the analyst, the fast car, the jewel), or the substance (cigarettes, alcohol, cocaine).

A third source of selfobject experiences derives from *ideation* associated with experiences that provide a powerful boost to vitalization and cohesion of the self. A child's belief that she is a beautiful, intelligent, loved little girl is never separate from actions–her parents and her own–but it is the activation of the self-image that can trigger the selfobject experience with or without an action pattern of display and applause. Religion employs this recognition in its promise of an enduringly available protective deity. Reliance on a conscious belief or a preconscious or largely unconscious fantasy ideation as a source of selfobject experience to relieve distress and raise self-esteem is not pathological, although the beliefs and fantasies and their enactments may be more or less maladaptive. The ideation assumes pathologic consequences when one is unable to realize that it is a means of creating an affect state of invigoration or cohesion that might otherwise be lacking. For example, a Don Juan fantasy does not assume pathologic consequences because the person gains social ease or phallic invigoration or heightened potency and orgastic excitement from it. The main pathologic consequence arises if a man persistently resorts to the fantasy (and its attendant behavior) as a means to relieve unrecognized distress from problems in any motivational system, not necessarily the sensual-sexual system. As long as the person's dominant motivation is to preserve the fantasy and the person resists every effort to create doubt about its validity or its compatibility with other goals, little attention can be given to the sources of distress. From the person's point of view, distress arises from the threat to dislodge the belief or illusion or unconscious fantasy that has become the source of a vitalizing experience he relies on to cope with stress from a variety of sources. Omnipotence and overidealization are frequent fantasy elaborations used in this way to create illusory but consistently re-creatable selfobject experiences, however brief and vulnerable. For patients we are able to help in analysis, a strong desire for sustainable selfobject experiences from more ordinary sources persists alongside the addictive search for alternative triggers recognized to be maladaptive.

Eating disorders illustrate that the three sources of pathological vitalizing experiences (repeated distress-producing lived experience; the inherent affect-regulatory and stimulatory property of an activity, object, or substance; and the regulatory and invigorating power of fantasy) may coexist in any individual. First, the memory residue of early pathologic patterns of feeding may unconsciously influence the person to re-create disturbed affect states as sources of feelings of being alive and of self-cohesion. For example, rigid adherence to fixed-time feedings regardless of signals of hunger may establish patterns of deprivation as familiar and valued. Concurrently or alternatively, the infant's signals of satiety may be ignored and overridden, with stuffing and frequent regurgitation as an intense experience. Added to establishing a fundamentally distorted, affect-laden pathologic pattern is the absence of an ordinary sense of recognition of hunger-feeding-satiety so that self-regulation cannot be attuned to inner signals. Thus, while others take for granted the relationship between hunger and satiety, for some people the timing and quantity of food and fluid intake may be fundamentally disturbed. In these people an alternative pattern of deprivation or overstuffing may resonate with their previously lived, affect-laden experience. Patients with this type of disturbance manipulate eating or deprivation patterns "to achieve a notable experience that would reestablish their groundedness in their bodies and thus provide a basis for reorganization at moments of extreme disharmony" (Krueger, 1988, pp. 43–44). Through the creation of these intense body sensations, these patients achieve a temporary state of the selfobject experience of aliveness.

Second, food intake, chewing, sweet tastes, and mildly stimulant drinks may serve as means to provide slight lifts (glucose kick, chocolate, caffeine) or soothing (the sensual elements of sucking, mouthing, rhythmical chewing) that can be used to relieve depression, anger, or frightening feelings from any source. The availability of food may then be desperately focused on as though food were an addictive drug. Hidden stashes of food may be protected like bottles by an alcoholic, and a whole secretive set of rituals developed. The binge eater describes eating to "fill feelings of emptiness and despair, to anesthetize herself to emotional pain; her binging actually enables her to feel and experience a part of her body as real and to focus the pain in a particular location (her stomach), which she can now master by purging" (Krueger, 1988, p. 44). Alternatively, the affect states associated with food deprivation as well as the means to reduce body weight – amphetamines, physical exercise to the point of runner's high – may become central organizers of the patient's affective life, blotting out all other sources of conflict and disturbed cohesion. Thus, even in the absence of an early lived experience of disturbed psychic regulation of food and fluid intake, later severe disturbances can occur. At any age, the inherent quality of food intake or deprivation to trigger affective rises or falls can result in the use or avoidance of food becoming a central means to escape from other difficulties.

Third, eating and body size and shape are elaborated symbolically into a multitude of representations and fantasies that draw on motivations from all five systems. In the eating disorders, three characteristic fantasy elaborations are found frequently. One centers on intake or its restriction. To eat is equated with being loved and with loving, and to refuse to eat is equated with rejecting attachment, achieving separation, control, and independence–the intrapsychic mastery of disturbances in attachment motivation. In another fantasy elaboration or pathogenic belief, fat is equated with ugliness and undesirability, while thin is equated with beauty and becoming loved and admired. In a third fantasy, body bulk is associated with body armor and impenetrability. Heaviness can thus serve as an equivalent both of antagonism without overt anger and of withdrawal without fright. In a whole series of situations involving controversy, rivalry, and sexuality, the fantasy of having a body with an impenetrable armor can create the illusion of security without the need to consider the primary problems. The fantasy of eating or rejecting "love," of achieving all forms of admiration and being sought after by thinness, or of invulnerability to penetration and danger by fatness becomes the means to achieve a selfobject experience of vitality and cohesion while a variety of more basic problems become inaccessible to awareness, their disturbing affects warded off.

Let us apply the concept of a selfobject experience to the therapeutic exchange. Each patient brings to treatment a previously organized repertoire for seeking and sometimes realizing self-cohesion and self-vitalization through a variety of adaptive and maladaptive means. Each patient starts with a hope of evoking in the treatment selfobject experiences of his or her own conscious and unconscious design sometimes in the form of a curative fantasy (Ornstein, 1984). Depending on prior experience, patients will seek to obtain from the treatment a response to needs in any or all of the five motivational systems. For some, the conscious and unconscious focus will be on the attachment potentials of the relationship with the analyst. For others, the focus will be on the exploratory-assertive potentials for understanding the nature of a problem. Invariably, aversive responses will be activated to ensure the protection of established selfobject experiences or to provide vitalization through the intensity of negative affects. Sensual enjoyment derived from the comfort and stability of the setting, even the vocal tones of the exchange, will be looked to for their soothing, tempering effect. At other times, the same sensual aspects of the treatment may be treated as equivalents of foreplay in pursuit of sexual excitement. Physiological requirements may occupy center stage at any time – in states of hunger or physical illness or because the office over- or underheats – and call for active recognition as a primary response.

From the beginning of an analysis, a patient's conscious and unconscious willingness to pursue those selfobject experiences that result from successful exploration of his or her motivations competes with the desire to obtain selfobject experiences from such nonexploratory approaches as advice, reassurance, special arrangements and concessions, arguing, seductive exchanges, submitting, rebelling, and the like. Also competing against immersion in an exploratory treatment are the lures of short-term methods, prescription medications and nonprescription substances, and enactments of every sort. Contributing to inducing and encouraging the patient's pursuit of selfobject experiences within the analysis despite the uncertainties of an exploratory approach are a number of familiar features. The analyst's concern, reliability, consistency, patience, honesty, directness, and resilience in the face of antagonism and withdrawal, challenge expectations of a patient that, inevitably, past empathic failures will be repeated. To whatever extent these traits of the analyst constitute a *new* experience, they open hitherto closed-off paths for belief that someone acting as a caregiver can help to facilitate self-vitalization. Supported by the traits we note, the analyst invites the analysand's trust and confidence in being understood by an empathic perception of the analysand's motivations and experience.

Two important results can be attributed directly to the analysand's awareness of the analyst's success in empathic listening. First, the analysand is encouraged to expand the moment-to-moment experience in depth. Feeling the full affective intensity involved in painful aversive experiences leads to a sense of relief and release long associated with crying and anger. We regard the selfobject experience that analysands derive from expanded affective expression to be the result of increased acceptance of their emotions shared as signals of distress rather than a catharsis of drive discharge. Second, the empathic mode of perception plays a crucial role in permitting and understanding the restoration of self-cohesion after those inevitable disruptions that occur from perceived empathic failures within the treatment. Recognition of the disruption, searching for its triggering cause, and acknowledging the analyst's contribution as perceived by the patient permits "self-righting" (Lichtenberg, 1989a) to occur.

The analyst's personal traits and empathic responsiveness provide an ambience in which patients feel safe to reveal their private selves. As long as an empathic ambience prevails, analysands feel confident that they are being understood, their individuality appreciated, and their resilient self-righting from disruptions and depletions encouraged and consolidated. The personal qualities and empathic responsiveness of the analyst draw patients into the treatment and sustain its continuance during periods when difficulties arise.

Once a patient becomes involved, the resultant immersion in the experience triggers transference responses that are crucial for lasting change.

We identify two processes involving transferences that lead to the reorganization of symbolic representations. The first is the analyst's assisting the analysand to recognize the manner of his or her response to the analyst's perceived benevolence or malevolence. The second is the patient's edge of awareness or unconscious appreciation of contrasting perceptions of the analyst. One perception of the analyst arises when an affectively loaded transference fantasy, belief, or interaction dominates the analysis. The patient's other perception of the analyst derives from the analyst as empathic listener-observer-interpreter of the transference (Lachmann, 1990).

One perception may involve the full affective sense of being specially preferred and loved by the analyst. The other perception recognizes that the analyst interprets the meaning of being special, ends the session at a prearranged time, and charges a fee. One perception may involve the full affective sense of the analyst as hated and hating, blamed and blaming, deprived and depriver. The other perception recognizes that the analyst listens to and interprets what he or she can identify as triggering acts involving hate, blame, or deprivation, thus making the experience open to shared consideration and reflection. The one representation involving self and analyst is largely organized in a primary-process mode; the other, largely in a secondary-process mode, the discrepancy probably appreciated largely unconsciously in both modes for full effectiveness. In summary, we believe that analysands' ultimately most significant selfobject experience derives from a sense of persistent change in their perceptions of themselves and others. We attribute this change to brief but frequently experienced moments of contrasting dual perception during the analysis.

Let us now consider certain situations in which no expectation of a selfobject experience on the part of the patient can be activated. We will exclude those in which analysts are unable to live up to the traits and empathic listening normally required, that is, instances in which persistent errors in management and failures in empathic listening and understanding require a change of analyst. Many situations arise in well-conducted analyses in which the analysand may be in an altered mental state that, by its nature, precludes the analysand's expectation of a selfobject experience. A frequent example of a state change is a protracted chronic or deeper, more acute depression. Another is a recurrent intense state of panic. Another is an obsessional state that interferes with spontaneity of thought or action. In each situation in which a patient's affective-cognitive state precludes realization of a selfobject experience from expanding awareness and insight, use of an appropriate medication is indicated.

We propose, therefore, that medication is called for when a disturbed cognitive-affective state precludes the patient's realizing a selfobject experience. A clinical example will illustrate. O, an intelligent, attractive woman had become completely alienated from her abusive family during her mid-teens. She lived a marginal life and married a silent, indifferent, sometimes cruel man. With great perseverance she continued her education and eventually completed advanced training in a difficult profession for which her aptitude was limited.

Beginning in her preteen years, she had become preoccupied with what she came to call her "addictive" attachments to men that always ended unsatisfactorily. In all these attachments, she repeated a similar pattern. The first phase was her pursuit, her willingness to do anything needed to captivate, engage, and win the interest of the man. In her excitement state, she was a bundle of energy and in hypomanic fashion screened out all awareness of danger. Once the conquest was made, she became hyperaware of slights, hurts, and disappointments from the man who had fallen painfully short of her idealized expectations. Now she derived emotional stimulation from two sources. First, she experienced intensified reactions to every up and down in the relationship. When the man indicated interest, she would become exhilarated, full of fantasies of the future. When he indicated a lack of interest (almost always the presence of another woman), she would experience vengeful, murderous fantasies. Second, she would energetically elicit from a coterie of friends, and, if possible, from the analyst, a shared belief in the suffering she was being subjected to at the hands of her abusive unappreciative partner. She would skillfully partial out information about her intentions to her analyst and other listeners so that vital information was always being withheld or "swept under the rug."

The final phase involved the denouement of the relationship. Once she or her partner initiated a breakup, she would oscillate dramatically between delight in her escape and panic at her abandonment. Once her panic began, she would reinstitute her pursuit, buttressed by expressions of abject apology for real or imagined faults and failings. Frequently she would already have instituted another pursuit before the final ending, but, if not, she would experience a period of intense depression during the interval.

The interpretative approach during this long period of the analysis consisted largely of identifying the motivational needs being served by her pathological addictive relationship, especially the short-term but, to her, all-important selfobject vitalization she obtained in this way. The treatment was greatly enhanced by her intelligent, lively pursuit of understanding what she was doing and how it related to her childhood. The three facets of an addiction came into awareness: first, the stimulant quality of the complex components of the behavior itself; second, the use of the behavior as an all-purpose solution to, and mode of denial of, problems arising in any other aspect of her life; and the self-sustaining, self-soothing experience she derived from an unconscious fantasy and belief system integrally associated with the behavior. Her fantasy/belief system went back to early childhood, when she pictured the arrival of a romantic male rescuer similar to that depicted in Woody Allen's *Purple Rose of Cairo,* in which the hero actualizes off the screen. Each successive man would briefly be the embodiment of this fantasy, only then to be the recipient of her disdain and contempt and her vengeful fantasies.

Analytic interpretation led to a detailed, emotionally vivid appreciation of the changing but recurrent sources of self-vitalization of each facet of the addictive pattern. With an awareness of the consequences both of continuing the pattern and of giving it up, O determined to break off her last unhappy affair and not begin anew. With the support and understanding of the analyst and friends, she was managing her depression, loneliness, shame, and regret. Then another unexpected blow fell when a crisis in her work that had been simmering for years suddenly erupted and she lost her position amidst condemnation by her employer. O was shattered, and her depression intensified. She now evidenced a physiological disruption, with insomnia, anorexia, and an inability to pull herself out of bed. She came to her hours to report her state but could do little more. With her agreement, the analyst referred her to a colleague, who prescribed antidepressant medication and carefully monitored the dose and effects. As O slowly responded to the medication, the analytic hours were spent in exploring the possibilities for her to pull together the broken threads of her professional life. Gradually her hope in the future returned, buoyed by her pride in having broken with her addictive pattern and survived once again, despite very difficult circumstances. O was able to plan for professional retraining closer to her interests and capacities and determined to complete her treatment.

9

Defense, Conflict, and Abuse

Self psychologists are repeatedly asked, why do you leave out sexuality and aggression, conflict, defense, and resistance? We can claim that in the conception of three of our five motivational systems—one dealing directly with sensual and sexual development, one with aversive antagonistic responses, and one with exploration and assertion—we have refuted the charge of omitting, ignoring, or downplaying sexuality and aggression. We now approach defense and resistance as *experiences* that arise as patterns of regulation of the aversive motivational system. The experience of the patterns of defense and resistance is subject to empathic exploration by analyst (and analysand). We view conflict as an *experience* of tension and dissonance that arises when competition between motivational systems or contrasting motives within a system cannot be resolved into a smooth transition. We view deficit as an *experience* of perceived inadequacy of empathic support and the sense of dysfunction related to the empathic failure. In instances of abuse, self-cohesion and the seamless transition of emotional-cognitive states cannot be maintained.

To facilitate a discussion of defense and resistance, conflict and deficit, we present an hour taken from the exploratory psychotherapy of T, a 28-year-old graduate student. He entered treatment to "improve his relationships" and to "learn more about himself." During several hours leading up to this session he had mentioned that he might not be able to remain in treatment because of the cost.

T: I've had financial trouble this week. My air conditioner broke down and it cost me $1000.

A: Oh no! [The analyst reported that her exclamation was emitted spontaneously in response to the content and the concern for the treatment it had triggered in her, not, she quickly realized, in response to the patient's affect, which was matter-of-fact reporting.]

T: [after a brief silence] It's OK because I know the repairman real well and he'll get it fixed . . . I had put away enough money for a breakdown, but I just didn't think I'd be hit with that big an expense.

A: [realizing her confusion about T's affect] How do you feel about it?

T: Sad . . . and I can't make plans yet for how Dana [his fiancée] and I are going to afford the expenses next year when she starts law school because her parents haven't come forward yet with what they will contribute.

A: You're uncomfortable with the lack of planning.

T: And having to be dependent. That's worse . . . It's important to be independent. Dana's parents talk about all the self-sacrifice they go through and I don't want to hear it. My family gave us kids a lot but they don't talk about it. When I was a kid I wanted to put on a puppet show with my best friend and charge admission. My dad loaned us the money to make the stage and charged us interest on the loan. I learned that if you borrow money it costs you, but if you save money, you make money.

A: So to be independent is very important.

T: Independence means freedom. That's why after my long bout with mono I went on a tough wilderness survival program. When you're all alone in the wilderness you learn responsibility–how to deal with life-and-death decisions. That experience made me different from other people. Remember, I told you the other grad students were panicking about the oral exam. Well, I didn't feel nervous. I was *eager,* not nervous.

A: So your wilderness survival experiences have given you a unique perspective. When you've dealt with life-and-death decisions you know what real nervousness is.

T: Yes . . . [laughing] Maybe I can work on money next. The situation with Dana and her parents doesn't have to make me nervous. Oh, I asked my mom about my memory of the first house we lived in before my sister was born and mom said I had it right. She said I played a lot by myself, that I was either close to her or off alone. In nursery school, the teacher told mom I wanted to sit on her lap all the time and that maybe I needed more attention. Mom said she laughed and told her, "Why he sits on my lap half the time so I don't think so."

A: What do you think?

T: I don't know. My mom says I got lots of attention, so maybe I wanted it in school too.

A: Yes, that could be . . . or maybe it didn't feel enough . . . maybe you felt that you needed to be held a lot.

T: That reminds me how I got teased when I was little and pleaded with mom to hold my hand or pick me up. I was sensitive about it – embarrassed when they'd say, "Don't you ever get enough!"

The exchange between T and the analyst can be viewed either from a perspective that asks primarily how T's psychic functioning is to be explained or from a perspective that asks what he is experiencing. Let us examine two segments of the hour from each perspective. In the opening dialogue T is making a statement about an unexpected financial drain that triggers in the analyst the expected response of alarm, but in T only unemotional, factual reporting. He is put off by the analyst's exclamation and explains to her the basis for his calm acceptance. She recognizes they are misattuned emotionally and asks him how he feels. He answers "sad," with little affect and no direct follow-up.

From the perspective that seeks to explain T's psychic functioning, he would be described as using the defense mechanism of isolation. He has separated his thoughts from his feelings. From this perspective the analyst's task is to draw the patient's attention to the employment of this mechanism, help him recognize that he has a need to protect himself from his dystonic emotion, and thereby promote the entering into consciousness of the warded-off affect. Two benefits would be expected to derive from this approach. The patient would repair the disunity of thought and feeling. He would learn also that when threatened by a dystonic emotion, he resorts unconsciously to this particular mechanism to prevent experiencing an affect frightening to him when he was younger but that he is now old enough to tolerate.

From the perspective of inquiry into T's experience, the analyst would note the absence of concern in the content of his communications. She would surmise the anxiety that would be aversive to him. But her interest would be in the nature of *his* experience from his point of view. She could not know this from their initial colloquy. Her interest in his feeling, demonstrated by her question and her listening stance, allows her to follow the initial meanings of his assertions about independence and the training he received in financial management. Now the analyst could form a working hypothesis. From T's point of view, he was experiencing a businesslike acceptance of the vagaries of equipment costs and was proud to demonstrate to himself and to her that he had learned this "independent" approach to money management. The meaning, from his standpoint, a meaning not in full awareness but experientially available, is that he is demonstrating his success as a planner. At that moment he is not experiencing himself as having isolated anxiousness, as an outside observer might surmise. The motivation dominant at *that* moment is based on his exploratory-assertive attempt to achieve efficiency and competence in planning for reverses. He derives pride from doing so. In his experience, his affect and content are well coordinated. Possibly encouraged by the analyst's expression of affect, later in the hour he acknowledges that he is saddened by the drain on his resources.

The second episode in the hour deals with another source of emotion – T's taking oral exams in graduate school. He states that, unlike other students, who were nervous, he was eager. From the standpoint of psychic functioning, the analyst could assume T was using denial to cover his fear. She could buttress this assumption by his association that after a long and debilitating illness he had employed a denial-in-action by volunteering for survival training. She would then have drawn his attention to his conflict between wanting to be independent and fearless and his natural concerns about health and exams. He keeps these concerns out of awareness by denying them. In fact, the analyst does deal directly with the disavowal at the end of the hour when she suggests to T that in contradistinction to his accepting his mother's version, he may have *felt* that his mother's holding was not all he needed.

From the standpoint of his inner experience, T was emphasizing to the analyst and to himself the dramatic lengths to which he had gone to experience himself as prepared, even eager, to face dangerous situations on his own. Guided by this perception of him, the analyst acknowledges to him that she has heard the full significance to him of his mastery experience in the wilderness, his life-and-death perspective. In our view, the empathic understanding and responsiveness conveyed by this acknowledgment are responsible for the two important associations T makes subsequently. First he returns to the theme of the initial part of the hour and, comforting himself with humor, admits to "nervousness" about money. Then he begins the final key associations to his childhood dependent attachment struggle with his mother. As he speaks about this important embarrassing memory from his early life, he approaches the subject through a series of distancing rhetorical forms (Schafer, 1976) – first, "Oh, by the way, it just occurred to me"; second, "I'm just reporting what others – mother, the nursery teacher – have said"; and third, the conjectural mode of "maybe."

The analyst now has a choice. She can either describe the use of the distancing rhetorical forms to T or attempt to disregard their effect for the present. The first path would lead into an analysis of defensive measures and their place in an aversive motivation. This path would be taken if the distancing forms were still rigidly maintained because of the dominance of self-protective aversive needs. The second path is more direct and economical. It would be taken if the analyst believed she sensed that the patient would be able to join her in exploring his dependent attachment struggle without feeling overwhelmed by embarrassment or forced into compliance. Whatever path the analyst followed, she would examine the sequence of subsequent exchanges to evaluate the effect.

The analyst followed the second route and responded directly to the rhetorical devices first by asking T to give *his* thoughts and second by offering him her perception of his childhood needs and the feeling state that accompanied it, "Maybe it didn't *feel* enough." T responds to the analyst's gentle pushing aside of his aversive indication that he wants to hide behind his mother's account. He describes his sensitivity and embarrassment in response to the family's teasing about his neediness, an aversive experience that contributes to his counterdependent attitudes that are the main theme of the hour.

DEFENSE MECHANISMS AS COMPONENTS OF THE AVERSIVE MOTIVATIONAL SYSTEM

Assumption 1: The psychoanalytic conception of defense and defense mechanisms requires redefinition in a theory of motivational systems.

We believe that the defense concept as a whole is better described as a broad set of pattern responses that characterize and express aversive motivation. In this way the question that has often preoccupied analytic consideration of defense – is this or that defense adaptive or maladaptive? – is replaced by the more immediate clinical questions, what triggered the aversive response, what form (antagonistic, withdrawing, or both) did the aversive response take, were others able to respond in a manner that promoted self-righting, or did the aversive response become organized as an aversive state? We believe that defense mechanisms do not refer to a specific group of psychic apparatuses but are simply modes of cognition, regulations of affect and memory that are used by the self-organization to express aversiveness. We would replace the general concept of defense or a defensive organization (Lichtenberg and Slap, 1971, 1972) by the aversive motivational system and regard defense mechanisms as uncoded pattern regulators of the fundamental level of unconscious mentation (see Chapter 4).

THE EMPATHIC MODE OF PERCEPTION VS. DEFENSE INTERPRETATION

Assumption 2: An inherent contradiction exists between the empathic mode of perception and the traditional treatment of defenses by confrontation and interpretation.

In psychoanalytic treatment, defenses and defense mechanisms tend to be dealt with from the perspective of an outside observer. Within this perspective, the analyst has learned a set of disguises, distortions, and deceptions that the patient unwittingly is practicing that keeps him from being aware of something he is afraid of knowing and of revealing to the analyst. If he himself knew, the patient would suffer anxiety, shame, and guilt; if the analyst knew, the patient would suffer embarrassment, humiliation, and guilt as well as the exposure of secrets that would portray him or his family in an unfavorable light. The analyst, having learned to decipher the code for hiding and deceiving, and being able to guess the secret before the patient can, makes his privileged knowledge available in a tactful and timely fashion. The patient can then learn to recognize cues to alert him that he is again repressing, displacing, isolating, reversing, projecting or denying, and learn to accept the analyst's reminders that he is doing so once again. Thus, while defense interpretation is generally thought of as making conscious the unconscious part of the ego, it is doing so only in a particular manner. It is not bringing into awareness unavailable memories, fantasies, or beliefs; it is teaching a patient to recognize patterns by which he regulates trends in his approach. It is comparable to teaching someone to recognize physiological signs of hypertension that lie outside of any coded awareness. It says to the patient, I know what is going on in your mind, what you are doing, and why you are doing it. So, if you want to know, you must learn to be an outside observer like me and catch on to what you do to interfere with your and my penetrating further in our understanding.

The interpretation of defenses, as we have outlined it and in various modifications (Gray, 1973), has proved useful, but the analysand's sense of agency and of trust may be diminished. Making defense interpretations often places analysts in the undesirable position of presuming to know – often mistakenly – the patient's reality (Schwaber, 1983). Defense interpretation carries with it an inherent pedagogic reconditioning, because it deals with the means of regulating and organizing experience, patterns of regulation that lie in the uncoded, nonexperiential realm. But our main argument is that, whereas for analysts knowledge of defensive (aversive) patterns of all sorts is necessary, interpretation of defense mechanisms is neither necessary nor optimal. The basis for this argument was hinted at over 50 years ago by Ferenczi (1932):

> If the patient notices that I feel real compassion for her, and that I am eagerly determined to search for the causes of her suffering, she then suddenly not only becomes capable of giving a dramatic account of the events, but also can talk to me about them. The congenial atmosphere thus enables her to project the traumata into the past and communicate them as memories. A contrast to the environment surrounding the traumatizing situation – that is, sympathy, trust – mutual trust – must first be created before a new footing can be established:

memory instead of repetition. Free association by itself, without these new foundations for an atmosphere of trust, will thus bring no real healing [p. 169; Haynal and Falzeder, 1991].

Analytic interpretations can help patients create trust in two different ways. Interpretations that lead patients to believe that their analysts know what is going on in their minds when they themselves do not know, especially their forms of self-deception, help patients to trust their analysts' knowledge and encourage belief in their omniscience. Interpretations that lead patients to believe that their analysts know what is going on in their minds when they too recognize or are close to recognizing it, especially their motives and feelings, help patients to trust their analysts' close attentiveness to and appreciation for their perspective. While both types of interpretations promote trust, we believe that analysts who convey to their analysands their empathic awareness of analysands' intentions, emotions, and beliefs from the analysands' perspective also convey inherently (not necessarily in tone or content) a greater compassion, a greater sharing of the human state than does the inherently oppositional stance (regardless of tone or content) of the penetrator of deceptions and the searcher for hidden secrets.

When analysts can convey to patients that they can see themselves from the patients' perspective, without what Ferenczi (1933) called "*professional hypocrisy*" (p. 158), they help their patients to create mutual trust in the ability to confront what is aversive. The question of trust is central to discussions of disruptions in which the patient has experienced the analyst as failing by commission or omission. Such exchanges concern the analyst and the analysand's memory of a shared event and are not a continuation or a repetition of a pattern of behavior of the patient alone. Alternatively, an interpretation that the patient brought the disruption about by this or that defensive operation for this or that defensive reason may help the patient to learn about his masochism, counterphobic inclinations, or other pathology as seen by the analyst. However, such interpretations risk a lowering of trust, induction of shame, and the resort to further aversive measures.

Remarkable parallels can be found between Ferenczi's comments about the therapeutic effect of the analyst's compassion and forthrightness and Levin's (1991) account from the standpoint of neurophysiological functions.

> During the course of a psychoanalysis a number of mechanisms will be tapped that seem conducive to learning. Although we cannot be exhaustive, we note the following: (1) personal and emotional input alerts the nervous system to ready itself for input; (2) timely soothing activities of the analyst probably reduce critical brain stem gating in the analysand so that the hippocampal/limbic and vestibulocerebellar systems are functional and contributory to the overall information processing of the brain; (3) the analysand identifies new information processing methods based on a modeling after the analyst's methods (including,

more specifically, how and when the analyst uses which hemisphere) and a judgment as to the adaptiveness of the viewpoints and assumptions implicit in the analyst's modus operandi; (4) some critical bridging occurs between the hemispheres that has the function of undoing repression and disavowal; (5) some analytic interpretations will result in the restoration of information (stored but inaccessible) by means of its replacement with "earlier versions"; (6) some of these "earlier versions" will come from the cerebellum under the stimulation of the analyst's interpretations and reconstructions; (7) in the analytic process the analyst and analysand will make use of their vestibulocerebellar systems to provide and communicate empathy; and (8) there is the possibility that some critical memories will be recovered by the assumption of postures or the reenactment of subtle action patterns that were part of the experience around which those memories were originally organized [pp. 78–79].

DEFENSE AS AN ORIENTATION
TO INTRAPSYCHIC DYNAMICS

Assumption 3: The optimal use by analysts of the knowledge of defense and defense mechanisms lies in analysts' orienting themselves to their patients' inner states. Knowledge of cognitive and affective regulation to effectuate motives in any of the systems is as fundamental to an understanding of psychic functioning as the neurophysiological conception of feedback and feedforward pathways is to an accounting of brain functioning. In our case example, the analyst was able to orient herself at first to her misattuned response and taking, the external position, consider the possible use of isolation of affect. Later she used her assumption that T was employing denial to obscure dependent wishes as the basis for her final suggestion that he might have felt he needed more. In other cases, the analyst can use recognition of a defense such as repression to alert the patient to whatever result affects the patient's awareness, for example, the patient's frustration or indifference to having forgotten an important meeting. At other times, the analyst can confirm a patient's sense, during the hour, of letting immediate contents or feelings "slip away" as a recognizable experience.

RESISTANCE AS AN INDICATOR
OF INTERSUBJECTIVE DYNAMICS

Assumption 4: Unlike defense, which is an intrapsychic concept, resistance is intersubjective. When T tried to hide behind his mother's account of his simply wanting to continue the satisfying attention at school, he was mounting a resistance to exposing his embarrassment to the analyst at having been teased for never feeling he had enough. On the intrapsychic side, we can presume that the analysand struggles with a belief that he was a shame-worthy, needy, clinging, dependent child in his mother's eyes. Thus, what was revealed during this hour was his resistance to embarrassment before the analyst. What was not revealed was the shame he may have felt about himself. While we may conceptualize shame felt toward the self as intrapsychic, a person, even when alone, is apt to experience, consciously or unconsciously, the imagined presence of others. What matters in the clinical situation is making the correct inference as to which is the dominant drift of the patient's orientation since many issues that emerge during analysis are Janus faced, sometimes pointing inward to the self as though intrapsychic and sometimes pointing outward to the analyst or others.

THE EFFECT OF SELF-STATE ON THE INTERPRETATION OF DEFENSE AND RESISTANCE

Assumption 5: When applied to any clinical situation, neither defense nor resistance can be considered independent of an assessment of state. Emde, Gaensbauer, and Harman (1976) define states as "a constellation of certain patterns of physiological variables and/or patterns of behaviors which seem to repeat themselves and which appear to be relatively stable" (p. 29). This definition applies to the state changes of infancy (alert wakefulness, quiet wakefulness, drowsiness, crying, REM and non-REM sleep).

As it applies to our use we define state as a constellation of relatively stable repeated patterns of motivational variables and patterns of self experience characterized by specific forms of activity, cognition, affect, and relatedness. When a transition from one state to another occurs, the new state acts to reorganize the prior behaviors, cognition, affect, and relatedness and to resist changes to other states. For example, a panic state is characterized by either frozen inaction or desperate retreat; paralyzed cognition; intense, overwhelming fear; and a breach in relatedness. A panic state involves an extreme manifestation of the aversive motivational system in which the experience of self as able to organize and integrate the current state with other states is compromised. Instead of a smooth transition, panic episodes arise as precipitous shifts from normal states. In contrast, an intimacy state, the state of a person's sharing a period of closeness with a friend, is characterized by a variety of activity levels varying from sedentary quietness to lively verbal or physical interaction; thinking that is ordered by common interests; feelings of affection, appreciation, and security; and a sense of connection that draws on a history of prior analogous experiences with the same person or other people. An intimacy state involves an ordinary manifestation of the attachment motivational system in which the self is experienced as flexibly able to organize and integrate the current states of motivational dominance with other states in a seamless transition. We suggest that for the patient T either a direct interpretation of his use of isolation and denial or an interpretation of his experience would be effective. This seeming paradox is resolved by the properties of T's state. An essential experience of a selfobject ambience was operating in the background. Thus, in the foreground T could be depended on to be accessible either to learn about the cognitive-affect regulations he was imposing on his access to awareness or to use an empathic understanding of his state of mind to expand his awareness.

Patients who are distressed by their habitual ways of responding and relating will often be appreciative of the analyst's help in recognizing how they limit their self-knowledge and block the progress of the treatment. But patients who are in altered cognitive and affective states often experience traditional defense interpretations as criticisms and unwelcome penetrations and intrusions and thereby as a trigger for resistance. In the most obvious examples, patients during states of panic, "narcissistic" rage, and severe inner, preoccupied depression cannot comprehend interpretations of defensive activities that are "causes" of their state. The presence of someone who will bear with them can enable them to accept an empathic reference to how their state feels to them. This simple reflective response facilitates self-righting, increases the value of the analyst, and stimulates trust in the potential for further help.

In narcissistic and borderline disorders (Lichtenberg, 1987b; Stolorow et al., 1987) special conditions of state limit the receptivity of patients to defense interpretation. When a patient oscillates between a state of manic expansiveness and depressed depletion or a state of awed adoration and depreciating denunciation, attempts to interpret splitting often fall on deaf ears. Under these circumstances, a patient in one state may have a very limited capacity to recall his or her experience in the other state. Such an incapacity often lasts for long periods during the treatment. Exploration of the experience a patient is having during a state, whether expansive or deflated, adoring or depreciating, is more apt to arouse the patient's interest. Approaching the state as a defense against another state is more likely to arouse resistance (defensiveness) until the patient indicates awareness of the discrepant states. Then the experiences of transition between states and what triggers the change are a more effective area of focus than the defensive activity involved. We will consider the impact of state on the self and the motivational systems again when we discuss abuse and distortion later in this chapter.

CONFLICT AND DEFICIT

Conflict has been cited as the preeminent conceptual basis of a fundamental theory of psychoanalysis (Brenner, 1976). In our view, the living human organism can be viewed, psychologically and neurophysiologically, only as in a constant state of dynamic tension. We hold that the motivations of each system are constantly intensifying, becoming dormant, and competing for dominance (Chapter 4). The self as a developing center for initiating, organizing, and integrating experience and motivation is likewise constantly involved in intrapsychic and intersubjective dynamic tensions. We define conflict as the constant competition for dominance between and within motivational systems and the dynamic tensions present in the self and between the self and others. We do not define conflict as the inter- and intrasystemic tensions of id, ego, and superego since we do not use the tripartite model. Parenthetically, neither in the tripartite model nor in our model of motivation patterned in the form of systems can a circularity of reasoning be avoided: we hypothesized structures or motivational-functional systems that have competing aims and then seemingly derive a proof of the centrality of conflict from them. We believe it is the other way around. Conflict, or, as we prefer, ubiquitous dynamic tension, is a priori an assumption, and the structural or motivational constructs are derivative of that assumption.

What is the empirical evidence for a self psychological assumption of conflict as a ubiquitous occurrence, a sine qua non of the human condition? Let us return to our clinical example of T. T tells his analyst that he is not feeling conflicted about his expensive repair. We learn that he is proud to have prepared himself. We can easily infer from his memory of the puppet show that he had been conflicted between wanting his father to help him directly with the cost while wanting to please his father by learning about money. That some of this conflict still lurks near the surface of his consciousness becomes evident in his later reference to his worries about financial help from Dana's parents. T is also in a struggle between joining his mother in her cover story about their relationship during his early years and revealing to the analyst the nature of his needy attachment. The struggle (intersubjective conflict) with his embarrassment about revealing to the analyst his "never getting enough" comes into consciousness although not specifically verbalized. A struggle (intrapsychic conflict) with his sense of shame about the discrepancy between the self he wished to be and the needy, pleading self he felt compelled to act on as a child can be hypothesized but not confirmed by this material. We can add to our empirical evidence of the ubiquity of conflict in the form of dynamic tension the mix of motivational strivings surrounding the analyst's "Oh no!"—her sympathy (not her empathy [Olinick, 1984]) for T, her self-interest, aroused by the threat to the continuity of the treatment; her puzzlement and quick, self-critical (mild shame/embarrassment) reappraisal as she let herself become aware of their discrepant affect states; and her restored aim to explore empathically the affect she recognized T evidenced, not the affect she would have expected.

Having stated our position on the ubiquity of conflict, sometimes conscious, sometimes partly or wholly unconscious, what can we say about deficit? T's mother and he take different stands. The mother is reported to have said that she gave him so much lap time that he was spoiled (a theory of pathology based on overgratification). T, with prompting from the analyst, remembers that he *felt* he hadn't gotten enough (a theory of pathology based on deprivation). A drive theorist might engage this argument by saying that libidinal urges are insatiable: by overstimulating her son, the mother encouraged his innate potential for distortion and rendered him a compulsive seeker for gratification and a distorted claimant of deprivation. A self psychologist might say that the issue is not lap time but empathic success or failure as measured by the presence or absence of vitalizing selfobject experiences. Thus what the analyst sensed (drawing on prior associations and intersubjective experiences) to be T's edge-of-consciousness evaluation of his childhood experience was a *feeling* of deprivation. The exploration by the self psychologist would focus on the feel of the lap time rather than the frequency itself. Did T sense his mother as perfunctory and cold? Did he picture her as ashamed of her cuddling or guilty for drawing sensual pleasure from her little boy? Did she seem to him to be embarrassed before her stern husband for babying the child? Once we begin to ask these questions about the quality of an attachment experience, the formulation of a deficit in empathic relatedness becomes as generalized an explanatory claim as the ubiquity of conflict. In fact, at this level of abstraction an argument about the preeminence of conflict or deficit becomes irrelevant: any child who experiences a sense of persistent empathic failure will be extremely prone to organize motivations along conflictual lines; and any child who organizes motivations along conflictual lines will be extremely prone to experience, expect, and provoke empathic failures and hence feel that his caretaking was deficient.

The concept of deficit proposed by Kohut (1977) has a more specific meaning as a structural deficit based on empathic failures. In this view empathic success results in development's going forward in accordance with its natural design for the individual whereas empathic failure leads to developmental arrest. A mother's own hyperanxiousness can result in her failing to be empathically sensitive to her child's fears. The child cannot internalize the means to regulate his fear (Tolpin, 1971). In treatment, reexperiencing the failure in small doses can make up for this deficiency in structure. Then, drawing on the analyst's support, the patient can, by transmuting internalization, fill in the deficient structure.

We hold that Kohut's proposal retains elements of the structural hypothesis and utilizes the theory of internalization advanced by Freud (1917). With the shift of emphasis in the clinical theory of self psychology to a consistent employment of the empathic mode of perception, these structural theory holdovers no longer appear cogent. In the treatment situation, we attend only to that which is or can be brought into awareness; that is, we listen empathically to the patient's experience. If patients' communications lead us to perceive them as *experiencing conflicting motivations* or a *sense of deficit,* we understand and interpret from the perspective of conflict or the experience of deficit. Thus the stance our emphasis on self- and motivational systems points to clinically is that experiences of conflict and deficit are ubiquitous human *experiences,* and when either is dominant in a therapeutic situation it is addressed. Our theoretical understanding of self- and motivational systems leads us to reject Kohut's suggestion that empathic failures in early life result in *absent* structures, which then are built during analysis by transmuting internalizations.

Rather, we offer two perspectives on positive analytic change. One perspective notes the analysand's experience of newness – newness of ambience, of patterns of reciprocal responsiveness, and of problem-solving approaches that in their aggregate constitute a constructive (corrective) emotional experience (Marohn and Wolf, 1990), and new intersubjectively organized expectations of mutuality and responsivity (Lachmann and Beebe, 1992). Another perspective notes the activation, reorganization, rearrangement (Wolf, personal communication), and transformation of existing alternative patterns. In developmental terms, the motivational systems of a patient for whom analysis is possible could not have achieved self-organization and self-stabilization without some of the necessary responsiveness of caregivers. The changes during analysis occur in the dialectic tensions and hierarchical arrangements within and between systems. In neurophysiological terms, new pathways are not laid down during treatment, but existing pathways begin to be more reliably activated while other, more commonly used, existing pathways are inhibited.

Self psychology has also employed the concept of arrested development for patients who have restricted the use of their potential for attachment, exploration and assertion, effective antagonism in controversy, and sensual and sexual love. The proposal of a developmental arrest conforms with the frequent clinical finding that during analysis, as a result of the supportive elements of affirmation and idealization, the analyst's reliability, and increased understanding, self-righting occurs in a fashion that both analysand and analyst experience as development proceeding in accordance with its "design" (Kohut, 1977, 1984). Our emphasis is on the significance of this experience of progress along a developmental path – a very invigorating sense of success – rather than on a mechanistic metaphor of "arrest." Many such hope-giving, self-righting experiences are the result of improved regulation of self- and affect states in each of the motivational systems.

REGULATION, ABUSE, AND DISTORTION

When technique is conceptualized in the manner we have described, a theory of self- and motivational systems accommodates a concept of both conflict and deficit as experiences. We hold that a more paradigmatic, nonexperiential overview concept is that of *regulation*. Intrapsychic regulation is inherent in the development of each motivational system through self-organizing, self-stabilizing, dialectic tension and hierarchical arrangements as well as shifting dominance between systems through dialectic tension and hierarchical rearrangement (Chapter 4). Mutual regulation is inherent in the intersubjective perspective: self-cohesion is exquisitely responsive to the empathic responsiveness of caregivers and others, while self-initiating, organizing, and integrating influences the potential for caregivers and others to be empathically responsive. Regulation of state lies at the heart of our theory. In infancy, transitions of state are intimately related to the ascendance and fading out of the patterns of each motivational system. Success in regulating smoothness of transition between states is a principal indicator of the organization and stability of the emergent and core self as well as caregiver success. The centrality we ascribe to self-vitalization from selfobject experiences is a regulation-of-state concept. Infants seek the sense of control over their environment they obtain by being able to re-create a prior state. A sense of agency, of efficacy, of animation accompanies re-creation of a familiar state. These affects can be further augmented by pleasurable affects triggered by physiological needs being met, intimacy in attachment relationships, competence in exploration and assertion, and sensual and sexual sensations. But state regulation also occurs when a repeated organized state involves negatively toned affects of hunger, pain, ineptness, disappointment, anger, shame, sadness, and fear. Then such selfobject experiences as seem to the child or adult to be possible to extract from an unempathic environment derive from the ability to re-create the familiar intensity of the dystonic state. The intersubjective aspect of the repetition of familiar states, whether pleasurable or dystonic, is that once states are established as having strong affective tonality, the interpersonal components can be activated by the person in either role—agent or recipient, lover or loved, abuser or victim.

The regulatory effects of positive and negative tonalities are the same in that both lead to an inclination to re-create the affect state, but they are different in the plasticity of the repetition. Patterns that fulfill physiological, attachment, exploratory, power, and sensual-sexual needs are repeated with the pleasure of their re-creation but if blocked in one area are relatively easily shifted to another. Clinically we make the assumption that the patient for whom eating provides the selfobject experience of satiety and taste will change his diet if health needs require it. But clinically we also make the assumption that the patient who uses food or cigarettes to re-create an optimal state of tempered rage, depression, or loneliness will adhere addictively to the pattern. In the clinical example of T we observed evidence of two relatively inflexible patterns. One was his quest as a child for the intersubjective state of wresting reassuring affection from a reluctant caregiver (mother and teacher), a repetition that often characterized his relationship with the analyst. The second was his determined pursuit of experiences that provided him with the temporary conviction of independence.

T's case brings us to another issue involving regulation: was his disregulation the result of distortion of perception and cognition or of empathic failures or abuse? This question evokes the familiar conflict and distortion versus empathic failure and deficit argument. To extract ourselves from this unproductive dichotomy, we put the proposal in a different manner: empathic failures as experienced establish expectations that the situation will recur. Analogous events are scanned for indication that by active or passive means the familiar experience of failure is being re-created. Thus distortion, that is, selective perception and cognition based on expectation, is as ubiquitous as a sense of conflict and of deficit. But selective perception and cognition do not answer the question, do analyst and analysand form an approximation of actuality (Chapter 3)? The response to this question has been discussed at the theoretical level in debates about narrative versus historical truth (for example, Spence, 1982). At the practical level of individual case discussion, many analysts have tended for years to follow a duplicitous tack. In theoretical discussions analysts have propounded a theory that drive distortion governs perception and thereby symptom formation, whereas in considering clinical material, they describe, for example, a patient's mother as cold and compulsively clean and the father as unavailable or seductive. The leader of a case conference would treat such descriptors of the parents as causally related to the patient's memories and the basis for transferences, while at the same time teaching the necessity to adhere to a belief that the internalized representations are largely the result of drive distortion. Similarly, the assumption that distortion determines transferences is used to divert attention from the analyst's direct contribution to triggering or intensifying a transference configuration.

In our discussion of model scenes and the search for clinical truth (Chapters 2 and 3), we approached the complexity of the manner in which lived experience is recorded in memory. We believe that evidence from child observation supports the hypothesis that children experience empathic responsiveness and failure reasonably predictably and that uncontrollable drive pressure is not an ordinary, expected experience. Considerable variance in lived experience does exist, and many intrapsychic and intersubjective factors influence it. For example, an inherent readiness for soothability will permit one infant to extract a selfobject experience from the same environment from which another, less soothable infant will experience failure. Then the expectations of each will differ, and the experiences they will seek to re-create will differ with very different effects in success in regulating self-cohesion.

The regulation of state we have been discussing affects personality and plays out in episodes of daily life recorded in memory. The self initiates, organizes, and integrates the motives present in these episodes and their shifting dominance. Generally effective regulation of state occurs either in the direction of a smooth experience of competing motives or in the less flexible tilt toward an aversive organization of angry, shame-filled, depressive, and fear states that are relatively circumscribed, as in most psychoneurotic illnesses. But a serious misfit between caregiver and infant, as well as traumatic experiences and abuse at any time of life, can lead to more severe failures in organization and regulation.

Recent reconsideration of the nature of infant attachment revealed by the Ainsworth Strange Situation tests (Ainsworth et al., 1978; Main and Solomon, 1990; Lyons-Ruth et al., 1991) indicates that a significant number of 12- and 18-month-old children evidence attachment to their mothers that is disorganized and disoriented. On their mother's departure, these children may get into chaotic states of distress. They may call frantically, bang on the door, collapse on the floor, and cry bitterly. Then, on the mother's return, they may go into an equally chaotic state of rejection – running away, shrieking and pushing away, slowed "underwaterlike" physical movements, or prolonged total freezing, often with dazed expressions.

When a population of preschool and kindergarten children were studied, a large majority of those with many incidents of hostile-aggressive behavior were found to have been disorganized and disoriented in their earlier attachment relationships. This early disturbance had undergone transformation into organized aversive-antagonistic, controlling behaviors by the age of five. In school these children displayed hostile-aggressive behavior toward peers and exhibited a variety of other problems. Some showed depressive affect, irrational thinking, and violent scenarios in free play. Some reversed roles with their parents, treating them with controlling and punitive or caregiving responses. A second finding that bears on the source of the infants' dysregulated state is that a large percentage of their mothers evidenced depressive states as well as other psychiatric problems. Lyons-Ruth (1988) notes that although the depressive state may be a very important predictive variable, the critical mediation lies in the mothers' mix of hostile-intrusive and withdrawn behaviors. Lyons-Ruth adds that depressed mothers are but one subset of a larger group of mothers with hostile behavior who themselves had markedly adverse family histories and whose own mothers were very often alcoholic or psychiatrically hospitalized.

These findings can be looked at from the vantage point of the self-organization and motivational systems. The researchers are careful to distinguish between *behaviors* they call disorganized and disoriented and adult *state* disturbances, which are inevitably more complex. Nonetheless, when considered from the standpoint of the self, these are inabilities of the child at 12 and 18 months to regulate a state transition that other children of the same age can regulate. The disorganized, disoriented behavior and affect expression of 12-

and 18-month-old children indicate a failure of the emergent core and subjective self to organize a consistent strategy, even an avoidant one, to deal with brief separations. The hostile-aggressive behavior of preschool children indicates that the self of the older child is able to use symbolic representations, based on an expectation of hostile intrusiveness and lack of kindness and concern, to organize consistent patterns of aversive responsiveness. The child is likely to vacillate between states of disorganized, uncohesive self-experience and dominance of the aversive system as the self's primary mode of an organized response. Lyons-Ruth (1988) found that the negative effects are additive when a child has both the vulnerability of an early self-state disorganization and disorientation and a mother who is depressed, hostile, and intrusive. Children who are prone to disorganization into chaotic states have to cope with a home environment in which the caregivers are unable to help them regulate state transitions, and often the children cannot regulate their own transition out of aversiveness either.

Major regulatory disturbances in the ability of the self to organize and integrate experiences are receiving increasing attention in the focus on multiple personality disorders, dissociative states in borderline and narcissistic patients, posttraumatic stress disorders, and bipolar disorders.

Studies of cases of multiple personality disorder (Kluft, 1984; Putnam, 1988; Ganaway, 1989; Ross, 1991) document an unusual form of severely disturbed regulation of self-experience and the relationship between abuse and distortion. These patients' dramatic creations of disparate self-organizations, with complete disconnection after momentary shifts, lie at the opposite end of the spectrum from the ordinary, seamless integration of self-experience. It is as if a dominant motivational system and self based on memory from any age operates as having a separate, unintegrated existence. The potential for this peculiar form of self-narrative creation is believed to lie in a possibly inherited inclination to dissociate and experience autohypnotic trances. Patients with this inherited inclination are extremely hypnotizable and given to easy revivification of memories with or without hypnosis. They can become totally absorbed or focused in some area while unaware of even extreme logical incongruity. They seem to share some of the traits of the disorganized, disoriented infants in that some of the infants are dazed and seemingly entranced, and others become totally absorbed with a toy or a speck of dust and are apparently unaware of their anxious concern for their mother a moment before. Ganaway (1989) states that multiple personality disorder "patients typically have begun to establish a matrix of dissociated self states by early childhood" (p. 209). Thus, both the infant group and the highly hypnotizable group demonstrate a readiness to shift from a normal state of attentiveness to an altered state, although any relationship between the extremes of each is totally conjectural.

Among the highly hypnotizable group who develop multiple personality disorders, a consistent finding is that abuse occurred in most cases. The multiple personality patients describe hazy or vivid memories of abuse of all kinds, often with highly specific details. In an example provided by Ganaway (1989), during a therapy session with Sarah, Carrie (a previously unknown five-year-old alter ego personality) emerged and relived

> in vivid detail her participation in a bizarre ritual abuse mass murder on a mountainside not far from her childhood home. After witnessing 12 little girls from her Sunday school class bound, raped and brutally murdered, this alter . . . was spared by the cult leader (identified as a member of her church) and was taken to his home and later released [p. 21].

The psychiatrist, who neither validated nor invalidated these memories as factual, later learned that the rape-murder stories were created to absorb the terror the patient had felt when her grandmother had read murder stories to her when babysitting. This patient had perceived her parents and sister as chronically abusive but had revered her grandmother as her only nurturing, protective figure. "It had been preferable to screen out the unthinkable reality that even her grandmother had been emotionally abusive by ingeniously creating an alter who would remember the crime stories as actual experiences witnessed by or participated in by the patient" (p. 21).

Ganaway's case provides us with a typical example of an abusive situation that is dealt with by a creative defensive measure, a compromise formation in the traditional sense. It may be similar to the abuse suffered by T in the embarrassing, shame-evoking teasing he received for his needy clinging. Cognitive processing is retained and a cover-story fabricated to cushion the blow. In both cases, the patient protects the illusion of a idealized, protective caregiver: Sarah, by inventing Carrie, who removes the disturbing event from grandmother to an "actual" occurrence; T, who submissively joins his parents in their demeaning of him. In many other instances of multiple personality disorders, however, the abuse, if experienced as more massive or intensive, paralyzes the cognitive capacity to sort out and give meaning to the event in keeping with ordinary sequential logic. The perceptual-cognitive disruption and the unmetabolizable negative informational overload produce a traumatic state of fragmented self-cohesion. The response to massive or intense abuse is shock similar to that of traumatic events occurring in adulthood such as automobile accidents, rape experiences, and battlefield explosion episodes, but without the definition these types of calamities have in an adult mind.

Ferenczi (1933) observed:

> When the child recovers from such an attack, he feels enormously confused, in fact, split—innocent and culpable at the same time—and his confidence in the testimony of his own senses is broken. Moreover, the harsh behavior of the adult partner tormented and made angry by his remorse renders the child still

more conscious of his own guilt and still more ashamed. Almost always the perpetrator behaves as though nothing had happened, and consoles himself with the thought: "Oh, it is only a child, he does not know anything, he will forget it all." Not infrequently after such events, the seducer becomes over-moralistic or religious and endeavours to save the soul of the child by severity [pp. 162–163].

The narrative that traumatized people construct, whether the often fantastic accounts of multiple personality patients about satanic cults, UFO invasions, kidnappings, and demonic possession, or the possibly more fact-based flashback memories and nightmares of acute traumas, are largely efforts to fill gaps in the continuity of experience. A frightening narrative and the response it can elicit are less disturbing than the anxiety-evoking deficit of the gap in continuity of experience. The theme or content of the constructive narrative may draw on many sources – newspaper accounts, popular occult preoccupations, illusions shared with close friends, myths, and movie and TV horror stories. In addition, the rendered version will also be tailored to appeal to the listener. But capturing a therapist's interest, involvement, and confirmation is secondary to a more primary need to satisfy an inner need for a causal explanation. Abused people know that something is awry with them and that something had gone awry in the past. If this is a one-time or rare occurrence, especially if overwhelming, even a reasonable account of what happened may be unavailable. If the abuse was repeated, expected, and anticipated, the victim would know the "what' – my father made me do sexual things with him – but not necessarily be able to follow the track from the "what" through the emotional impact of those experiences to the symptomatic disruptions in their attachment, sensual-sexual, and aversive motivational systems. As Ferenczi (1933) noted:

If the shocks (of sexual attacks) increase in number during the development of the child, the number and the various kinds of splits in the personality increase too, and soon it becomes extremely difficult to maintain contact without confusion with all the fragments, each of which behaves as a separate personality yet does not know of even the existence of the others. Eventually it may arrive at a state which – continuing the picture of fragmentation – one would be justified in calling atomization [p. 165].

As a result of such experiences, acutely and chronically abused children have two sources for distorted accounts of their experiences: one is the ordinary inexplicability (depending on age and cognitive maturation) of such puzzles as sexual differences, bodily sensations, procreation, illnesses, aging, and death; the second is the particular calamity or chronic abuse that has inexplicably happened to them.

Normally, in environments in which soothing and restoration of dystonic states are possible, the self can preserve a sense of unity and seamless transition of motivational states. When abuse enters this picture, the self is markedly limited in the capacity to initiate, organize, and integrate motivation and experience. In some instances of abuse, especially acute traumatic abuse, the self-organization undergoes a temporary loss of cohesion; cognitive-affective paralysis occurs and with it a gap in information processing. After self-righting occurs, the person is apt to be left with a vulnerability to dissociative self-states. Distorted accounts will then serve as Band-aids to repair gaps in continuity but will simultaneously convey a subjective sense of truth. The direct effect of abuse, whether acute or chronic, can be noted in the development of the motivational system most involved. We expect sexual abuse to involve the sensual-sexual system primarily and the attachment and aversive systems as well, and physically assaultive abuse to involve the aversive system primarily and the attachment and sensual systems. Abusive, painful, ineffective, or inconsistent physical care, especially that involving physical states such as asthma, constipation, or feeding disorders will affect physiological regulation primarily; abusive interference with or attacks on the child's intellectual competence will expectedly affect the exploratory and assertive system primarily. If the self, by innate potential and the support of others, can maintain or regain cohesion, the motivations of the five systems can be experienced as integrated, even though the patterns of motivational functioning will be rigidly hierarchical, inflexibly organized, and conflictedly regulated. Alternatively, if the self, by innate limitations or the compellingly disruptive nature of the abuse, is unable to remain or regain consistent cohesion, motivational shifts within and between any of the five systems may trigger a dissociative state and self-fragmentation.

At an abstract level of generality, the self and the motivational systems have a mutual feedback regulatory reciprocity. The more or less successful development of motivations of each of the five motivational systems is integral to the development, maintenance, and restoration of the cohesiveness of self-organization, which, in turn, is integral to the initiation, organization, and integration of motivations from the five systems and their smooth (nondisruptive, nondissociative) transition.

10 _____

Values and Morality

As analysts we have been trained to value a "nonjudgmental" stance toward the analysand's productions. In consequence, values and morality may be sidestepped, relegated to the periphery of treatment, or focused on when they have been viewed as troublesome manifestations of a strict superego. In this chapter we address values and morality as they are articulated in the five motivational systems. Informed by empirical studies, we explore the emergence of altruism, shame, and guilt and their transmission within families and through peers. We recognize a place for analysts' and analysands' values and morality in the analysis of all motives and in the construction of model scenes. Treatment implications include a consideration of the place of "actuality" of the analyst's values and the potential for expanded awareness by both analyst and analysand from the analyst's "wearing" the attributions of the analysand.

THE DEVELOPMENT OF VALUES:
CHILDHOOD OBSERVATION

At 17 months, 10 days, Katie, taking her babysitter by the hand and pointing to the exact spot where the driveway, a favorite area for walking, met the forbidden street, said emphatically, "No." One week later Katie was pushing a toy on wheels. She stopped in front of an electric outlet with a plastic protector. She looked longingly at the forbidden focus of interest, tilted her body toward it, then stopped, said "No" in a matter-of-fact tone, and then resumed pushing her toy.

Four days later, Katie was sitting in her feeding table. She had eaten hungrily and then began to play with her remaining food. She lifted the plate. Her mother removed the plate saying matter-of-factly, "No, Katie, we don't play with food." Katie made faces with her aunt and then indicated an interest in the food, pointing and saying "Uh." Mother put the plate back, inviting her to eat more. As Mother looked away, Katie, eyes glued on mother, a speculative expression on her face, lifted the plate, testing to see if she could get away with throwing it down. Her mother turned toward her and again removed the plate, distracting Katie with a promise of a favorite fruit dessert.

At 18 months, 7 days, Katie, alone in the family room, knocked an object off a table she was not to climb up to. She went to the kitchen and pulled her mother to come with her, saying "Uh oh, Katie no, no!"

Jerie, age 20 months, 19 days, defiantly demanded to have an object her mother had taken from her. Shortly afterward, Jerie fell. She got up crying, her hand on her forehead, saying "Boo-boo, mommy." Her mother explained to the observer that Jerie had bitten a child on the forehead the day before and had been talking about it ever since. As her mother spoke of the incident, Jerie's face changed from an expression of mild distress to a pained look, with downcast eyes and body immobility unusual for this very active child.

HISTORICAL BACKGROUND

According to Haynal and Falzeder (1991), Freud's personal view of morality can be summarized by

> a saying of Vischer's that he liked to quote: "As to morals, that goes without saying." . . . He could not and would not take up an analytic stance toward people for whom morals were not self-evident but passed judgment on them . . . in accordance with the morality that was self-evident to him as man, doctor, professor, father of a family and founder and leader of a new movement in the Vienna of his time [p. 8].

If for Freud-the-man morality was self-evident, Freud-the-scientist sought the origin of its compelling force in biology and found its presumed hold on mankind in ontogenic and phylogenic cataclysmic events. Ontologic development compels the male child, through love of his mother as an expression of sexual drive, to erect taboos against incest and patricide. He (and civilization) are rescued from these moral transgressions by the fear of retributive castration (plus the loss of his needed idealized father and the potential humiliation of trying to perform a sexual act for which he is biologically unprepared). Freud (1905) also proposed a Lamarckian phylogenetic prohibition based on guilt over patricide (and possibly cannibalism) of the primal horde of sons. An agency, structure, or set of prohibitive functions–the superego–arose as both cause and result of the resolution of the Oedipus complex, leaving mankind to fight a lifelong battle over sexual and rivalrous urges.

Three main challenges to this widely accepted formulation of the origins and functions of the superego have arisen within psychoanalysis. The first, starting with Ferenczi's (1925) discovery of "sphincter" morality, states that conflictual issues involving guilt and shame arise much earlier than the oedipal or postoedipal period, during the preoedipal period. Katie and Jerie illustrate the early acquisition of morality. A second challenge came from studies of survivors of the Holocaust and other tragedies. Survivors often experience depression and other disturbances as a consequence of guilt over their continued existence in the face of the losses others suffered (Loeb and Auerhahn, 1985). The significance of this finding is that it presented a form of "existential" guilt that was neither oedipal nor sexual nor even the result of childhood experience. The third challenge came from Kohut's (1977) shifting significance from Freud's "guilty" man to that of "tragic" man. Kohut's view does not directly challenge the existence or time of origin of the superego but, rather, the importance ascribed to it as a prime factor in mankind's ills. Kohut suggested that the central preoccupation of people in the second half of the 20th century is a sense of apathy, boredom, and dissatisfaction rather than guilt and superego (moral) conflict. People who suffer from a lack of empathic responsiveness are left not only lonely and isolated but also subject to altered states of self. The tragedy is that they are unable to reach the full potential of growth of which they are capable. Instead they suffer from shame, embarrassment, and humiliation and are inclined to pursue selfobject experiences in any form (Chapter 8). The issues they are dealing with are not the great moral issues of incest, parricide, and punishment but rather of preserving self-cohesion. Again, the preeminence of childhood oedipal-superego conflict comes into question. Survivors' guilt is a disturbance of adults; preoccupation with preserving self-cohesion may begin in infancy and extend throughout life.

We believe that the Freudian and Kohutian views envision two different childhood experiences. In the Freudian view, a relatively large family lived in confined quarters; children slept in the parents' bedroom and witnessed parental intercourse. They slept with one another and often had access to the parental bed. They were frequently confronted with pregnancies, infant and childhood death, and actual castration threats to inhibit masturbation as well as sexual overexcitement. In the Kohutian view, children are raised in small

families, have their own rooms, are tended by babysitters, and see their
working parents for "quality" time. They receive neither the warmth to
temper excitement nor the stimulation of attentiveness to feel affirmed in their
accomplishments. The moral issue shifts from an overconcern with guilt and
the need to lift archaic repression to a preoccupation with fragmented and
depleted self-states and the need for empathic responsiveness. Kohut's view
moves away from the biologic ontology of a decisive oedipal complex toward
a focus on empathic success and failures in a self-selfobject matrix. Stated in
this way, the arguments between traditionalists (oedipal-derived superego),
object relationists (survivor guilt), and self psychologists (a self highly vulnerable to shame and embarrassment) seem broadly philosophic. What do
developmental studies and clinical experience tell us about values and morality?

Damon (1988) states:

> It is doubtful that children are capable of taking on the entire, complex system of
> parental values in one fell swoop by the age of five or six. Moral development is
> more accurately characterized as a gradual process that entails continual addi-
> tions, modifications, and revisions of the child's values and behavioral standards
> [p. 23].

Kagan (1979) writes, "The appearance of internal standards is not a late
development that occurs after the child learns to fear adult punishment, but is
present early in ontogeny. These first standards are concerned with task
competence" (p. 1053).

The historical background verifies that values and morality touch on a
philosophy of the nature of man, the sociology of child rearing, and the
psychoanalytic theory of development. Our approach centers on values and
morality as they are organized within each of the motivational systems.

VALUES AND MORALS IN A NEW LIGHT

Assumption 1: Values, rules, and ethical and moral codes develop as *an integral
component* of the patterns that compose each motivational system rather than
as separate systems or structures.

Assumption 2: Values, rules, and ethical and moral codes in each motivational system are experienced variably as external and internal and as derived
from a personal authority, a general authority, or an immutable source.

Assumption 3: Violation of values, rules, and ethical and moral codes may be
experienced as fear of punishment, shame, humiliation, embarrassment, and
guilt with great variation for any individual and between individuals.

Assumption 4: Because of the considerable variation in what may be considered as a value, a rule, or an ethic or moral in each of five motivational systems and the variation in response to violations that may be experienced by each of two participants in an analysis, great care is required to respect the individuality of the analysand's perspective.

Assumption 5: The analysts' values and morals as recognized by themselves and particularly as recognized and imagined by the analysands constitute an important factor influencing the treatment.

THE DEVELOPMENT OF VALUES AND MORALS

Altruism as a Foundation

Zahn-Waxler and her group (1979, 1982, 1990) discovered that, beginning around 18 months of age, toddlers become alert to the distress of others and often attempt some remedial action. This observation suggests that altruistic concern about the distress of others is an innate emergent potential that adds an underlying capacity for empathy to attachment experiences. The researchers also observed that the toddlers frequently indicated that they regarded themselves as responsible for the distress although the children's judgment about the event might be faulty. Zahn-Waxler et al. regard these findings of guilt and concerns about responsibility to be significant indications of an adaptive check to aggressiveness, an encouragement to undo harm and thereby restore social harmony. These authors have tracked guilt and altruistic responses in older children in an effort to discover factors that promote or detract from adaptive relational patterns. For example, when five- to nine-year-old children were presented with vignettes to elicit narratives about interpersonal conflict and distress, "Children of well mothers showed prototypic expressions of adaptive guilt involving themes of responsibility and reparation, especially at the older ages. In contrast, themes of children of depressed mothers often were aberrant, distorted, and unresolved" (Zahn-Waxler, 1990, p. 51). In another study (Zahn-Waxler et al., 1984), a small group of male children of fathers or mothers with bipolar illness lacked, by age 2, the cautionary restraint or cooperative attitude of a control group. Instead they were sometimes inappropriately aggressive, hitting or grabbing from an unfamiliar adult. Following separation from mother, they were particularly likely to attack playmates but also were apt to adopt a passive stance to the aggressiveness of other children.

These studies reflect the reciprocal relationship between child and care-givers through which the child's emergent, core, subjective, and symbolic representational selves absorb and elaborate values, rules, ethics, and morals.

A guiding parent must have available strong and clear affective responses of a directive nature because young children are much more able to perceive emotional responses than they are to understand cognitive explanations. At the same time, children's inherent potential for altruism and their desire for order and guidance are best encouraged when children sense an empathic response to their needs. Effective responsiveness to physiological requirements and affirmations of attachments, exploratory-assertive efforts, and sensual and sexual needs, as well as guidance and acceptance of aversive antagonism and withdrawal, are very difficult for a depressed, angry, fragmented, or depleted parent. Thus it was not surprising to find children of depressed mothers inclined to attribute failure at school and in social interactions to themselves. They also see themselves as the cause of their parents' maltreatment, and they worry about causing other bad things to happen. These children feel that they deserve to be punished, berate themselves when sad, and frequently feel shame.

Mothers are generally the principal caregivers and therefore the primary conveyers of values in the first years. As development takes place in each of the motivational systems, values accrue to each functional pattern. Babies who eat, sleep, and eliminate in accordance with their mothers' expectations are told they are good. Physical substances and objects in daily life themselves are either good or bad. Food is yummy and "good for you," or "that's bad; don't put it in your mouth." Feces are "a good BM" or "smelly and yucky." A baby's efforts to make eye contact and to touch and later smile with her mother are received with affirming joy or as an unwelcome pull on a depressed, angry, or dissociated mother. A baby's physical appearance is "pretty like me" or "robust like daddy" or "too fat like me" or "skinny with big ears like his father's family." A baby's exploratory efforts are encouraged by providing him with appropriate toys and opportunity, discouraged when he is regarded as too active or destructive. A baby may, in desperation, derive whatever self-worth she can from exploration and assertiveness when attachment opportunities are too infrequent. Each act of antagonism and withdrawal will evoke a value judgment–don't display anger, it's naughty and destructive; or be angry with others, not me; or he's got his own mind and stands up for what he wants; or she's shy just like me, but she'll grow out of it; or she's a scared little wimp, and we won't tolerate that in our family. Sensuality may be welcomed in one form, such as cuddling, and vigorously discouraged in another, such as thumb sucking. Genital touching may arouse extreme censure or tense "ignoring." A mother (or father) may expose an unclothed body to the child's gaze and then look askance at the child's "voyeurism." And approval or disapproval of each pattern in each motivational system may be limited to a particular action–"Don't hit your brother"–or be broadened to the entire self–"You're an angry, hostile child" or, worse, "In our eyes you don't exist, we can't look at or talk to you." Children are inclined to personalize a value judgment as a way of organizing experience. Thus a mother can carefully focus her criticism on the *actions* of the child, or she can criticize (and thereby damage) the child's self. While the values that are being transmitted can be made explicit by the verbal statements of mothers, we believe crucial communications of values, especially in the preverbal period but essentially throughout life, lie in the nonverbal, largely affective aspects of communication. A mother's saying, "Don't take your brother's toy away from him. You're being mean" communicates a value and a moral judgment, but a vocal tone that conveys neither conviction nor an "I mean it" affect and no indication of readiness to physically intervene to back up the statement undermine the support necessary for the child to make a moral choice.

Values and Morals in the Aversive Motivational System

Traditional conflict theory posits continuous tension among drives and values and morals. We account for the frequent occurrence of tensions in a different way. We recognize that an aversive reaction may arise whenever needs are not met or when empathic failures occur. We do not, however, regard the aversive system as primarily a development of defensive efforts implicated in pathological formations. We hold that four critical developments of the aversive motivational system in the preverbal and early verbal period play a role in the earliest regulation of values. First, in infancy the functioning of the aversive system involves primarily signals that indicate to the caregiver the young infant's state of distress, the need for removal of the cause of that distress if possible, and calming and soothing. From these experiences, infants draw as a fundamental value a sense of trust (Erikson, 1959) that their distress will commonly be responded to. Second, infants and young toddlers, in carrying out agendas of their own, learn that their anger, triggered by frustration, can be instrumental in buttressing assertive efforts. Thus, the forming self can appreciate as a core value that anger can provide power needed at times to overcome obstacles. The third development is necessitated by infants' extremely limited capacity to judge danger to self and others. In many contacts with toddlers, caregivers induce or support children's aversive responses in situations of emotional and physical danger through physical restraint and affect-laden communication. The fourth developmental task is learning to engage in and regulate controversy. Like Katie, with whom we opened this chapter, toddlers learn the value of "no" as a restraint needed to prevent the dangers of the street and to avoid disapproval. Because of the child's developing assertiveness, buttressed by anger at obstacles and the caregiver's imposing of limits to protect the child and others, many parent–toddler exchanges involve antagonistic outbursts and conflicts over agendas. A critical feature of intrafamily confrontations is that at the end both partners can reestablish a positive attachment rather than endure rage or avoidance and a persisting injury to self. Learning to engage in and regulate controversy in this way inculcates the values of autonomy (Erikson, 1959), restraint, reconciliation, reparation, and forgiveness.

The vitality that accrues to the values and morals that guide choices within the aversive (and other) motivational systems derives from the liveliness of underlying intuitive, empathic, reciprocal resonance between child and caregivers. Stated in a self-psychological framework, the value and moral component of all motives constitutes a potential selfobject experience (see Chapter 8) or is mere compliance, a flat, ritualized duty. Shame, embarrassment, and guilt are not inherently pathologic, nor are they associated inevitably with unresolved conflict. Rather, they are potential regulators, contributing to the vigor and intensity of experience, as in the example of Jerie. We recognize the significance of the values, ethics, and morals that constitute the regulatory component of the sensual-sexual system (Freud's core of the superego), as we do the significance of the cognitive ability to form such abstract concepts as justice and equity (Kohlberg, 1981). We do not, however, believe that the concept of oedipal resolution or cognitive abstractions provide the basis for an adequately broad vision of the development of a lively sense of moral guides. Rather than approaches that emphasize postoedipal internalization, we point to parent–child and peer–peer reciprocity as both the means and the experience of gaining values and morals.

Transmitting Values Within Family Life

Notwithstanding that mothers are generally the principal caregivers and therefore the primary conveyers of values in the first years, our theories often overstate the solitary focus of the mother–child relationship. Infants and toddlers will turn from mother to father, siblings, and other family members to get the responses necessary for the development of each of the motivational systems. Moreover, children learn values (for good or bad) from the interplay of the emotional life of the family as a whole. Observations of one- to two-and-a-half-year-old children revealed that affectionate interactions between others were most often responded to with affection and overt signs of pleasure, although jealous responses particularly with siblings were also common. Alternatively, expressions of anger between parents or between a parent and another child, especially if a physical attack was involved, caused the observing child, even at a year old, to become distressed. Repeated exposure to anger between parents increased the likelihood of a negative emotional response. The children who were repeatedly exposed to fighting parents were themselves inclined to become involved in the conflicts (Cummings, Zahn-Waxler, and Radke-Yarrow, 1981).

The emotional life of parents, whether affectionate and effectively prohibitive or depressed, hostile, and ineffectively prohibitive, has a particularly strong influence on very young children. Young children are sensitive to parental emotion because they are simultaneously empathic and altruistic, cognitively limited in comprehension, egocentric in perspective, and unable to express their feelings in words. Thus, many children raised in high-risk environments are very likely to value avoidance, rejection, and antagonism as a necessary self-protection. Individual variation is considerable. Many children raised in high-risk environments are prone to depression, as would be expected. Researchers have found, however, that some children raised in similar environments were constructively committed to helping others without themselves becoming depressed. One group of resilient adolescents of affectively ill parents were unexpectedly mature individuals who valued empathic, concerned relations with and toward others (Beardslee and Podorefsky, 1988).

Differing childrearing practices affect the inculcation of values and acceptance of rules. As we have stated, before the age of two, children generally ignore a verbal command to discontinue a desired act unless the command carries a strong emotional overtone and is reinforced by the parent's physical presence. On the other hand, a parent's continually strident anger loses the ability to arouse attention and creates an atmosphere of disorder, antagonism, and withdrawal. Maccoby and Martin (1983) found that contrary to expectations based on theories of "spoiling" children through gratification, relative permissiveness alone did not contribute to aggressiveness. Permissiveness, however, particularly in the form of ignoring the child's behavior until it impinged on the parent, combined with a severely punitive response, adversely affected the child's moral values and behavior.

Hoffman (1967) contrasted assertion of power, withdrawal of love, and "induction" as ways parents transmit values. Power assertion teaches that might makes right, especially when a rule has little intrinsic value for meeting the motivational needs and desires of the child. When the parent is absent, the child tends to revert to prior patterns. Disapproval, disappointment, and withdrawal of love activate a child's struggle between loss of a desired goal and loss of parental affection. Compliance is therefore contingent on an attachment need rather than on development of a fully autonomous moral belief the child considers his or her own. Induction is a two-part approach to teaching moral beliefs. First, the parent must control the child's behavior through the use of minimal necessary force. Second, the parent must explain to the child the rationale for the standard. With small children this may best be done by activating their altruistic concern for the welfare of others. With older children persuasion, argument, and reasoning can bring in more abstract appeals to fairness and justice.

At times, parental practices may encourage flexibility and pragmatism. In the words of A. S. Byatt's (1990) poet hero, "if I urge that we receive Truth only through the Life/or Liveliness/of Lies/there's no harm in *that*/since we all take in both with our mother-milk/Indissoluble/it is the human case" (p. 186). Each time a mother makes believe that she is eating the baby's food to induce him to accept it, she is also teaching the practical value of some deceptions, the foundation for the moral acceptance of "white lies." On the other hand, other parental practices are liable to lead to deceit and self-serving manipulation. Damon (1988) notes that bribing children with large rewards turns children's intrinsic motivation to perform into a seeking for the reward itself. He also notes that for a parent to tell "a child that he stopped hitting his sister because he loves her when the real reason was that his father grabbed him and sent him to his room" (p. 63) teaches the child to mistrust the perceptions or purposes of the parent and does little to encourage moral instruction. Clinically we are familiar with children being told falsely that something would not hurt, would taste good, and was for their benefit. Many patients describe being tricked into hospitals, being left while parents go out or on trips without being forewarned and emotionally prepared, and lied to about the sources of parental discord and divorce. Clinically we are aware that parents who themselves were manipulated often find it difficult not to repeat their own abuse. They are especially ill equipped to help children over the pitfalls of the cognitive limitations grouped by Piaget (1932) under moral realism: they place the consequences of an act above the intention behind it; they assume punishment will inevitably follow a wrongdoing; they assume unquestionably that moral rules are immutable givens. Thus, authoritarian parenting tilts toward retention of moral "realism," whereas authoritarian but deceitful and manipulative parenting tilts toward cynicism accompanied by slavish obedience or rebelliousness.

THE INFLUENCE OF PEER RELATIONS ON VALUES AND MORALS

Children are not dependent solely on parental authority for their values and moral guidance. The powerful influence of peer relations has been emphasized by psychological research. For learning values, rules, and moral behavior, peer relational play has the great advantage of being coincident with exploratory and assertive motivation. Children have the opportunity to observe on their own how rules contribute to efficacy pleasure and then to practice being rule maker, learner, and enforcer. Attachment motives are components of peer moral learning but are not central, as they are in learning from parental authority. "During infancy, children discover by chance that other infants share an interest in toys and that joint play with the same toy is more fun and more interesting than solitary play" (Damon, 1988, p. 32). They delight in and insist upon the symmetry and predictability of taking turns. While conflicts over toys outnumber episodes of spontaneous sharing by small children, a toddler who witnesses another child's distress may be moved to share as an altruistic gesture. Many factors play a part in learning to share: being confidently in control leads to offering a turn or toy to the other; being outside the activity leads to insisting on being shared with; being in the presence of an adult who encourages and demonstrates sharing stabilizes the children's learning. Until the age of four, sharing is largely for the fun of ritual, to obey commands, and to imitate. After four, sharing is done with a firm inner sense of obligation and is regarded as a matter of being right or wrong, fair or selfish. Children's verbal statements of codes of fair distribution, turn-taking, and sharing frequently do not translate into actions. Being the recipient may determine one approach, being the giver, another; and fairness may be obligatory within one's group (boys yes, girls no, or our team, not theirs).

By the early years of elementary school, fairness is increasingly determined by the belief that everyone should be treated the same, except that those who do something well should be rewarded and those who are at a disadvantage through no fault of their own should be given special consideration. By the end of elementary school, preteens can juggle competing claims of equity, merit, and benevolence and devise compromise solutions.

While the sharing of toys, turn-taking, justice in distribution, and rules of procedure in games all develop as component values and ethical codes of the exploratory-assertive motivational system, the morality of friendship involves primarily attachment motivation. In early childhood, friendships form through simple contiguous association and are maintained through the reciprocal advantages that having a companion provides. When acts of injury occur, apologies and forgiveness and the giving and taking of reparation may restore the friendly affect state. Because having a friend adds vitality to play, children are highly motivated to learn the rules of procedure needed to preserve the envelope of friendship as a background to the inevitable agenda clashes, controversies, and moments of cruelty. In fact, many issues that color the therapeutic relationship have their origins in successful or unsuccessful childhood and adolescent friendships. Will my friend let me have my say in our discussions? Will my friend accept my sharing my fantasies, my secrets, and not tell? Will my friend try to sort out what happened between us and not lie about it to protect himself or herself?

As children, especially adolescents, learn moral reciprocity, kindness, co-operation, and a sense of justice from their peer relations, they match these standards against their parents' demands for respect and the observance of prescribed social rules. An authority demanding compliance will be challenged on the grounds of the appropriateness of the moral rationale. Many arguments between adolescents and their parents, school, and religious authorities parallel the extensive disagreements between psychologists about the extent to which values, rules, and morals are considered as conventions of human thought or as immutable laws to govern human conduct, such as justice, fairness, and the welfare of others (Gabennesch, 1990a,b; Helwig, Tisak, and Turiel, 1990; Shweder, 1990). For our purposes it is sufficient to say that at all ages, people will respond to values and rules as either man-made and changeable or as a universal truth (religious or natural law) and therefore immutable. For example, 73% of four and five year olds and 40% of six year olds considered poor table manners to be as wrong as stealing (Damon, 1988), a finding that supports the power of convention against the moral imperative of honesty. Helwig et al. (1990) counter by saying that a wide body of studies strongly supports the thesis that, regardless of age, children and adolescents make clear distinctions between the two domains of convention and morals. One factor influencing the selection of domain is "ethnocentrism, the ubiquitous tendency to view the central institutions of one's own culture (and subcultures) as normal, natural, superior, and perhaps universal" (Gabennesch, 1990a, p. 2050). Even within the domain that might be more broadly considered moral, variations exist. Gilligan (1982) found convincing evidence that boys gravitate toward the morality of justice, whereas girls gravitate toward the morality of caring. Gender inclinations, however, clearly do not preclude females from forming a full moral code of justice or males from caring, empathy, and altruism. Charity, mercy, and forgiveness, as well as awareness of the feelings of others, are more apt to be both individual proclivities and situationally triggered than restrictively gender determined. From our perspective, Gilligan's report of differences between the moral judgments of boys and girls do not reflect absolute differences in morality. When attachment motivation is dominant, boys and girls can be empathic. When exploratory-assertive motives are dominant, boys and girls can evoke justice values. We understand the gender differences noted by Gilligan as differences in motivational priorities.

In arguing for the widespread tension between conventionality of interpretation of values and their reification into universal morals at different ages in different societies, Gabennesch (1990a), suggests that

> it may be useful to consider the great cultural changes in the United States between 1960 and 1980 to be a ripple effect of the demystification of the social order induced when such events as the civil rights and antiwar movements focused the attention of young people on the fact that major social formations can be all too human [p. 2058].

Television presents a view of life that serves as the background for the development of values in children – and in the clinical situation – whether in the planned, constructive decency of Sesame Street; the Simpsons' breaking every code of good taste, ethics, morals; or the evening news' portrayal of stock brokerage thievery and street violence. Yet each individual interprets the same events differently. An official of a stock brokerage firm caught in a blatant abuse of the laws explained that he had to do what he did to face the competition of his job. A resident of a crime-ridden, economically depressed southern Illinois town stated that he remained there despite its faults and dangers because it was home and he would like to try to make it better. The headmaster of a school in Kenya in which 70 girls had been raped and 19 killed in a marauding raid on their dormitory by boys defended the boys by stating they they hadn't meant to harm the girls, only rape them.

GENDER AS A FACTOR IN VALUES

Research findings on infants and toddlers (Robinson and Birigen, in press) indicate that within the context of mother-child emotional communication, males and females follow distinctly different trajectories of emotional development. For males, the value-laden dimension is toward separateness and independence; for females, toward skill in the realm of interpersonal relatedness. What mothers and their sons and daughters value in each other's responses becomes, by the time the children are 18 months old, a two-way street. Within the first year, mothers favor their son's more autonomous *activity* and daughter's more sensitivity in their *interrelatedness*. By 14 months, boys are more likely than girls to remain apart from mothers and more apt to be involved in conflicts over will. By 18 months, sons indicate that they value mother more highly when she is less directive and intrusive while daughters show a more positive response to mother when she involves herself and directs the play. By 24 months, boys withdraw from a negatively expressive mother while girls are relatively unaffected. During the toddler period, girls are more inclined to remain within an aversive engagement, increasing their skills in conflict responsiveness. Robinson and Birigen (in press) believe that girls get a complex dual message from their mother: they are rewarded with positive affect when they distance themselves but get indications of mother's more sensitive attachment when they are more controlled and close. These studies provide strong indications that within the first few years of life distinctly different values are set for what mothers prize in their sons and daughters and for what sons and daughters prize in their mothers' responses to them.

Lewis (1991) found that "positive specific attributions were higher for 3-year-old boys than they were for 3-year-old girls; however negative specific attributions were higher for the girls" (p. 103). Lewis relates these findings in studies of toddlers to the manner in which males and females respond to academic performance. "Women are socialized to blame themselves for their failures, but not to reward themselves for their successes; the reverse is true for men" (p. 103). In addition, women are likely to make internal attribution for their failures and external attribution for their successes, whereas men are likely to do the reverse. Lewis also reports,

> When a female child shows anger, parents use a variety of techniques, including direct punishment and love withdrawal, to inhibit her behavior. But when a male child exhibits aggressive behavior, his parents make little or no effort to inhibit his behavior; indeed, they may even actively encourage such behavior [p. 100].

Women thus are more apt to experience shame in response to both problem-solving failure and the expression of anger.

Our emphasis on the need to reconsider values as experienced by the individual is further borne out by research on girls' evaluation of their genitals. Psychoanalytic theory has long held that girls invariably feel ashamed of their genitals and that any later association to the absence of a penis will trigger a recurrence of that painful affect. Mayer (1991) confirmed Erikson's (1950, 1964) studies that boys and girls prefer towers and enclosed spaces, respectively. Mayer states

> psychoanalysts have tended to emphasize both the generally depressive tone with which girls respond to the fact of gender difference as well as the implications of that depressive response for later female development. Roiphe and Galenson (1981) share this emphasis and concur as well in the generally held explanations for that response in terms of the girl's basic experience of lack insofar as she discovers she is without a penis. In this context, it seems noteworthy that, among almost all of the girls I interviewed, *the affective tone with which they responded to the enclosed space was highly positive. Not only did they strongly associate the enclosed space with femininity: equally to the point, they strongly associated it with pleasure and with attractiveness. They were relaxed and happy—indeed, enthusiastic— as they pursued their thoughts about the enclosed space and its association with things female* [pp. 505-506, italics added].

Mayer asks:

> Are the origins of that pleasure to be found entirely in vicissitudes of an early depressive response to gender difference? Can we regard it simply as a defensive or compensatory strategy developed for dealing with an early depressive response? Or may it point to a possible developmental line in which the experience of femininity is pleasurable from the beginning, and in which the perception of gender difference means, for the girl, valuing what she *has* in the way of femaleness, at the same time that she reacts to the discovery of what she *doesn't* have in the way of maleness? [p. 506].

Alternatively,

> from ages eight to ten, the associations from the boys I interviewed appeared to include heightened manifestations of castration anxiety as well as a broadening of strategies to deal with it in their self-reported broadening of interests to include other than tower-like things [p. 507].

Mayer uses her findings to raise a serious question about how values may become distorted in psychoanalytic theory:

> I believe that the marked anxieties expressed by many of the boys concerning preferences for the tower and wishes to be masculine have a certain indirect relevance to the concept of primary femininity – or rather, to understanding one aspect of the relative inattention given to concepts like primary femininity over the years since psychoanalysts began trying to understand women. The anxieties expressed by those boys lend themselves readily to projection onto anyone who is *not* male – with familiar possibilities implied for theory, so that girls may come to be viewed as centrally preoccupied with the lack that the boy views as fearful, and femininity is actually defined to reflect that preoccupation [pp. 509-510].

SHAME AND GUILT

Shame in Infancy: Tomkins's Hypothesis

Tomkins (1987) proposed that any barrier to the ongoing experience of interest-excitement or enjoyment-joy that dampens but does not eliminate the interest or enjoyment may activate shame. If Tomkins's hypothesis is correct and shame is an innate response triggered when interest and enjoyment are partially interrupted, especially if the interruption is abrupt, then shame would be a frequent component of the lived experience of the preverbal child. As each motivational system becomes activated, interest is triggered. In many situations, varying degrees of excitement and joy follow, sometimes generated principally by the infant's own activities, more often by the added participation and encouragement of a caregiver. A mother's active participation in feeding, or social contact, or toy play, or rocking will support the infant's interest. Further, the mother's indications of approval and attuned inclusion will enhance the experience toward the particular form of vitalization we call a selfobject experience. But often parents need to interrupt a feeding, social contact, toy play, or rocking to take care of another need of the baby or of their own. When this happens, infants can easily be observed having an aversive response. With some infants, the response may be anger and thrashing about in attempts to resume, but others react with a postural change – slumping the head, lowering the eyes, tilting the head – that may well be experienced as the affect of shame or shame-sadness.

Because anger or some other affect may occur when interest and enjoyment are interrupted, Broucek (1991) argues that Tomkins's hypothesis should not be treated as a formula. We agree that shame triggered by an interruption of interest and enjoyment need not be regarded as an invariable occurrence; but that if it occurs often in infancy it is an experience important to the development of all children. By following this speculative line of reasoning further, we propose the following:

1) Shame as an *affective* (nonreflective, non-self-attributive) experience may be part of the daily life of every infant. 2) Caregivers interrupt infants' rising interest in throwing food, biting the nipple, or pulling on an earring and thus automatically trigger an affect that at least some of the time may be experienced as shame. 3) Shame, then, may be an important aspect of the "socializing" of infants during the period when the self is forming. 4) Shame inhibits interest and excitement and therefore can be considered a counterpart to affirming and confirming responses. 5) Whether shame as a lived experience is a useful component of regulation of undesired behaviors and mounting excitement or a pathologic inhibitor will be determined by the frequency with which caregivers activate shame, the length of time infants are allowed or required to remain in a shame state before reparative efforts occur, and the balance between affirmation to encourage and shame to interrupt. 6) An affirmation/shame balance may be generalized from the lived experiences of the preverbal period and will form a component of fundamental unconscious mentation. 7) In each motivational system shame may serve "the function of fostering conformity or deference to standards of conduct valued by the group" (Ferguson et al., 1991, p. 827) as those values apply to the activities of the system. Alternatively, shame may be interwoven into the fabric of the developing self in such a way that, when shame is triggered, the developing child is vulnerable to rapid diminution of interest/excitement and enjoyment/ joy and is prone to a fragmented and depleted state of self.

Lewis (1991) believes that embarrassment rather than shame is an affective response in the period before a self-attribution of failure can be made. Embarrassment requires only the awareness of being pointed at or referred to. Lewis regards embarrassment as an innate response of the 18-month-old infant to being exposed and looked at. Embarrassment emerges "when the child becomes objectively aware of herself" (p. 88). Embarrassment at being exposed to scrutiny, even to being complimented, follows this initial pattern. Lewis distinguishes shame and embarrassment by body pattern. In shame, the posture is one of hiding, with a pained, downcast expression; in embarrassment, the pattern is of looking and then averting the other person's gaze, accompanied by smiling.

SHAME AND GUILT
IN AN INTERSUBJECTIVE CONTEXT

Many authors (e.g., Lewis, 1991; e.g., Schore, 1991) argue for the more readily confirmable view that shame begins as an affective response of verbal children (after 18–24 months) who can recognize their caregivers' view of them (as object) and then view themselves similarly. Lewis (1991) writes, "It is the objective self-awareness mode that is associated with the emotions of shame, guilt, and pride" (p. 61). Lewis continues,

> success or failure in regard to abiding by standards, rules, and goals provides a signal to the self. This signal affects the organism and allows individuals to reflect upon themselves. This reflection is made on the basis of self-attribution. The self-attribution one makes determines the nature of the resulting emotion. . . . Many events are capable of eliciting shame or guilt. No particular stimulus has been identified or is likely to be identified as the trigger for shame and guilt [p. 66].

We share Lewis's view that for a child of two years or older, the event or situation itself does not determine whether or not either shame or guilt will be triggered or which response, shame *or* guilt, it will be. The self's evaluation (not the event) determines whether a violation of values or morals has occurred and, if so, whether the violation elicits shame or guilt. For example, a child who has agreed to share an ice cream with another child and who eats more than her half may decide that the other child did that to her yesterday, so they are even and no offense has occurred; she has only pride in holding her own. Or she may decide that she has violated a rule of fairness to which she subscribes, and she may feel ashamed of having let her excitement at the taste get the better of her. Or she may be moved by the distress of her friend as she watches the treat disappear and feel guilt for his distress. But she could feel ashamed of hurting him – a violation of her values, or guilty about cheating – a violation of her morals.

Both experience and observation indicate that shame and guilt are best regarded as different affective responses. Shame may be an innate response triggered when interest and excitement are interrupted, and it may therefore be an integral component of the regulation of specific motivations of infancy in all five systems. With each motivation the representation of a balance between affirmation, supporting interest and excitement, and shame, inhibiting interest and excitement, is generalized and abstracted out of repeated lived experiences. Guilt may be an emergent response that coincides in development with reactiveness to the distress of others at about 18 months. Guilt would then begin as a response centering on the attachment motivational system and act as a trigger to inhibit aversive antagonism. With later development, guilt may be triggered more generally in response to self-attributions of transgressions of any sort in each motivational system (overeating or not eating enough, soiling, winning at contests, sensual and sexual activities, running away or attacking, etc). In the fundamental stage of the development of guilt, a balance forms between altruistic (empathic) feeling, supporting prosocial behaviors, and guilt, inhibiting antagonism and aggression.

When we encounter shame and guilt clinically, the distinctions presumed to be fundamental to the initial links of shame to interest and excitement and guilt to altruism and prosocial behavior are far from clear cut. Shame and guilt are, to most people, distinguishable affective experiences. Wolf (1991, personal communication) suggests that a physiological component of the affective response distinguishes shame from guilt by blushing in the former and blanching in the latter. Wolf believes that the reddening of the skin surface is consistent with shame's being a response to an external evaluation and the blanching (or constriction of the blood vessels) that goes with guilt being a response to an internal evaluator. Although this distinction may have an evolutionary significance, we believe that both shame and guilt are triggered sometimes by the negative evaluation of a real or imagined other and at other times by the negative evaluation principally of the self. Which viewpoint is taken is crucial. Is the offense a shameful violation of values and standards – moral values and standards included – or a guilt-inducing violation of morals – injury to people and destruction of objects – included? The same trigger often can be evaluated either way.

Within the psychoanalytic literature, a principal focus on values and morality has centered on a revived interest in shame (Wurmser, 1981; Nathanson, 1987; Morrison, 1989; C. Goldberg, 1991; for works that bridge infant research and analytic theory, see also H. B. Lewis, 1987; M. Lewis, 1991; and Broucek, 1991). We note four trends in these works. First, observation of children fails to support the conceptual clarity proposed by Peirs and Singer (1953) that shame is elicited by preoedipal conflict while guilt is a response to postoedipal conflict involving a newly formed and consolidated superego (see Furer, 1972). Second, while guilt appears to be (along with anxiety) the preeminent affect associated with pathologic conflict, shame has equal, or in many instances, greater importance. Third, shame has come to be spoken of sometimes as a generic affect for what might be embarrassment, humiliation, or a downcast mood hard to distinguish from sadness. Fourth, efforts have been made to restore clarity of distinction between shame and guilt by linking shame to lowered self-esteem (narcissistic disturbance), triggered by failing to live up to *values*, and linking guilt to internal condemnation, triggered by failing to live up to *morals*; but contradictions in usage and, more important, in experience lead us to question the validity of these distinctions.

Tomkins (1987) makes the provocative assertion that discouragement, shyness, shame, and guilt are identical affects in that they reflect an identical innate program. As the separate names indicate, these affects are experienced differently because of separate coassemblies of perceived causes and consequences, all reflective of situations in which an aroused state of interest or excitement is brought to a halt. In Tomkins's view, discouragement is associated with temporary defeat; it could be a temporary failure in regulation of physiological requirements (going off one's diet), in attachment (a date fails to show up), in exploration and assertion (losing a queen in chess), or in seeking sensual and sexual satisfaction (an episode of premature ejaculation). Shyness is experienced when an expectation of familiarity is breached, that is, when the established norms and forms of attachment and affiliative experiences are replaced by "strangers." Shame, as a quality of affect experience rather than a general designator of the innate program, is associated with feelings of inferiority or with failures to meet standards of accomplishment set by others (become potty-trained) or by the self (successfully solve a puzzle problem). Guilt is the affect experience of having committed a moral transgression (hurting another or committing a "sin" by masturbating). Nathanson (1987) suggests that guilt is shame coassembled with fear of reprisal based on memories of prior punishment. For Broucek (1991), "Shame is *innately* connected to the sense of self and to sexuality" (p. 23). He adds, "Shame is about the self and its social context and is reflective of a disturbance in the sense of self as well as a disturbance in the nature of the relationship with the other" (p. 21). Shame originates from the infant's experiences of interpersonal inefficacy; from experiences of being treated as an "object," that is, dehumanized; and from being unloved, rejected, or scapegoated by important others.

Zahn-Waxler et al. (1990) regard guilt as a discrete, separate emotion. "Guilt refers to thoughts and feelings of remorse and responsibility that accompany real or imagined wrong doings. . . . As the main affect in conscience, it checks aggressive impulses and encourages people to undo harms, hence, restoring social harmony" (p. 51).

Beginning at age five and increasingly by age nine, children can express in words the features they associate with shame and guilt.

> Feelings of guilt were aroused by moral norm violations. Guilt feelings were also seen as involving an approach-avoidance conflict with respect to the victim, self-criticism, remorse, desire to make amends, and fear of punishment. Feelings of shame resulted from both moral transgressions and social blunders. Younger children associated shame with embarrassment, blushing, ridicule, and escape. Older children additionally characterize shame as feeling stupid, being incapable of doing things right, and not being able to look at others [Ferguson, Stegge, and Damhuis, 1991, p. 827].

Shame in the Clinical Situation

A number of authors call attention to shame that has been bypassed (H. B. Lewis, 1987), substituted for (M. Lewis, 1991), or disavowed and gone underground (Morrison, 1989). They present clinical examples in which overt experiences of ridicule, defiance, boredom (Wurmser, 1981), anger/rage, contempt, envy, and depression (Morrison, 1989) are the outcomes of unacknowledged shame. Morrison (1989) states, "I regard shame as a central ingredient to the experience of low self-esteem" and "frequently a necessary stimulus to depression" (p. 113). He argues that because of the searing quality of shame and accompanying sense of helplessness, any other aversive emotion may be more readily allowed into awareness. M. Lewis (1991) notes that persons who undergo repeated shame experiences are likely to substitute either depression or rage. He adds the provocative suggestion that a patient who is consciously shamed and who acknowledges the shame is rarely seen clinically. "Here, the shame becomes so intolerable that instead of employing a defensive emotional substitution, the self disintegrates" (p. 149), resulting in borderline, psychotic, or multiple personality disorders.

We share the view of Broucek, Goldberg, H. B. Lewis, M. Lewis, Morrison, Nathanson, and Wurmser that shame is a far more important affect than had been appreciated and that the clinical situation and "patienthood" is itself an experience that triggers shame. We also agree with their clinical findings that shame may be experienced fleetingly and then replaced by other affects, such as depression or rage, or reversed into contempt, hauteur, or superiority. Thus we must be alert to discovering shame in any consideration of values and the failure to live up to them. But we reject on clinical and theoretical grounds an *invariant* linkage of shame to loss of self-esteem, depression, rage, sexual excitement, or any other affective experience.

We recommend that the exploration of each associative sequence and its transference implications be approached with an open mind to the affects being experienced both within and outside of full awareness by the patient. For example, a dominant manifest affect may be depression or rage, bravado or hauteur. Nonetheless, prior experience with the particular patient's proneness to shame and the theoretical knowledge of the significance of shame for the condition under investigation may guide the analyst to a working presumption of its presence, however fleeting. Likewise, when shame or some other affect is dominant, the patient's proneness to fear and shyness, to anger and to being easily provoked, to sadness and discouragement, together with the analyst's theoretical knowledge of the vicissitudes of these affects for phobic, obsessional, or depressive conditions, may guide the analyst to a working presumption of the presence of these affects, however fleeting. That is, disturbances in self-esteem and self-cohesion may result from a failure to live up to one's values and morals, and the affect triggered by the failure often is shame but it may be guilt, fear, an angry blaming of others, or sadness, varying from person to person and for an individual depending on context and period of life. For the same person, failure to live up to expectations about a physiological requirement, such as overeating, having diarrhea in someone's bathroom, or oversleeping, may trigger shame, whereas failing in a love affair may trigger sadness, and failing in a work endeavor may trigger frustration and anger, and a successful sexual experience may trigger guilt. Although failure to live up to values in each motivational system may trigger shame consistently (or fear, or anger, or sadness), the range of aversive affective responses is so broad (see Chart 2) that this degree of restrictive response is rare in our experience.

VALUES AND MORALS IN THE CLINICAL SITUATION

Values and Morals That Guide the Practicing Analyst

What conventional values and moral codes guide analysts and therapists in their work? With few exceptions, such as Bornstein (1983), little attention has been devoted to this omnipresent issue. Building on experiences of their own physiological requirements, analysts place a high value on maintaining physical health. They are attentive to indications from the patient of a need to investigate failures of regulation of eating, elimination, sleep, exercise, and use of medical resources.

In dealing with the junction of their attachment motivation and that of the patients, the values of analysts are subject to strain. On one hand, analysts, of necessity, place a high value on the kind of attachment coincident with

Chart 2
Aversive Motivational System

Antagonism	Withdrawal	
cry	cry	shame
anger	startle	embarrassment
rage	fear	humiliation
sarcasm	panic	guilt
belligerence	shyness	moral masochism
sadism	o o o o	o o o o o o o
hatred	disgust	sadness
condescension	distaste	low-keyedness
vengefulness		apathy
		depression

"professionalism": concerned but dispassionate, consistent but flexible, non-judgmental but ethical. On the other hand, analysts, also of necessity, must immerse themselves in the relational world of their analysands, a relational world in which they become important persons. As in any attachment experience, analysts will at times like and at other times dislike their patients, like and dislike the way they are treated by their patients, like and dislike the way their patients treat their own spouses and children. They will tend to form "independent" opinions of people in the analysands' life – their parents, their spouses, and those involved in any dealings. Analysts may find themselves rooting for the patient to marry, or for a marriage to succeed, or for a breakup or divorce to occur. An analyst will, at times, hope a patient will stand up for her rights, at other times hope she will be willing to comply with rules or not fight criticisms. In the interest of professionalism, analysts will withhold and conceal their opinions and often facts about their emotional and physical state while feeling torn about the withholding, obfuscations, and deceptions of the analysand. If, in their attempt to maintain neutrality and abstinence, analysts are perceived as tilting toward aloofness, patients often feel "objectified" (Broucek, 1991) – a slot in the analyst's busy schedule, a filler in the revolving door of the office, a source of income. If, in their attempt to be empathic, analysts are perceived as tilting toward actualizing love and hate and rivalry and mentoring, patients often feel trapped in repetitions of unsuccessful attachments. We believe that a prime paradox in analytic work is that all these pitfalls must occur in an enterprise that so strongly evokes attachment motivations on both sides. Thus in our value scale for ourselves as analysts, we emphasize along with professionalism and our listening and interpretive skills, a willingness to expand the awareness of whatever attachment inclination may be dominant in us at any moment.

In instances where their view of a need or an event coincides with the patients', analysts can easily be affirming and can accept the patients' assessment that they hold a comparable (alter ego) perspective. But when a patient like P (Chapter 7) demands that the analyst respond with a direct assurance of caring, the analyst must juggle a variety of conflicting values. For analysts, an organizing value is to do that which will best further the analysis toward the goals of increasing cohesion of the self and of developmental progress along the lines of the patient's potential in each of the motivational systems. But what will further the analysis? That involves giving full value to the unpleasant state of uncertainty, that is to the recognition and acceptance by analysts that in any given instance they do not and often cannot know what is an optimal way to respond. Is it the analyst's responsibility to tell the patient by gesture and word that he does care for her as the analyst did with P? Should analysts take responsibility for their own contributions to difficulties that arise in the analysis? Analysts can observe the effects of their choices to act or not act, but they will never know the impact of the other possibilities. If self-righting occurs, if emotional intensity mounts without a fragmenting change in state, if associations expand, if perspectives about the matter under inquiry widen, if symbolic reorganization seems to be occurring, analyst and analysand can draw confidence from the interventions they are making with each other.

> A little-explored aspect of analysis is the analyst's regulation of his own action responses. When, and in response to what, does a given analyst feel called upon to act? By act, I mean a range of communicative responses. One action is making an interpretation and thus evokes understanding and further curiosity in the analysand. In another communication, couched as an interpretation, the analyst is moved to send a disguised message that such and such is good or bad. At the other end of the spectrum are the relatively infrequent direct messages calling for the analysand to do or not do something. I regard the disguised messages as likely to contain the more serious value judgments. A particular analyst's proneness to action in a certain area may key in a group of his analysands a tilt toward divorce, a tilt toward heavy drinking, or in other less troublesome instances a tilt toward intellectual scholarship or art collecting. I refer to something more than identification, I mean a value complicity that is based on an unrecognized communication of value judgments–where the grounds for it are fertile. What the analyst stands for, or is strongly against, that abuts an important issue in the patient's life will overtly or covertly make its appearance in the course of the intimacy that constitutes a well-conducted analysis. If overtly, it may become a stimulus for highly meaningful analytic progress; if covertly, it may become an unrecognized form of manipulation at the level of values [Lichtenberg, 1983, pp. 663-664].

Meissner (1983) provides a clear example of his approach to initiating a discussion when a patient reported an incident that breached his values. The patient, a young man, described becoming enraged at a fellow student and smashing in all the windows of his car with a brick. Meissner "was somewhat taken aback and shocked" (p. 590). On recovering, he asked the patient to examine what he had been experiencing that led to his "unusual" behavior. The patient asked Meissner if he wasn't shocked. Meissner acknowledged finding the behavior disturbing and inquired whether the patient had expected and wanted him to be shocked and offended. The patient agreed that he wanted to provoke a response. In the ensuing work, Meissner and his patient recognized that provoking a response was an enactment the patient had had repeatedly with his father as part of their warfare over disparate values.

Model Scenes That Illuminate the Analyst's Values: "Wearing" an Attribution

We believe that the technical principles governing the joint construction of model scenes can be usefully applied to bringing to full recognition the subtle and overt contributions and intrusions brought to the analysis by the analyst's values. The core of this approach is that the analyst accept and then explore the patient's attributions. We euphemistically refer to this approach as "wearing" the attribution as if it were a suit of clothes, a costume, or a role that is assigned to the analyst whether stimulated knowingly or not.[1]

Sometimes the analyst is required to help the patient bring the attribution into the foreground, for example when the representation is embedded in a dream image or displaced to a proxy figure outside the analysis. Often the patient will make a direct attribution, such as "You always get cross with me when I criticize shrinks" or "You think my wanting to change my job is because I'm greedy." We recommend that the analyst sincerely enter into the scene as being annoyed at the patient's slurs about analysts or believing the patient to be greedy. For the analyst optimally to pursue a search for himself as he is being perceived by the analysand, the analyst can oscillate his attention between the joint experience he and the patient shared relevant to the attribution and his introspective sense of his attitudes and values about slurs to his profession and greediness.

To use this method successfully, analysts must be conceptually and emotionally open to the pain (and sometimes joy) of discovering aspects of themselves they may only be dimly aware of (or defensively unaware of). With the analyst's encouragement, the patient is invited to enter with the analyst into an investigation of the attitude under question – what the analyst has done to trigger the attribution at this time, how the patient responds to the analyst's annoyance or criticism, where their values converge (I think we both are greedy) or diverge, and what meanings these convergences and divergences have. Since appraisals of causality and of "reality," actuality, and authenticity are inevitable components of mentation, both partners will be apt to include their feel for these factors in their associations. But with most patients, these factors need not preclude the attribution and its investigation from being explored in the "illusory" "playful" (London, 1981) mode ideal for more freely expanding awareness.

We can illustrate our recommendation through a reexamination of two clinical encounters. In the first, Silverman's (1987) female patient complains about feeling intimidated by a good-looking tennis pro:

> I couldn't understand anything he said. It was just like with my father all my life. He thinks he gives such good directions and clear explanations, as I said yesterday, but he doesn't. I get intimidated with men. I always feel that they

---

[1]We are indebted to Warren Poland (personal communication) for calling our attention to the use of a similar metaphor by Fliess (1942): "Technique requires [the analyst] to serve as what might be called a 'transference dummy,' to be dressed up by the patient, i.e. to be invested with the various traits of his infantile objects" (p. 215). As would be true of most analysts of his time, Fliess omits the intersubjective dimensions we emphasize.

know they have the knowledge. They have the brains, and I'm dumb. And I always feel like I don't know anything and I can't understand and I get intimidated. It's the same thing here. I keep feeling like asking you, "What does it mean?" I always feel like you know. I feel like asking you now. I know you've told me you don't know anything until I've told it to you, but I don't feel that way. I feel you're always a step ahead of me. You know, because you're smarter than I am and all the training and experience you have. (I speak: I don't think that's what it is. I think you feel I know because I'm a man, that as a woman you don't have the brains.) I get intimidated by men. [anxiously] Do you think I signal it to them and that drives them away? So they think, "Who wants her!" I think it started in a way when my father said to me, "Every man is going to want the same thing from you." I got so angry. Why? Why would he expect that of me? What right does he have? I heard R. and her boyfriend kissing just outside the door. She likes it! When my father said what he did, first I was mad at them for wanting sex eventually, and then I got mad if I thought they wanted to kiss on the first date. Then I started getting mad that they'd ever want to kiss. I got so angry. I'm such an angry person. (I speak: As you've said, you get mad to push away other feelings) [pp. 152-153].

We can easily follow the analyst's reasoning. He is certain that the patient is indicating to him that she believes he devalues women. The patient responds with associations that can be regarded as confirmatory. She wonders if she signals men to stay away. With mounting anger, she blames her father for devaluing her as someone who would be treated as only a sex object by men. The analyst interprets her anger as her defense against experiencing sexual desires.

What if the analyst had accepted her attribution that he was always a step ahead, if he had "worn" the cloak of being smarter, more highly trained, and more experienced, of being able to answer her question "What does it mean?" Of course, such a proposal places us in the realm of conjecture. For example, her associations could have moved in the direction of how she felt being with this smart, experienced man. Maybe she felt wonderful knowing she had his attention and interest and eventually his help. Maybe she felt constantly diminished, overshadowed by his brilliance. Or maybe she felt that he indeed did explain meanings to her that she appreciated, or that he didn't, and she was hesitant to tell him so.

And what of the analyst's reflections were he to regard himself as the trained, knowledgeable analytic guide, the "pro"? He might sense that he enjoyed this mantle more than he knew or that *he* felt that she was insincere in her praise and merely setting him up for failure and ridicule. Or that he did like to explain meanings to her in a clear way and enjoyed her appreciation, or that he was embarrassed that he could not make any greater dent in her confusion than the tennis pro?

The point we wish to make is that while the contents of this moment of experience for both analysand and analyst are speculations, the probability is great that both would be engaged in a potentially revealing exploration of an

important intersubjective aspect of the analysis. Moreover, this joint exploration would be at the instigation of the patient. Both participants would have
much to gain. The patient could expand her awareness of a significant
transference theme and implicit value judgments as they organize her experience in the immediate, affectively charged moment. The analyst could expand
his awareness of important aspects of how he and his actual and assumed
values are experienced by the patient, often in ways he himself may have
given less significance to.

Let us now consider the second example, the patient discussed in Chapter
7. The patient states that she is feeling critical of the analyst and then is
hesitant to express her thoughts for fear of hurting him. The analyst wonders
to himself about the meaning – is it protective, it is his telling her he will tape
the sessions.[2]

> P – Yeah, I think these things about you that are . . . [hesitatingly] . . . A – I
> understand that you don't want to hurt me, but we'll have to take that risk. P –
> I didn't like the car in your driveway. [Now, without hesitation] I was driving
> over on Friday and feeling so good about you, but as soon as I parked I saw a
> Cadillac in your driveway. I hate Cadillacs, I hate them [with high-pitched
> intensity]. A – Why? P – I like your other car, but I hate Cadillacs. Is it your car
> [intensely worried and questioning with an increasing pitch]? It's not your
> secretary's. Maybe it's your accountant's car. It's your car, isn't it? I can't stand
> it. It's probably a new car, and I've never seen it before. I hate it. A – So what does
> a Cadillac mean? P – It's an old person's car. It's the kind of car to me that
> someone drives who's very inactive; it's too luxurious. I like your other car I
> saw. When it was snowing you drove up, and it's great. You belong in that car.
> It's an expensive car, but I don't have a problem with that car. A – So, you felt
> that I sold the other car and bought the Cadillac. P – No, that you bought another
> car. It was too much. A – And your vision of me was . . . P – That you were just
> getting old, that you had too much money and you didn't know what to do
> with it, and . . . you were just heading into this conventional, American,
> materialistic way [pp. 469-470].

In this example, the analyst begins his part of the exchange in a manner
that conforms to ordinary procedural techniques. He helps the patient to
overcome a reluctance to tell him her thoughts by recognizing the basis for her
reluctance as her fear of hurting him. Then he enters into the spirit of an
intersubjective exchange in which her view of him as a person who can be
hurt is the basis for her emotional state at that moment: he *confirms* rather than
denies such a risk exists by saying *"We'll* have to take that risk." The patient
launches an impassioned attack on the analyst as a Cadillac owner. The
startled analyst asks about meaning, and the patient begins to develop a model
scene involving her fear of his attitudes and values – that he is inactive, too
taken with luxury. The analyst enters into the construct: "You felt that I sold

[2]*P* refers to patient; *A* to analyst.

the other car and bought the Cadillac." The patient accepts his entry – his wearing the costume she has fashioned – and corrects the detail. "No that you bought another car." The analyst asks her to continue to develop her view of his values that disturb her: "And your vision of me was." She continues: conventional and materialistic, and in later associations adds settled, old, on the way to the grave. Over the next several hours these exchanges move toward an expansion of understanding of her transference while allowing the analyst to examine a self he may or may not have recognized without his willingness to remain within her view of him and his values.

THE PLACE OF ACTUALITY OF THE ANALYST'S VALUES AND ITS ACKNOWLEDGMENT

We close this chapter on values and morality with our reflections on the thorny topic of reality. Much analytic energy has gone into the debate over answering questions involving self-revelation (see Stone, 1961 and Miller and Post, 1990). We believe it is necessary to unscramble three views that may seem mutually contradictory: 1) the actuality of the analyst's attitudes, values, and morality do matter; 2) the patient's view of the analyst's attitudes, values and morality (accurate or inaccurate) are exposed by the empathic mode of perception; and 3) appraising actuality and the analyst's overt acknowledgment of an actuality or disagreement with the patient's perception are often components of the exploratory work with the patient's attributions about the analyst. The exploration must go beyond appraisal and acknowledgment to a joint construction similar to that of model scenes.

To unscramble these views we must distinguish between the experience the patient has during an analysis and the investigation of that experience. An analyst's attitudes, say condescension or sympathy, disrespect or respect, will inevitably affect the experience both have, whether either is overtly aware of it or not. Knowing about the existence of those attitudes and their effects is a part of the exploration. The empathic mode of perception is key if the analyst is to sense into the patient's awareness of the impact he or she is having. The impact of the analyst may be based largely on the analyst's actual attitudes, values, or morality, or minimally on them. In investigating the patient's sense of the analyst, the distinction between "largely or minimally actual" needs to be set aside to expand empathic entry into the attribution. Once the patient spontaneously or with the analyst's help brings the attribution into the associative flow, the analyst's attitude toward the work at that point will heavily influence the subsequent course. If the analyst becomes concerned with clearing up the "reality" of the attribution, either by acknowledging (admitting) its accuracy or interpreting the distortion it involves, the work will center on agreements or disagreements about viewpoints and happenings. If the analyst becomes fully invested in the search for the self that is being revealed, checking out with himself any attitude, value or moral that needs to be appreciated further as a personal requirement, wondering what triggered the patient's attribution at this time, yet all the while "wearing" the role with the patient, a process will be set underway that will carry forward with great vitality.

The joint investigative process becomes the activity that occupies the analytic space and provides an impetus whether "actuality" becomes defined or not. The analytic work will take place in the illusory mode that accommodates the range from largely or minimally actual without a reduction or concretizing of the search for meaning. To illustrate, if Silverman were to conclude that he gave explanations in a confusing manner or did regard women as dumb sex objects or Fosshage were to conclude he was tilting toward smug materialism or was looking old, ill, and fragile, each might determine to use his recognition to alter his presentation, attitude, or values. If either were to recognize what he contributed to triggering the patient's transferential self-state centering on him, that would help him to make empathic entry in the patient's state of mind. But once the inquiry begins about the analyst, it can be deflected from the analyst to the father, as it was with Silverman's case. Alternatively, as with Fosshage's case, the inquiry may persist on the analyst's attitude and values. Statements about actuality become only components of this lively investigatory activity. The focus remains centered on the analyst as *perceived* with all the experiential expansion it is possible to construct mutually as long as both partners are able to remain in the illusory mode of an exploratory-assertive motivation that characterizes optimal analytic inquiry.

11

Toward a Theory
of Technique

In this final chapter we shall pull together the threads of our argument that our concept of self and motivational systems calls for a revised approach to technique. The relationship between theory and technique in psychoanalysis has been complex, even disorderly. Originally, technique was largely a matter of trial and error. The use of the couch was a carryover of relaxation hypnotic techniques, reinforced by Freud's dislike of being looked at continuously. Free association was Freud's brilliant, creative, empirical response to the need to gain information from the patient, a method he based on Breuer's and Anna O's experience with "chimney sweeping" through the talking cure and his own dissatisfaction with the unreliability of hypnotic inductions. Early experiments with the method proved remarkably flexible, flexible enough to remain applicable a century later. The use of the couch and free association have persisted as useful techniques despite consistent major revisions of theory (Lichtenberg and Galler, 1987). They have persisted as techniques because their original purpose of providing information remains central to the psychoanalytic method of exploration even though there have been continuous changes in the kind of information that each theory considers to be most important: for example, repressed childhood trauma and strangulated affect; unconscious fantasies; unconscious defensive structures and products of id, ego, superego conflict; separation-individuation disturbances; paranoid and depressive positions; fragmentation and depletion of self-structure; and a recent return to the focus on childhood sexual and physical abuse. Thus, to the extent that a technical procedure supplies desired information that is otherwise unavailable, it can be independent of the theory that gives conceptual meaning to that information.

Alternatively, changes in theory bring about changes in both the nuances and the form of technique. A theory that holds a positivist view of "objective" reality demands the analyst's neutrality and abstinence to avoid contamination. A theory that holds that the impetus for self-revelation requires the frustration of an ever-present inclination for drive discharge demands the analyst's vigilance against gratification. Since we hold a constructivist-subjective view of reality, our concern, of necessity, shifts from the danger of contamination to an exploration of how the inputs of analysand and analyst influence each other and contribute to or inhibit progress. Because we believe that many instances of feared gratification prove to be optimal responses that lead to more, not less, willingness to share self-revelation, we are freer to answer questions and interact in a variety of ways. Our concerns shift from vigilance against gratification to the motivations and vulnerabilities that are revealed when needs are or are not perceived by either analyst or analysand as being met by the other.

Our point is this: theory and technique are loosely coupled with each other. We have attempted in this book to take a theory – a complex proposal of five motivational systems buttressed by the weight of much empirical evidence – and illustrate its implications for many familiar components of preexisting analytic theory. At every step, implications for technique have been implied or stated. We are not attempting a coherent organization of technical modifications. Our strategy runs in a different direction. We are exploring the implications of our theory for the development of technical recommendations. Our goal is to provide the background for a technique that coheres as rationally as possible. In this chapter we bring the threads of theory and technique closer together.

BEGINNINGS

Our theory of self and motivational systems is an extension of self psychology. We follow Kohut's lead in moving from ego psychology to an exploration of self and self-states. In tracing the beginnings of the theory presented in this book, we start with the clarification of empathy and introspection as a general statement of limits of the domain of psychoanalysis (Kohut, 1959) and the further application of empathic listening as a specific principle of technique. Stated differently, the theoretical change from a tripartite structural hypothesis to a psychology of the self led to the formulation of an empathic mode of perception as a *central* principle in technique. We begin with a restatement of this technical proposal (Lichtenberg, 1981; Schwaber, 1981; Ornstein and Ornstein, 1985) and indicate the sequence of proposals that followed. First we restate technical principles that evolve directly from self psychology. Then we summarize the theoretical proposals that followed: model scenes, a reinvestigation of infancy, and a change in theoretical focus from an exploration of psychic structures, or self as structure, to an exploration of structured motivation. These considerations of the sequence of technical and theoretical hypotheses formed between 1981 and 1989 bring us to our current presentation.

The empathic mode of perception in psychoanalysis allows analysts to gain information by orienting their listening stance so as to be from within the perspective, the state of mind, of the analysand. Listening from within an analysand's perspective means perceiving and conceptualizing the *whole* context of how the analysand is sensing himself, how he is sensing others, how he senses the source of his affective-cognitive state, and what he feels is the range of his active and passive potential responses to this state. Thus, when in a shorthand way an analyst says that she has made a successful interpretation based on her use of empathic perception and that the patient has responded with convincing affirming, and confirming, associations, the analyst means more than that she is in touch with or attuned to the patient's feelings. The analyst means that she is in touch with the patient's whole experiential state in an articulated sense, having coordinates of self and others, temporal linkages, causal explanations, affective ranges, and conscious, preconscious, and often unconscious associative threads.

In taking an empathic position analysts employ (1) their empathy, (2) their intuition, and (3) their more "labored" cognitive reasoning.

Six principles of psychoanalytic technique (Lichtenberg, 1983a) follow from the understanding gained from this approach.

1. The empathic vantage point is central to analytic observation.
2. Analysts form their constructions by shifting their perception between what their analysands are experiencing in the foreground and what the analysands are experiencing in the background. Foreground refers to the immediate content and meaning of the associations the patient is relating; background references to the more general status of the receptivity that the patient presumes, on the basis of prior experiences (transferences), he or she will receive from the analyst. The relationship of foreground–background experiences is fluid. The principle of general receptivity is based on the self psychological premise that the analysand's experience of the analyst as providing mirroring, or as being a twinlike sharer or an idealized caregiver, provides essential background

support for constructive foreground analytic work. When a disruption of support occurs, the failure of the analyst to provide an experience of mirroring, twinship, or idealization becomes a foreground issue.

3. Symptomatic alterations in the sense of self must be recognized. These may be restricted to depletion and enfeeblement, or they may progress to a state of fragmentation.

4. There is a need to follow patterns in each hour and in each sequence of hours that indicate both subtle and gross fluctuations of patients' ways of sensing their states of self in relation to their ways of sensing the analyst and the analytic milieu.

5. The analyst's perception is geared to an appreciation of analysands' intentions as analysands would themselves perceive them.

6. There is a sequence for the interpretive effort of the analyst. Regarded overall, the aim of this sequence is to enable analysts to construct for themselves and for their analysands an "observation platform" on which both can stand and perceive the data of the analyst's empathy and the analysand's introspection.

When through empathic perception analysts are able to construct a verbally communicable understanding of their patients' state of mind, they offer this initial bridging interpretation as a way to affirm and confirm the shared state of emotion-laden comprehension.

Analysands who feel themselves successful in communicating their state of mind and who experience the ambience of the analysis as sustaining may then bring up aspects of a problem in a context of assuming or asserting some degree of responsibility.

Analysands who are now able to recognize and communicate the symptom, behavioral disturbance, or pathological wish from a self-originating perspective will often, in their associations, provide evidence of an alternative or variant (often potentially more normal) disavowed motivation. The analyst's perception of this nascent alternative self-aspect gives focus to a struggle-in-depth (current and often developmental).

The problem or disturbance may then be subject to a deeper, more causal interpretation guided by the nature of the material. If analysts' understandings of the patients' associations warrant it, their interpretation will focus on elucidating what the patient experiences as an intrapsychic conflict. Alternatively, if in the analyst's view the material warrants it, the interpretation would be made with respect to a disturbance in the patient's relationship with a caregiver that has led to an experience of a defect in self-regulation. Each problem – the conflict and the disturbance in self-state – could be interpreted sequentially. As analysts listen empathically to the flow of material, they are guided in their timing and choice of associative subject matter by their understanding of the form the difficulty takes in and out of the transference and by their reconstructions of antecedent forms and variants of conflicts or defects of self-regulation.

The metaphor of a shared "observation platform" led to a further exposition of the analyst at work.

> During those moments when analysands respond to feeling understood and to having their experiences articulated, they will provide associations from a perspective of working within a dialogue, with a shared aim of analyzing or exploring a feeling state, symptom, dream, or puzzling transaction. At these times, the analyst often has a rather unique experience, involving rapid shifts in vantage point. The analyst may fleetingly establish a mental scene in which, like an outside observer, he or she visualizes an affectively charged experience, fantasy, dream, or sensation the patient is describing. The analyst's empathy may shift between the patient and the others involved. The analyst's attention may then fall on how the analysand is experiencing the analyst, even though the patient's focus does not seem to be on the transference. The analyst's quickly oscillating attentiveness may again shift to his or her own response to the shared closeness. At times the analyst may move away from the more emotional side of empathy or introspection and suddenly see, from the shared platform, a whole vista of the experience of the hour, the prior hours, and the already-made reconstructions of the past. From this sudden coming together, the analyst may construct a new set of integrations. This new formulation will facilitate the analyst's ability to subject the problem to a deeper, more penetrating inquiry. This process illustrates the optimal unity of the analyst's primary- and secondary-process functioning. The analyst may then be prepared to offer the new formulation to the patient. To do so, however, the analyst will first return to a state of intuneness with the patient's state of mind in order to get clues as to the optimal timing and phrasing of the interpretation [Lichtenberg, 1983b, pp. 232–233].

The shared "observation platform" metaphor opened a path to explore those special moments during a successful analysis. From this exploration a number of crucial issues required reconsideration. Our introspective awareness of ourselves as analysts indicated that we used experiential models to identify the sources, patterns, and meanings of the events, transferences, and role enactments being puzzled over. We recognized that analysts often order the complex information before them through the use of particular experiential models we call model scenes. Based on Freud's account of psychosexual development, scenes of children feeding, toileting, observing primal scenes, and enamored of the opposite-sex parent have been the most powerful source of experiential models. Each new emphasis in theory brought more models into focus—destructiveness, separation, attachment, rapprochement, mirroring, and idealization, to name a few.

Our experience with the model scenes available forced us to acknowledge a number of problems. First, we became aware of how much we relied on a *joint* construction, a pooling of awarenesses. Frequently the relatively "cool" period of shared reflective awareness followed a "hot" period of intense transference feelings, often with an actual or potential disruption in the continuity of working together. After a sense of safety and an exploratory motive were restored, the task was to look back at the preceding shared experience and understand what we could of its triggers, motivations, and meanings. We found that trying to force the pattern of the experience into one of our existing configurations (oedipal or preoedipal) was always possible, sometimes extremely illuminating, and sometimes forced and unconvincing. Especially when the motivation was the focal point under investigation, sexual or aggressive drive seemed a procrustean bed, an unsatisfactory limiting of choices.

Adding the seeking of object relations or of experiences of mirroring, twinship, and idealization as goals provided a welcome broadening of the possible explanations but led to mixing theory bases. Alternative leanings toward classical, object relational, or self psychological theories became factors pulling at the analyst. The preferred theory of one analytic group might be difficult to integrate with some clinical material yet wonderfully applicable to others. Moreover, each theory provides model scenes of sufficient ambiguity that a creative devotee could make convincing fits. In conferences using clinical examples, we often hear what we believe is a distinctly separate motivational system presented as an outgrowth of another. An object relational (attachment) problem may be presented as an outgrowth of a sexual drive distortion. A sexual problem may be presented as insignificant and only an outgrowth of an object relational or self-selfobject failure. Or both relational and sexual problems may be regarded as the result of an empathic failure or the product of a compromise formation. In addition, these terms are often used simplistically with little specificity or careful linking to lived experience.

An additional problem lies in how to reconcile differences in formulations. Each commentator may seem to have his or her expectation confirmed and can present a convincing exposition. We conclude that, first, single or dual explanatory theories lend themselves to reductionistic misuse because of the success their followers achieve from the plasticity of the metaphors they employ, and, second, when alternative formulations are offered, it is virtually impossible to convince a follower of one school of the salience of an alternative explanation. Our assessment of the problems of 1) having a restricted choice of motivational explorations in our core theories and a limited number of agreed-upon model scenes derived from them and 2) the inability to adjudicate between competing contradictory formulations leads us to seek solutions both within and outside the clinical experience.

Looking outside the clinical situation, we reviewed the findings of contemporary developmental studies of cognition, affects, attachment, innate and learned behavioral response patterns, and state changes. We took as our guide two leads: Stern's (1985) suggestion that we view infancy afresh rather than begin with the premise that infant studies are to be reviewed through the prism of existing psychoanalytic theory; and Kohut's (1977, 1984) dictum that each individual grows in accordance with his or her design. Each instance of infant observation and research was examined afresh to learn from it something about a "design" for development. The extensive examination of the burgeoning literature on infancy led to a reevaluation of existing theories (Lichtenberg, 1983a), many of which were unsubstantiated or contradicted by the evidence at hand. The picture of the infant changes dramatically when we realize that a neonate actively seeks stimuli and has well-ordered states that coordinate with parental caregiving.

The new view of infancy places in question all analogies between the stages of early development and the pathological states of autistic, psychotic, borderline, and neurotic patients. Normal stages of development are not pathologic states either never outgrown (fixated) or regressed to. On the basis of studies by Sander (1975, 1983), Ainsworth et al. (1978), Emde (1981, 1988a, b), Stern (1985), and others, we abandoned models of dual drives and psychic structures for a conception that portrayed development in a regulatory (systems) model. Each developing system self-organizes, self-stabilizes, and exists in a constant state of dialectic tension and a flexible hierarchical organization. Returning to our belief that psychoanalytic models are essentially models of structured motivations, we sought the fundamental sources of motivational needs in response to which systems would form. We concluded that five systems could be distinguished—each based on a discrete need, each involving characteristic recurrent experiences, each prepared for by innate response patterns that interdigitate with intuitive caregiver activities. We assumed that such systems would give rise to experiences that would be powerful sources for model scenes regularly found in the clinical situation.

To bridge the systems in their formative stages in infancy and the model scenes of adult psychoanalysis, we had to track the development of the systems through continuities and transformations that mark the passages through childhood and adult life. The fundamental needs formed in the neonate for the psychic regulation of physiological requirements, for attachment, for exploration and assertion, for aversive reaction, and for sensual enjoyment persist through life. As development proceeds, numerous changes occur. Physiological regulation becomes more self-directed and unified under needs for health and exercise. Attachment to individuals broadens into affiliation with family, school, religion, and country. Exploration and assertion become increasingly complex with education and "life-smart" strategies for work and recreation. Aversive patterns undergo a wide range of transposition from gross withdrawal, flailing about to the subtleties of defense mechanisms. Sensual enjoyment becomes a forked road leading sometimes to soothing and calming, sometimes to a centerpiece of affection, and sometimes to the rising tide of sexual excitement and the pursuit of orgastic release. In each system, needs become symbolically represented as desires and wishes; memories become the foundation for rekindling rich scenes in conscious and unconscious fantasies, beliefs, and context. The universe of experience expands from a kaleidoscope of sensations, affects, and actions to an ordered world of planned perceptual-cognitive behaviors, to a realm of verbally organized inner and relational communication. Looked at in this way, each system is a rich universe of model scenes for each individual based on his or her lived experience at each stage of life. The imagination of the analyst or the analysand is removed from any procrustean restriction but retains a general schema for organizing the data of the clinical exchange.

The problem of reconciling or ruling out alternative or conflicting formulations of clinical data remains and possibly even increases as we add the complexity of five motivational systems. The findings and assumptions from our beginnings do not offer us a solution to this problem, only a perspective from which to address it. The concept of a developing self and motivational systems tells us that the idea of an intrapsychic perspective is a very useful fiction for theorizing but a grossly inadequate mode of accounting for lived experience. A baby's self and motivational systems develop because the baby is securely embedded in the intersubjective realm of caregivers. By caregivers we refer to a broad group of others: mother, father, siblings, grandparents, pets, housekeepers, babysitters. They all have a direct and and indirect impact on the baby. The direct impact involves their empathic-intuitive ability to read the shifting needs of the baby. Their attunement to the baby's needs is made possible by sensitivity gained from matching their motivational systems with the baby's. The indirect impact involves the manner in which those in the baby's world-at-large interact with each other and the supportive or troubled ambience this provides.

What does this tell us about assessing clinical data? The analyst cannot be an outside observer appraising the patient's associations "objectively." Analysts use as much objectivity as possible, but, then, so do analysands. What each does with the other, or fails to do, triggers a perception in the other that affects the tilt toward "subjectivity" and "objectivity." The thoughts and feelings, fantasies and beliefs of each are influenced in form, content, and availability to awareness by the other. Thus, the record of an analytic experience must reveal the mutual influencing of analysand and analyst if the evaluation of any formulation of dynamics or underlying process is to be made. A protocol that tells about the patient, even if verbatim, is inadequate for us to begin to resolve alternative hypotheses. The parallel between a developing child embedded in the reciprocity of emotions, attitudes, and actions with caregivers and an evolving patient embedded in the reciprocity of emotions, attitudes, and actions with an analyst must guide us in investigating analytic questions.

To summarize: from our prior investigation of infancy and the psychoanalytic experience, we conceptualized an empathic mode of perception; moments in which patient and analyst stood together on an "observational platform"; model scenes constructed by analyst and analysand; five motivational systems; and the need to regard analytic exchanges from an intersubjective perspective. In this book we have expanded each of these concepts in the expectation that we can build a solid foundation for a theory of technique.

LAYING THE FOUNDATION

We use the model scene concept to integrate many of our findings. Constructing a model scene is a time-honored technical procedure. What we add is the relation of model scenes to the mode of representation of lived experiences, motivational systems, and the intersubjective mode of analytic exchanges. Our view of development is that infant and caregiver function together to organize the infant's world into perceptual-affective-action states. The infant re-creates these states in the repetitive modes that characterize physiological regulation, attachment, exploration and assertion, aversive responses, and sensual enjoyment. The sense of familiarity that arises from the re-creation of feelings of hunger passing to satiety, awake to asleep to awake, intimacy, interest, and sensual enjoyment creates, along with agency and body coherence, a sense of self. The self-re-creating familiar affect states, exercising volition both in conjunction with others and when alone in the patterns of the five motivational systems constitute "lived experience." Lived experience is recorded in episodic and procedural memories. The recurrence of similar experiences through the 24-hour-cycle of an infant, child, and adult day guarantees memories with similar themes built around similar motivations.

The innate and learned responses of each motivational system contain invariant features in their fundamental schemas. Lived experiences are recorded in memory by abstracting their invariant features and from them forming generalized prototypic representations. The narrative envelope that contains the representation of the themes and variations of lived experience builds an accounting of who, what, where, when, and how into a temporal structure of beginning, middle, and end. The relative sophistication of the elements of who, what, where, when, and how depends on cognitive capacities, but, by the age of two to three, the central features of this organization can be recognized in speech and dreams. The richness and variation increases from the simplicity of early schemas, to scripts like the somewhat stereotypic accounts of three- to six-year-olds, to complex imaginative stories with elaborations and subtle deceptions for fuller effect.

The finding that lived experience is remembered in narrative envelopes has direct significance for analytic technique. First, the lived experience on which the narratives are based is intersubjective. Caregivers immerse the infant in a world of communicative sights and sounds guided by the caregivers' expectations and procedural predilections and by their responses to the baby's temperament. The ghost of others shadows into the agency of the self, even when the lived experiences and the memories abstracted from them are experienced primarily as the infant's being alone. Thus, mutuality of influence, of one person's dominant motivational system allowing an intuitively empathic responsiveness to another's, is built into the human experience. This fundamental relatedness of self to others provides the basis for treatment. The negative effect is that prior experiences of an aversive nature, of having the potential for the expectation of mismatched responses, is also built in. The path to awareness and communication is burdened with suspicion, deception, and resistance. The fact that episodic memory formation is similar for analyst and for patient allows each to meet the other in a world of both shared communication and shared obfuscation. We have found that model scenes constructed by analyst and analysand together facilitate the movement from periods of shared obfuscation to moments of shared communication.

A second influence of the manner in which lived experiences are represented is the analysts' increasing use of the concepts of schemata (Wachtel, 1980; Fosshage, 1990; Parens, 1991; Slap and Slap-Shelton, 1991), scripts (Nelson, 1986), and role-relational models (Horowitz, Fridhandler, and Stinson, 1991). We see these concepts as attempts to depict in structural or relational terms the narrative envelopes in which episodic memory is recorded. Emde (1991) states:

> [S]cript representations are affective themes that are as much interpersonal (guiding real interactions) as they are intrapsychic (guiding expectations and goals). . . . Scripts evoke a metaphor from the theater with actors involved in dramatic encounters. I believe this metaphor is apt; represented experiences are dynamic, sequential, and goal-directed as well as expectant of final outcome scenes [p. 33].

Speaking of repeated excessive unpleasurable experiences, Parens (1991) writes "The more frequent and intense such experiences, the more these become internalized, shaping the hostile destructive trend in aggression and stabilizing hostility-imbued self-object-experiential representational schemas" (p. 88).

Role-relational models and person schemata have been described by Horowitz et al. (1991), who write:

> Recent schema theory . . . fits . . . readily with emerging neuroscience theory of network organization of information and parallel distributed processing in the brain. . . . On large and small scales, and in a variety of ways, the differently

specialized brain areas are connected with each other. Important information is associated with related information by means of the connections among neurons and their activation patterns [p. 182].

In our presentation of five motivational systems, we offer modes of organization of lived experience that build on easily identifiable basic needs. The descriptions of each system divide into levels of mentation. A fundamental level organizes experience into conscious and unconscious schemata of increasingly complex affective action agendas of self with others and self alone. Beginning at 18 months, a more fluid conscious and unconscious level of wish, desire, fantasy, and often contradictory beliefs and values develops. The division between fundamental and symbolic mentation correlates with precortical and cortical associational connections.

A significant feature of this way of conceptualizing motivation is that an organized sense of a volitional self develops before self-experience can be processed by primary and secondary (right and left cortical hemispheric) modes of cognitive-affective organization. Thus, we hypothesize that (1) consistency in the mode of organizing lived experiences in narrative envelopes provides continuity between fundamental and symbolic mentations and (2) the symbolic metaphoric renditions of the older child indicate the transformations that occur with later development. The universality of motivational patterns of physiological regulation, attachment experience, exploration and assertion, antagonism or withdrawal, and sensual and sexual experience guarantees that clinicians can organize their listening stance through the episodic potentials in each system. The individuality of events and ways of experiencing events guarantees that what is contained by the narrative envelope requires the full imaginative creativity of both analyst and analysand to decipher any particular experience in a therapeutic manner. Model scenes are high-level envelopes for deciphering lived experiences coded in both early and full symbolic representation modes. We believe that analysts already committed to using schemata, scripts, and role-relational models will find considerable organizing and explanatory value in the episodic representational potentials that evolve from the five motivational systems.

A third influence on technique of the episodic organization of lived experience lies in the clinical finding that coherence of narrative presentation has a beneficial effect on treatment. Empirically we recognize that understanding is facilitated when a child in analysis can present or construct a coherent event in symbolic play. In both child and adult analysis we and the patient profit greatly when the patient presents an organized rendering of who, what, where, when, and how. The cues we use to unravel repressed or disavowed motives, fantasies, and beliefs often remain meaningless fragments unless incorporated into a relatively coherent narrative of an event or a dream. No matter how symbolically rich a patient's association or an isolated dream element may be, we cannot empathically enter the state of mind of the patient without an episodic schema or representation in which to place the symbol. Empirically, we have tended to regard the ability of patients to relate their experiences in coherent narratives rich in affects as an important facet of psychological mindedness and a major contribution to most successful therapist–patient matching.

A recent study (Levine et al., 1991) lends support to this empirical premise. The ability of adults to acknowledge and integrate contradictory experience and memories correlated with the feeling they had of being self-reliant and securely attached. Adults who spoke of their experiences in global, idealizing terms either contradicted or unsupported by actual memories tended to devalue or dismiss attachment relationships. Adults who were caught up in a dependent relationship with parents gave a confused, incoherent flood of episodic memories with no ability to generalize. They confused pronouns and indicated that they had had to parent their parents from early childhood. Adults who had been abused and traumatized evidenced cognitive disorganization, disorientation, and irrationality when discussing their experiences of loss and trauma. Based on the studies reported in Main and Goldwyn (1992), Levine et al. suggest that "adult attachment classifications are determined not by the actual events of an adult's childhood, but instead by how the memories and feelings about these experiences are organized" (p. 456).

Our essential orientation is toward experience. Our approach is to recast constructs used in theorizing in the light of lived experiences and to apply our motivational system theory to clinical experience. A motivational theory must, however, not only incorporate but also extend beyond phenomenology. We recognize that our proposal can be regarded as "a radical revision of the theories of motivation that have been the cornerstone of classical psychoanalytic thought" (Leichtman, 1991, p. 530). A radical revision is justified only if there are problems with the existing theory. Gill (1991) states:

> [T]he theory of motivation remains a major weak point in psychoanalysis. It ranges from the somatic, as in sexual discharge, to the seemingly psychologically autonomous motive of striving for self-cohesion. I am impressed by the literature that proposes several sets of motivations in hierarchical relationship, without that hierarchy necessarily being the same for all people or even for the same person in different phases of development [p. 17].

Our goal has been to provide a theory of motivation supported by a wealth of empirical data and the earlier theoretical proposals of others that we have reorganized and reintegrated into five systems.

The significance of coherent narrative envelopes, schemata, and episodic memories highlights the importance of helping patients to relate their past, current, and immediate experience in organized renderings of who, what, where, when, and how. Then the analyst as listener and the patient as self-reflector can step into the analysand's shoes and "be there" with some degree of attuned feeling. Helping may take the form of merely indicating our empathic sensing, but often we can encourage patients by asking for examples or further elucidation of the unfolding story. Our openness to amending our account encourages equal openness. Moreover, working within the verbal exchanges to fill in the who, what, where, when, and how allows both analyst and patient to integrate better the expanding information. When causal connections are sought, they can be grounded more firmly in a shared informational base of scenes and scenarios. The best of our instructional clinical vignettes and the lasting integrative power of Freud's case histories lie, we believe, in the evocative quality they exhibit as narratives. Working to help patients develop their skills as narrators of their shared experience and ours allows us to follow Freud's lead as storyteller. We add that we now recognize the value of coherent narration as more than communication; coherent narration gives to all our motivations and relationships and to our sense of self a greater organization, integration, and cohesion.

We have chosen to employ a systems orientation rather than one of psychic structures. Even though organized and stabilized, systems remain dynamically in flux, like lived experience. Our optimal human adaptation calls each motivational system to have periods of hierarchical dominance if each system is to develop effectively. But our optimal adaptation also calls for continuous dialectic tension between systems as alternative needs or opportunities arise within the person or from changes in external situations. And to add further flexibility, sometimes we require the highest level of functioning of the system and other times more automatic procedural responses. Each person has different tendencies for dominance by one or another system; each person changes in the tendency for any system's dominance at one or another time of life. In chapter four we illustrated the range of potentials in the exploratory-assertive system and drew comparisons with other systems. A detailed life span portraying each of the other four systems could be constructed.

To use the motivational systems concept clinically, we must learn to think in unfamiliar terms or the unfamiliar usage of familiar terms. For example, analysts who regularly organize their patients' associations in terms of object relations would be comfortably at home when the dominant motivational system is attachment. When the dominant motivation, however, is exploratory-assertive, they might be so strongly inclined to seek relational or aggressive aspects that they would find it difficult to track the associations for goals of learning with efficiency and competence.

Along with unfamiliarity and the "retraining" needed to use a different conception, a further problem lies in the self-consciousness that theory (any theory) creates in the user especially when the user is learning to apply it. An analyst using our proposal might ask: do these associations indicate that the patient is dealing with an attachment motivation, or is another system dominant? This inevitable awkwardness is similar to another analyst's asking, is this an id–ego or ego–superego conflict or a father or mother transference? Or, what are the components of this compromise formation? Or is the patient indicating that he is locked in the paranoid-schizoid position or moving into the depressive position? With all these ways of organizing our listening, we eventually become as intuitively sensitive to useful landmarks as we are to driving from our office to our home. Even with familiar tasks, our level of awareness shifts back and forth from procedural (on automatic pilot) mentation to full cognitive appraisal. We have found that once we began to use this approach, we could generally easily identify the dominant motivational system and whatever other motivational strands were active. We became alert to shifts in dominance. Those shifts which indicate aversiveness cue us to expect a possible disruption to exploration.

With familiarity we no longer require conscious designatory recognition or labeling as such. We sense our orientation largely from the affects we are empathically sharing. Often, however, we may be confused or mystified. In our uncertainty we may resort to more focused rational thought to identify the active motivational thrust. Frequently an acceptance of and longer immersion in uncertainty offer more potential understanding than trying to puzzle-solve intellectually. The other side of uncertainty is certainty and with it another danger. Imposing any theory onto the reading of associations destroys the delicate balance necessary for optimal openness to the individuality of the patient. The empathic mode of perception purposefully aims to preserve that balance by staying as close as possible to the lived experience, simultaneously being related and occurring. But, as Schwaber (1987) warns, an analyst believing he has entered the state of mind of an analysand has no assurance that he has. Our approach offers, therefore, no more certainty than any other. The safeguards lie in our willingness to offer our understanding relatively freely and to be guided in our follow-up interpretations by the prior exchanges.

Four of our concepts add further complexity and yet greater guidance to our search for orientation in mapping the inner world of the analysand and our own as well: the selfobject experience, the intersubjective context, the perspective of state, and the wearing of attributions.

In conventional terminology, the selfobject experience represents an intrapsychic perspective. The trigger may be what another person does for or to one or what one does for oneself. In analysis, the vitalization of a selfobject experience may be triggered by direct intervention, such as a successful interpretation, or more indirectly as by providing an empathically perceived listener. The sense of an empathic response may arise from the analyst's actual understanding or from the patient's assumption of it. As Kohut (1971) indicated (see chapter 8), the self-selfobject experience during analysis is not a relationship in the ordinary sense, it is the inner sense of self-cohesion being maintained, enhanced, or restored. As a practical advantage, retaining the intrapsychic perspective compels us to consider all responses of the patient from the patient's point of view. The patient's expectations, the motivational need around which the narrative envelope formed, will determine the affective-cognitive response to any input.

We can orient ourselves cognitively by following the cognitive organization of the patient's associations, but we achieve a greater depth of empathic entry by attending to affects. As Tomkins (1962, 1963) states, affects amplify experience, making good things better and bad things worse. As Kohut (1977, 1984) puts it, strong affects tend to promote cohesion of the self. As we suggest, the vitalizing effect of selfobject experiences occurs when needs are met in each motivational system, building an adaptive inclination to repeat. Thus, in tracking the patient's responses to events, to their own fantasies and beliefs, and to our interventions, we can sense often subtle, sometimes overt, indications of vitalizing selfobject experiences of successful physiological regulation, intimacy, competence, power, and sensual pleasure. But when his or her needs are not experienced as being met, the patient will seek the short-term vitalization, even exhilaration, of any pattern regardless of its maladaptive potential. In the short run, consciously or unconsciously, the patient may seek a selfobject experience of an intensified sense of self by provoking a violent argument, drug usage, sexual cruising, refrigerator prowling, and the like. Looked at from the standpoint of the motivational system involved, the wishes and desires involved may be manifold: involving the analyst through provocation, getting vengeance through "acting out," self-soothing through food or drug intake. But to orient ourselves more thoroughly we must also consider that, from the viewpoint of the patient, he is using the self-soothing, or vengeance, or arguing for the purpose of maintaining or restoring cohesion in the most reliable way he feels he has available at the moment. Adaptation in the service of self-cohesion is first and foremost intrapsychic.

However successful we may be in orienting ourselves to the patient's intrapsychic experience and gleaning his understanding of his motivation, we are still outside looking in. And being outside looking in, we do so with our own sensibilities and expectations. In analysis, two sets of expectations and "prejudices" meet, assist, and thwart one another. Each partner in the dyad knows from personal life experience how to reveal and to conceal, how to open the path to awareness even if a motive is shameful and guilt producing, *and* how to deny and disavow motives, deceiving self as well as other. Each partner has the same possibility of creating transferences. But the experience of analysis is not best described as two intrapsychic realms coming together like two billiard balls coming near to each other, or even colliding, but having no effect on the shape of each other. Each partner influences the shaping of the other, and analysis requires the recognition and interpretation of that mutual influence.

An example is the effect of the analyst's pattern of verbal interventions. For instance, one patient expressed deep appreciation of her analyst's prolonged listening before he spoke. She had never felt so free to follow her own thinking and be listened to. Had the analyst spoken more, she would have felt intruded upon, competed with. Since the patient's way of organizing her experience of the analyst's listening coincided with the analyst's long pauses between comment, an ambience of mutual ease developed during this opening phase of the analysis. But even if the analyst was inclined to want to work more actively and frequently, he might have decided to accede to the patient's wishes and comfortably altered his style. Alternatively, if he felt controlled and restricted, he might insist on interpreting the patient's "need" to control him – as he experienced it.

In any case, analyst and analysand will each be influenced by the other, and this influence is a valuable source of information. An analyst might say to the patient, "You have a need to be listened to without interruption because you fear competition" and be accurate intrapsychically about the patient. He might, but probably wouldn't, say, "I find it limiting, frustrating, and controlling to not feel free to offer helpful comments when I deem it appropriate." He would be accurate intrapsychically about himself. Or he might say, "You and I are experiencing tension about when I speak or how much I say. I can be more aware of your feeling interrupted, and we both can try to understand more about how it affects you." The analyst might then be accurate about the intersubjective context.

The intersubjective context provides an indispensable orientation for appraising experiences during analysis. As the patient's self-cohesion and interest in exploration wax and wane, recognition of the patient's sense of the analyst's contribution provides cues and clues to the triggering event. The analyst must center her listening to the patient's associations but must integrate with it her own activity and responses. While an indispensable perspective, the intersubjective context can be misused. In some case conferences, the pendulum at times seems to have swung to make analysis not only a two-person psychology but a two-person exploration. To a degree, for an analyst to expand his self-knowledge is advantageous to both participants. But as Anna Ornstein asked (personal communication, 1992), "Whose analysis is it anyway?" when the focus of the exploration appeared to be shifting too far from the patient. Stolorow, Brandchaft, and Atwood (1987), who have made pioneering explorations into intersubjectivity, have stated the focus in this way:

> "Making the unconscious conscious" refers to the interpretive illumination of the patient's unconscious organizing activity, especially as this becomes mani-

fest within the intersubjective dialogue between patient and analyst. We refer here to the ways in which the patient's experiences of the analyst and his activities are unconsciously and recurrently patterned by the patient according to developmentally preformed themes [p. 12].

To further define the relationship of the intrapsychic and intersubjective perspectives during analysis, we have described the optimal state of mind of analysand and analyst. In this optimal state, the analysand is closely in touch with his own needs, wishes, and desires. He attends his inner monologue with a relative sense of safety, even if the message is his sense of aversiveness. He is sensitive to the intersubjective context of the analysis, the analyst's presence, listening, and contributing. The optimal state of the analyst matches that of the analysand, but with some important differences. The analyst tries to remain primarily in close touch with the analysand's needs, wishes, and desires while maintaining a degree of awareness of his own. The analyst attends his inner monologue, which ideally is heavily influenced by the patient's current associations and related information from the patient's history, especially their joint experiences together. The analyst is also sensitive to the intersubjective context of the analysis but especially attends how he might be being perceived.

We add to the familiar intrapsychic and intersubjective perspectives an assessment of state. In most states during which analytic work takes place, dominance shifts between motivational systems with little or no disruption of the sense of self. Even when disruptions occur, self-righting will generally take place without the frame of the analysis being adversely affected. However, especially with patients with severe neurotic, narcissistic, or borderline conditions, state changes do occur in which the self is altered dramatically. Frequently encountered examples are states of panic, depression, anger-rage, paranoia, mania, drug or alcohol intoxification, anorexia, somnolence, insomnia, prolonged shame-humiliation-guilt. Then the intrapsychic dominance is replaced by an awareness of the temporary fixity of the disturbed state. The intersubjective focus on exploring the influence of the context shifts to the patient's immersion in his altered state and the analyst's preoccupation with what nonexploratory response will be most appropriate to the situation. The situation is similar to that of a parent whose child is having a temper tantrum. The parent has to stay with the child, remain as calm as possible, wait for the state to play itself out and self-righting to occur, and then as much as possible review the intersubjective context that triggered the state change.

The main feature of all the state changes we have described is that ordinary symbolic mentation is not possible. A therapeutic strategy that does not depend on exploration is required as a temporary measure. Each of the state changes calls for its own approach: medication, hospitalization, deconditioning, or work with other family members, under the guidance of either the analyst or an adjunctive person. We deliberately add the perspective of state because state and its effect on self determine whether an analyst can work in an exploratory mode. Using state as a guide, the analyst may recognize that he must function in a supportive containing mode within the analytic frame or, if a more altered state exists, he must modify his approach and adopt additional other strategies to make the treatment possible.

Wearing the patient's attributions is the final guide. Strictly speaking, expanding on the patient's attributions about the analyst is a technical procedure. We include it as a guide because we wish to stress the importance of a particular way analysts can orient themselves to aspects of themselves. In our own analytic work and in observing others, we note that analysts are by training expert uncoverers of hidden, repressed, and latent transference configurations. But with our emphasis on the shifting surface, we believe patients who come to feel safe enough to open the path to awareness will directly confront their analyst about their view of the intersubjective context. We have also observed that analysts often fail to exploit the great potential in these attributions for expanding awareness. Instead, the attributions are treated as distortions to be subjected to a reality reappraisal or ignored until such time as the patient "sees" through them.

We orient ourselves differently. When an analysand indicates he sees the analyst as angry with him or pleased with him, or more tired than usual, or as looking forward to his vacation and losing interest in the work, or as more invested in some exploration than in the patient, the analyst can expand his and the analysand's exploration. To do so, he must try to see himself as he is being experienced by the analysand. On one hand, the clues that the patient picks up about the analyst's feelings and character indicate expectations and areas of interest from the patient's past and often open associative pathways to his prior lived experience. On the other hand, the analyst, his attention hovering over the patient's attribution, can often gain unexpected information about how the patient regards the manner in which the analyst organizes his therapeutic approach. The analyst may expand his awareness of himself as he finds himself intuitively responsive to assuming a role or engaging in an enactment. These are moments when it can be accurately stated that the analyst facilitates an exploration of both partners without loss of focus on "Who's analysis is it anyway?"

OUTLINING A "USER-FRIENDLY" TECHNIQUE

We turn now to the implications for technique. The empathic mode of perception – empathy, intuition, and reasoned thought – leads in our view to a more "user friendly" mode of treatment. By "user friendly" we mean a less jarring, more natural humanistic experience for *both* analyst and analysand.

Since we are attempting to sense into the analysand's immediate state of mind, we attend the communicative flow for *that* purpose. Consequently, the way contents (associations, gestures, emotions) are dealt with changes dramatically. Our essential search is for the analysand's *lived* experience. Thus, we listen for and encourage the patient to reveal himself in ever richer descriptions of events and episodes, including those transpiring in the immediate present. This frees us from the burden of trying to outthink and outguess the patient for what is *not* being said. *The message contains the message.* Listening involves appreciating the nuances of the *delivered* message for what is stated, what is implied, what is consciously intended, and what might be unconsciously meant as well. Listening to a rendering of a dream, a symptom, or an event, that is, a lived experience, is akin to appreciating a work of art. A strong parallel exists in the suggestions of art historian Karen Wilkin (1991) to the viewer of a Caro sculpture.

> Typically, a Caro sculpture . . . reads . . . as an assembly of parts whose relationship is both logical and elusive, difficult to describe, but visually lucid. Much of the eloquence . . . resides in the way elements are placed, in the intervals between them, in how things touch, back off, and angle away from one another, in how they respond to gravity and resist it [1991, p. 2].

The change in theory we have recommended facilitates this approach to listening to the patient's communications to appreciate the lived experience they reference. We are not required to decode the message into either an oedipal or a preoedipal sexual or aggressive drive meaning, but to provide a wider base to account for motivation. A patient who is talking about his struggle with hunger and overeating needs to be listened to with respect to the regulation of that physiological requirement. The analyst need not struggle to translate that message into the form of a sexual fantasy. We say need not—maybe the associations will pull the analyst's listening that way. But if the analyst's prejudgment is that pay dirt in understanding motivation lies in uncovering an unavailable sexual (for example, fellatio) fantasy, she will be restless and bored while the patient "wastes" time with talk about food intake. Or if the patient talks about feeling frustrated because she isn't allowed to tackle problems involving higher math because of her male boss's prejudice, the analyst can listen *directly* to her sense of loss of an opportunity to expand and assert her skills. The analyst can appreciate that her goal may well be to experience a full sense of accomplishment and competence; he need not try to push the patient to the penis envy that he assumes is at the root of the patient's complaint.

Each motivational system has the potential for dominance at any time. The five motivational systems, with many variants within each, widen our potential to guide our intuitive appreciation of what is being said. We are better able to assess what is in awareness, what is close to awareness, and what may not yet be available to awareness. By working more closely with what is in and close to awareness, we stop insisting that patients change the venue of *their* associations to meet *our* theory. Both analyst and analysand have had to contend with an implicit devaluation of the message as presented spontaneously. An assumption has been that if she says now, she must really mean then; if he says boss, he must mean the analyst; if she is eager to tell me this, she must be defending against that. To avoid this catch-22, we don't have to assume an overly naive stance. To paraphrase a line of Hamlet, we can believe that there are more things in heaven and earth than are dreamt of in any speaker's immediate awareness. The source of the "more things" is the patient's delivered communication–verbal, gestural, and facial. From it we first seek the patient's intention as he would know it and then can identify and contrast other implied motives and messages.

Having a theory that is couched in ordinary language provides the advantage of accessibility. A theory that emphasizes emotions and common motives allows us *to think* more closely to the patient's speech. In our intuitively formed monologue we may think: he's saying that it's hard for him to get his breathing regulated for weeks after an asthma attack. Or she's telling me that she misses greatly the intimacy feelings she had with her daughter before she left for college. Or his mounting sexual excitement was interrupted by the phone call.

Having a theory that uses common terminology has the additional advantage that we converse with *each other* without transcriptions in and out of phenomenon-distant talk of id, ego, and superego, paranoid and defensive positions, and the like. Our attempt, following Freud, to construct a science-like language for our theory has evolved into schools of analysis each having its own jargon. Rather than making it easier for analysts to share their clinical experience, discussions often degenerate into arguments about what is meant by compromise formation or projective identification or a self-selfobject function.

As we have implied, defenses no longer are bugaboos to be extricated so that we can get to the real information. An indication to a mother of the experiences to which her baby is aversive is as valuable a communication as her baby's indication of what experiences he likes. When a patient withdraws, becomes affectless, sleepy, or avoidant, she is telling us that something has triggered a response of fear or sadness, shame, embarrassment, humiliation, or guilt. Or when a patient becomes argumentative, accusatory, scornful, or sarcastic, something has triggered a response of anger. Of course, the same applies to the analyst. Reflective awareness by the analyst of his own withdrawing or mounting irritability provides a wonderful way to follow subtle cues that he might easily miss. Once we listen to responses of withdrawal and antagonism as indicators of aversiveness (ours and the patient's) to be investigated, we become much better judges of when aversiveness is present and when it is not and another motivation is dominant. Then we stop being hypervigilant to prevent some defense or resistance from slipping by us. A greater danger to the treatment lies in the other direction: persistent pressuring of the patient about defensive avoidances is guaranteed to trigger an aversiveness that produces a false confirmation of "aggression-driven" resistance.

A third major change lies in the way we share responsibility for doing the work of analysis. Traditionally, analysts have construed their tasks to be 1) maintain abstinence and neutrality, 2) provide a blank screen, 3) decode inchoate messages from the unconscious, 4) analyze meanings largely from the transference, and 5) remain constantly vigilant to prevent countertransference conflicts from intruding. No wonder psychoanalysis has been called the impossible profession. In our view, the goal of both empathic listening and the interventions we make is not to block ourselves out of the picture until we can arrive at finished products of interpretation. Whenever we feel we can, we are free to make a surmise and offer it. The patient confirms or disconfirms, adds or subtracts. We follow him and he leads us. At some point, we or he may think there is a larger picture, a model scene. Once either formulates it, the other adds to the construct. Thus as analysts, we feel freer to use our associative flow to enlarge our view. At moments, we will inevitably find ourselves on what may seem to be a divergent path. We can never be certain whether our wanderings are parallel responsiveness in disguise or countertransference aversiveness, but the empathic mode of perception can provide a useful guide. As long as we can relatively freely resume empathic listening, we need not be terribly concerned, and certainly not self-punitive, about a brief lessening of attentiveness. A prolonged or recurrent inability to resume optimal responsiveness suggests either an unrecognized, intensified obfuscating inclination on our part, on the part of the patient, or on the part of both. The contents of our wandering associations may contain clues to the intersubjective state.

An investigative attitude and a sense of safety are twin goals of our technique. By helping the patient expand her awareness of her experience through our interest and questions, we encourage her to pursue a mode of inquiry. By conveying our understanding through frequent affirmative interventions, we encourage a sense of safety.

We are especially attuned to and supportive of patients' exploratory-assertive motivation as they attempt to master and problem solve. We acknowledge when we feel we have an understanding of what the patient is attempting to convey to us. If patients feel they are being understood, whether in their attempts to reveal themselves or in their attempts to convey their aversiveness to self-revelation, they will be more motivated to express their experience with emotional depth. Offering an appreciative awareness of where analysands stand at any moment in their thoughts and feelings implicitly validates their self-experience and establishes a mutuality of sharing the expansion of awareness. Altering our view in response to our patients' disagreement or modification validates their sense of effectiveness and competence.

While we attempt to base all our interventions on empathically gathered data, we vary in our introduction of our own perspective. An acknowledgment phrased as, "So what you are telling me is" or "What you're feeling is" or an "uh-huh" or a head nod indicates an attempt to stay within the patient's perspective. An explanation phrased as, "The way I understand what you are experiencing is" introduces more of the analyst's perspective. Finally, implicitly or explicitly using a discrepancy in the subjective experience of analyst and patient introduces directly alternative perspectives—"Your reaction (or your memory) is . . . my reading (or my memory) of it is . . ."

Once we have made an intervention, we pay close attention to the patient's response. We note and support the patient's use of the intervention to explore further the issue under consideration and assert further his or her own problem-solving effort. Alternatively, if the patient experiences the intervention as an empathic failure, we note the extent of the disruption in the patient's self-cohesion. We attempt to explore, and thereby repair, the empathic link through a shared understanding of the precipitants, from the patient's vantage point. Once self-righting from the disruption has occurred, we are often able to explore the here-and-now of these shared experiences. We find these explorations to be extremely rich in potential for the mutual expansion of awareness.

Fostering a sense of safety and an investigative attitude leads to an openness for affectively rich transference experiences and the willingness to explore, understand, and resolve their puzzling occurrence. The specific situation we regard as crucial for the reorganization of symbolic representations is thus established. The patient is embedded in a transference configuration that he is simultaneously telling to, and investigating with, an analyst sensed as a concerned empathic professional. We hypothesize that this discrepancy promotes an alteration in the tenaciousness with which the transference view is held.

Finally, we recognize that the contours of a technique that is "user friendly" are difficult to present when we detail one or another approach. We hope that we have suggested the ambience of the type of analytic experience we aim to achieve through our explication of self and motivational systems.

FINAL REFLECTIONS

We began with the assertion that psychoanalysis is a theory of structured motivation. We have attempted to demonstrate how a theory of self and motivational systems delineates the manner in which motivation and lived experience are initiated, organized, and integrated. The empathic mode of perception opens the path to awareness of the patient's dominant motivation and follows the thread of affects into the realm of current and past events. Using the prism of an intrapsychic and intersubjective perspective and an assessment of state, we are able to understand the impact of the techniques we employ on the therapeutic sequence. Guided by a sensitivity to his intentions and feelings and his attempts to ensure vitalizing selfobject experiences, we focus our attention on the message communicated by the patient. We attempt to tap the potential of each of the two partners to facilitate the expressive, relational, and exploratory efforts of the other.

We see all the activities of analysis – associating; remembering; exploring fantasies, dreams and unconscious beliefs, and values; and constructing model scenes – as reflections of here-and-now contextual conditions of the analytic ambience, organized under the influence of past lived experience. And we see the past lived experience to be organized by, and organizers of, five motivational systems. Then, building on the foundation of motivation systems, self, and lived experience, we postulate the outlines of a "user friendly" technique. By "user friendly" we mean a technique that increases the essential sense of comfort and safety of analyst and analysand with each other while promoting an attitude of joint interest, curiosity, and investigation. We offer the analyst a theory of motivational systems and waxing and waning of self-cohesion to help give coherence to the analyst's listening. We believe our theory is broadly experiential and richly humanistic and thus promotes by its application a sense of individuality. A technique that successfully investigates the structured motivation of an analysand must tap the unique capacities of analysand and analyst and thus enhance individuality.

References

Abraham, K. (1923), Contributions to the theory of the anal character. In: *Selected Papers*. New York: Basic Books, 1953, pp. 370–392.

Ainsworth, M., Blehar, M.D., Waters, E., & Wall, S. (1978), *Patterns of Attachment: A Psychological Study of the Strange Situation*. Hillsdale, NJ: Lawrence Erlbaum Associates.

Anthi, P. (1983), Reconstruction of preverbal experiences. *J. Amer. Psychoanal. Assn.*, 31:33–58.

Arlow, J. (1963), Conflict, regression, and symptom formation. *Internat. J. Psycho-Anal.*, 44:12–22.

_____ (1969a), Unconscious fantasy and disturbances of conscious experience. *Psychoanal. Quart.*, 35:1–27.

_____ (1969b), Fantasy, memory, and reality testing. *Psychoanal. Quart.* 35:28–51.

_____ (1991), Methodology in reconstruction. *Psychoanal. Quart.*, 60:539–563.

_____ & Brenner, C. (1964), *Psychoanalytic Concepts and the Structural Theory*. New York: IUP.

Atwood, G. & Stolorow, R. (1984), *Structures of Subjectivity: Explorations in Psychoanalytic Phenomenology*. Hillsdale, NJ: The Analytic Press.

Bacal, H. (1985), Optimal responsiveness and the therapeutic process. In: *Progress in Self Psychology, Vol. 1*, ed. A. Goldberg. New York: Guilford, pp. 202–227.

_____ (1990), The elements of a corrective selfobject experience. *Psychoanal. Inq.*, 10:347–372.

_____ & Newman, K. (1990), *Theories of Object Relations: Bridges to Self Psychology.* New York: Columbia University Press.

Balint, M. (1968), *The Basic Fault: Therapeutic Aspects of Regression.* London: Tavistock.

_____ (1991), Methodology and reconstruction. *Psychoanal. Quart.*, 57:539–563.

Basch, M. F. (1980), *Doing Psychotherapy.* New York: Basic Books.

_____ (1984), Selfobjects and selfobject transference: Theoretical implications. In: *Kohut's Legacy*, ed. P. Stepansky & A. Goldberg. Hillsdale, NJ: The Analytic Press, pp. 21–41.

_____ (1988), *Understanding Psychotherapy.* New York: Basic Books.

Beardslee, W. & Podorefsky, D. (1988), Resilient adolescents whose parents have serious affective and other psychiatric disorders: Importance of self-understanding and relationships. *Amer. J. Psychoanal.*, 48:145–169.

Beebe, B. & Lachmann, F. M. (1992), The contribution of mother–infant mutual influence to the origin of self and object representations. In: *Relational Perspectives in Psychoanalysis*, ed. N. Skolnick & S. Warshaw. Hillsdale, NJ: The Analytic Press, pp. 83–117.

_____ & Stern, D. (1977), Engagement, disengagement and early object experiences. In: *Communicative Structures and Psychic Structures*, ed. M. Freedman & S. Grand. New York: Plenum, pp. 35–55.

Bion, W. (1959), *Splitting and Projective Identification.* Northvale, NJ: Aronson.

Bornstein, M. (ed.) (1983), Values and neutrality in psycho-analysis. *Psychoanal. Inq.* 3:545–717.

_____ (1985), How infant and mother jointly contribute to developing cognitive competence in the child. *Proc. Natl. Acad. Sci.*, 82:7470–7473.

Brandchaft, B. & Stolorow, R.D. (1990), Varieties of therapeutic alliance. *The Annual of Psychoanalysis*, 18:99–114. Hillsdale, NJ: The Analytic Press.

Brenner, C. (1976), *Psychoanalytic Technique and Psychic Conflict.* New York: IUP.

Breuer, J. & Freud. S. (1893–95), *Studies on Hysteria. Standard Edition*, 2:1–305. London: Hogarth Press, 1955.

Broucek, F. (1979), Efficacy in infancy: A review of some experimental studies and their possible implications for clinical theory. *Internat. J. Psycho-Anal.*, 60:311–316.

_____ (1991), *Shame and the Self.* New York: Guilford.

Bucci, W. (1985), Dual coding: A cognitive model for psychoanalytic research. *J. Amer. Psychoanal. Assn.*, 33:571–607.

_____ (1992), The development of emotional meaning in free association: A multiple code theory. In: *Hierarchical Conceptions in Psychoanalysis*, ed. A. Wilson & J. Gedo. New York: Guilford, pp. 1–66.

Byatt, A. S. (1990). *Possession.* New York: Vintage.

Cummings, M., Zahn-Waxler, C., & Radke-Yarrow, M. (1981), Young children's responses to expressions of anger and affection by others in the family. *Child Devel.*, 52:1274–1282.

Damon, W. (1977), *The Social World of the Child.* San Francisco: Jossey-Bass.

———— (1988), *The Moral Child.* New York: Free Press.

Dorpat, T. (1990), The primary process revisited. *Bull. Soc. Psychoanal. Psychother.*, 5:5–22.

———— (1991), Primary process meaning analysis. *Bull. Soc. Psychoanal. Psychother.*, 6:3–12.

Dowling, S. (1982), Dreams and dreaming in relation to trauma in childhood. *Internat. J. Psycho-Anal.*, 63:157–166.

Ehrenberg, D. B. (1983), The interpersonal paradigm and the degree of the therapist's involvement. *Contemp. Psychoanal.*, 19:200–237.

Ellman, S. (1991). *Freud's Technique Papers.* Northvale, NJ: Aronson.

Emde, R. (1981), Changing models of infancy and the nature of early development: Remodeling the foundation. *J. Amer. Psychoanal. Assn.*, 29:179–219.

———— (1988a), Development terminable and interminable: 1. Innate and motivational factors from infancy. *Internat. J. Psychoanal.*, 69:23–42.

———— (1988b), Development terminable and interminable: 2. Recent psychoanalytic theory and therapeutic considerations. *Internat. J. Psychoanal.*, 69:283–296.

———— (1991), Positive emotions for psychoanalytic theory: Surprises from infancy research and new directions. *J. Amer. Psychoanal. Assn.*, 39:5–44.

———— Gaensbauer, T., & Harman, R. (1976), *Emotional Expression in Infancy: A Biobehavioral Study (Psychological Issues,* Monogr. 37). New York: IUP.

Erikson, E. H. (1950), *Childhood and Society.* New York: Norton.

———— (1959), *Identity and the Life Cycle.* New York: Norton, 1980.

———— (1964), The inner and the outer space: Reflections on womanhood. *Daedelus,* XCII:582–606.

Ferenczi, S. (1925), Psycho-analysis of sexual habits. In: *The Selected Papers of Sandor Ferenczi, MD, Vol. 2.* New York: Basic Books, pp. 259–296, 1953.

———— (1932), *The Clinical Diary of Sandor Ferenczi,* ed. J. Dupont. Cambridge, MA: Harvard University Press, 1988.

———— (1933), Confusion of tongues between adults and the child. In: *Final Contributions to the Problems and Methods of Psychoanalysis.* New York: Basic Books, pp. 156–167, 1955.

Ferguson, T., Stegge, H., & Damhuis, I. (1991), Children's understanding of guilt and shame. *Child Devel.*, 62:827–839.

Fliess, R. (1942), The metapsychology of the analyst. *Psychoanal. Quart.* 11:211–227.

Fonagy, P., Steele, H. & Steele, M. (1991), Maternal representations of attachment during pregnancy predict the organization of infant-mother attachment at one year of age. *Child Devel.*, 62:891–905.

Fosshage, J. (1983), The psychological function of dreams: A revised psychoanalytic perspective. *Psychoanal. Contemp. Thought,* 6:641–669.

_____ (1987), A revised psychoanalytic approach. In: *Dream Interpretation: A Comparative Study* (rev.), ed. J. Fosshage & C. Loew. Costa Mesa, CA: PMA, pp. 299–318.

_____ (1987), Dream interpretation revisited. *Frontiers in Self Psychology: Progress in Self Psychology, Vol. 3,* ed. A. Goldberg. Hillsdale, NJ: The Analytic Press, pp. 161–175.

_____ (1989), The developmental function of dreaming mentation. Clinical implications. In: *Dimensions of Self Experience: Progress in Self Psychology, Vol. 5,* ed. A. Goldberg. Hillsdale, NJ: The Analytic Press, pp. 3–11.

_____ (1990a), Clinical protocol and the analysis response. *Psychoanal. Inq.,* 10:461–477.

_____ (1990b), Towards reconceptualizing transference: Theoretical and Clinical Considerations. Presented at meeting of Division 39, American Psychological Association, New York.

_____ (1992), Self psychology: The self and its vicissitudes within a relational matrix. In: *Relational Perspectives in Psychoanalysis,* ed. N. Skolnick & S. Warshaw. Hillsdale, NJ: The Analytic Press, pp. 21–42.

Freud, A. (1936), *The Ego and the Mechanisms of Defense.* New York: IUP, 1966.

_____ (1965), *Normality and Pathology in Childhood.* New York: IUP.

Freud, S. (1893–1895), Studies on hysteria. *Standard Edition,* 2:1–306. London: Hogarth Press, 1955.

_____ (1899), Screen memories. *Standard Edition,* 3:301–322. London: Hogarth Press, 1962.

_____ (1900), The interpretation of dreams. *Standard Edition,* 4 & 5. London: Hogarth Press, 1953.

_____ (1905), Three essays on the theory of sexuality. *Standard Edition,* 7:135–243. London: Hogarth Press, 1953.

_____ (1911), The handling of dream interpretation in psychoanalysis. *Standard Edition,* 12:89–96. London: Hogarth Press, 1958.

_____ (1911–1915), Papers on technique. *Standard Edition,* 12:89–171. London: Hogarth Press.

_____ (1914), Remembering, repeating and working through. *Standard Edition,* 12:145–156. London: Hogarth Press, 1958.

_____ (1915), Repression. *Standard Edition,* 14:146–158. London: Hogarth Press, 1957.

_____ (1917), Mourning and melancholia. *Standard Edition,* 14:237–258. London: Hogarth Press, 1957.

_____ (1918), From the history of an infantile neurosis. *Standard Edition,* 17:7–122. London: Hogarth Press, 1955.

_____ (1921), Group psychology and the analysis of the ego. *Standard Edition*, 18:69–143. London: Hogarth Press, 1955.

_____ (1922), Two encyclopedia articles. *Standard Edition*, 18:235–259. London: Hogarth Press, 1955.

_____ (1933), New introductory lectures on psycho-analysis: Dreams and occultism. *Standard Edition*, 22:31–56. London: Hogarth Press, 1964.

Furer, M. (1972), The history of the superego concept in psychoanalysis. In: *Moral Values and the Superego Concept in Psychoanalysis*, ed. S. Post. New York: IUP, pp. 11–61.

Gabennesch, H. (1990a), The perception of social conventionality by children and adults. *Child Devel.*, 61:2047–2059.

_____ (1990b), Recognizing conventionality: Reply to Shweder and Helwig et al. *Child Devel.*, 61:2079–2084.

Ganaway, G.K. (1989), Historical versus narrative truth: Clarifying the role of exogenous trauma in the etiology of MPD and its variants. *Dissociation*, 2:205–220.

Gardner, R. W., Holzman, P. S., Klein, G. S., Linton, H. S. & Spence, D. P. (1959), *Cognitive Control: A Study of Individual Consistencies in Cognitive Behavior.* (*Psychological Issues*, Monogr. 4). New York: IUP.

Gedo, J. (1979), *Beyond Interpretation.* New York: IUP.

_____ (1984), *Psychoanalysis and Its Discontents.* New York: Guilford.

_____ (1986), *Conceptual Issues in Psychoanalysis.* Hillsdale, NJ: The Analytic Press.

_____ & Goldberg, A. (1972), *Models of the Mind.* Chicago: University of Chicago Press.

Ghent, E. (1989), Credo: The dialectics of one-person and two-person psychologies. *Contemp. Psychoanal.*, 25:169–211.

Gill, M. (1963). *Topography and Systems in Psychoanalytic Theory.* (*Psychological Issues*, Monogr. 10). New York: IUP.

_____ (1982), *Analysis of Transference, Vol. 1.* New York: IUP.

_____ (1984). Transference: A change in conception or only in emphasis? A Response. *Psychoanal. Inq.*, 4:489–524.

_____ (1991), Merton Gill speaks his mind. *The American Psychoanalyst*, Quarterly Newsletter of the American Psychoanalytic Association 25(1):17–21.

_____ & Hoffman, I. Z. (1982). *Analysis of Transference. Vol. 2.* New York: IUP.

Gilligan, C. (1982), *In a Different Voice: Psychological Theory of Women's Development.* Cambridge, MA: Harvard University Press.

Glover, E. (1929), The screen function of traumatic memories. In: *On the Early Development of the Mind.* New York: IUP, 1956, pp. 108–111.

Goldberg, A. (1988), *A Fresh Look at Psychoanalysis: The View from Self Psychology.* Hillsdale, NJ: The Analytic Press.

_____ (1991), *The Prisonhouse of Psychoanalysis.* Hillsdale, NJ: The Analytic Press.

Goldberg, C. (1991), *Understanding Shame*. Northvale, NJ: Aronson.

Goldstein, W. (1991), Clarification of projective identification. *Amer. J. Psychiat.*, 148:153–161.

Gray, P. (1973), Psychoanalytic technique and the ego's capacity for viewing intrapsychic activity. *J. Amer. Psychoanal. Assn.*, 21:474–494.

Greenacre, P. (1949), A contribution to the study of screen memories. *The Psychoanalytic Study of the Child*, 3/4:73–84. New York: IUP.

_____ (1971), *Emotional Growth, Vol. 2*. New York: IUP.

Greenberg, J. & Mitchell, S. A. (1983), *Object Relations in Psychoanalytic Theory*. Cambridge, MA: Harvard University Press.

Greenson, R. R. (1967), *The Technique and Practice of Psychoanalysis*. New York: IUP.

Grotstein, J. (1981), *Splitting and Projective Identification*. Northvale, NJ: Aronson.

Hadley, J. (1989), The neurobiology of motivational systems. In: *Psychoanalysis and Motivation* by J. Lichtenberg. Hillsdale, NJ: The Analytic Press, pp. 337–372.

Hala, S., Chandler, M. & Fritz, A. (1991), Fledgling theories of mind: Deception as a marker of three-year-olds' understanding of false belief. *Child Devel.*, 62:83–97.

Hartmann, H. (1964), *Essays on Ego Psychology*. New York: IUP.

Haynal, A. (1989), The concept of trauma and its present meaning. *Internat. Rev. Psycho-Anal.*, 16:315–322.

_____ & Falzeder, E. (1991), "Healing through love"? A unique dialogue in the history of psychoanalysis. *Free Assoc.*, 2:1–20.

Helwig, C., Tisak, M. & Turiel, E. (1990), Children's social reasoning in context: Reply to Gabennesch. *Child Devel.*, 61:2068–2077.

Hofer, M. (1990), Early symbiotic processes: Hard evidence from a soft place. In: *Pleasure Beyond the Pleasure Principle,* ed. R. A. Glick & S. Bone. New Haven, CT: Yale University Press, pp. 55–80.

Hoffman, I. Z. (1983), The patient as interpreter of the analyst's experience. *Contemp. Psychoanal.*, 19:389–422.

Hoffman, M. (1967), Moral internalization, parental power, and the nature of parent-child interaction. *Devel. Psychol.*, 5:45–57.

Holt, R. (1967), The development of the primary process. In: *Motives and Thought: Psychoanalytic Essays in Honor of David Rapaport*, ed. R. Holt. (*Psychological Issues*, Monogr. 18/19). New York: IUP, pp. 344–383.

_____ (1976), Freud's theory of the primary process present status. *Psychoanal. Contemp. Sci.*, 5:61–99.

Hornik, R., Risenhoover, M. & Gunnar, M. (1987), The effects of maternal positive, neutral, and negative affective communications on infant responses to new toys. *Child Devel.*, 58:937–944.

Horowitz, M. (1972), Modes of representation of thought. *J. Amer. Psychoanal. Assn.*, 20:793–819.

_____ (1979), *States of Mind.* New York: Plenum Press.

_____ Fridhandler, B., & Stinson, C. (1991), Person schemas and emotion. *J. Amer. Psychoanal. Assn.*, 39:173–208.

Izard, C., Haynes, O. M., Chisholm, G. & Gaak, K. (1991), Emotional determinants of infant-mother attachment. *Child Devel.*, 62:906–917.

Jacobs, T. (1971), *The Use of the Self.* Madison, CT: IUP.

Jones, J. (1981), Affects: A nonsymbolic information processing system. Unpublished manuscript.

Kagan, J. (1979), The form of early development. *Arch. Gen. Psychiat.*, 36:1047–1054.

Kernberg, O. F. (1975), *Borderline Conditions and Pathological Narcissism.* New York: Aronson.

_____ (1976), *Object Relations Theory and Clinical Psychoanalysis.* New York: Aronson.

Klein, M. (1952), *Development in Psycho-Analysis,* ed. J. Riviere. London: Hogarth Press.

Kluft, R. P. (1984), Treatment of multiple personality. *Psychiat. Clin. N. Amer.*, 7:9–29.

Kohlberg, L. (1981), *Essays on Moral Development, Vol. 1: The Philosophy of Moral Development: Moral Stages and the Idea of Justice.* San Francisco: Harper & Row.

Kohut, H. (1959), Introspection, empathy, and psychoanalysis: An examination of the relationship between mode of observation and theory. *J. Amer. Psychoanal. Assn.*, 7:459–483.

_____ (1971), *The Analysis of the Self.* New York: IUP.

_____ (1977), *The Restoration of the Self.* New York: IUP.

_____ (1982), Introspection, empathy, and semicircle of mental health. *Internat. J. Psycho-Anal.*, 63:395–408.

_____ (1984), *How Does Analysis Cure?* ed. A. Goldberg & P. Stepansky. Chicago: University of Chicago Press.

Kris, E. (1956), The recovery of childhood memories in psychoanalysis. In: *Selected Papers of Ernst Kris.* New Haven, CT: Yale University Press, 1975, pp. 301–340.

Krueger, D. (1988), *Body Self and Psychological Self: A Developmental and Clinical Integration of Disorders of the Self.* New York: Brunner/Mazel.

Krystal, H. (1974), The genetic development of affects and affect regression. *The Annual of Psychoanalysis,* 2:98–126. New York: IUP.

Lachmann, F. (1986), Interpretation of psychic conflict and adversarial relationships: A self-psychoanalytic perspective. *Psychoanal. Psychol.*, 3:341–355.

_____ (1990), On some challenges to clinical theory in the treatment of character pathology. In: *The Realities of Transference: Progress in Self Psychology, Vol. 6,* ed. A. Goldberg. Hillsdale, NJ: The Analytic Press, pp. 59–67.

_____ & Beebe, B. (1989), Oneness fantasies revisited. *Psychoanal. Psychol.*, 6: 137–149.

_____ _____ (1992), Representational and selfobject transferences: A developmental perspective. In: *New Therapeutic Visions: Progress in Self Psychology, Vol. 8.* Hillsdale, NJ: The Analytic Press, pp. 3–15.

_____ _____ (in press), Reformulations of early development and transference: Implications for psychic structure formation. In: *The Interface of Psychoanalysis and Psychology*, ed. J. Barron, M. Eagle & D. Wolitzky. Washington, DC: Amer. Psychol. Assn.

_____ Lapkin, B. & Handelman, N. (1962), The recall of dreams: Its relation to repression and cognitive control. *J. Abn. Social Psychol.*, 64:160–162.

Leavy, S. A. (1984), Discussion. In: *Empathy II*, ed. J. Lichtenberg, M. Bornstein & D. Silver. Hillsdale, NJ: The Analytic Press, pp. 249–253.

Leichtman, M. (1991), Review of *Psychoanalysis and Motivation. Bull. Menn. Clin.*, 55:530–531.

Levin, F. (1991), *Mapping the Mind: The Intersection of Psychoanalysis and Neuroscience.* Hillsdale, NJ: The Analytic Press.

Levine, L., Tuber, S., Slade, A., & Ward, M. (1991), Mothers' mental representations and their relationship to mother infant attachment. *Bull. Menn. Clin.* 55:454–469.

Lewis, H. B. (1987), Shame: The "sleeper" in psychopathology. In: *The Role of Shame in Symptom Formation*, ed. H. B. Lewis. Hillsdale, NJ: Lawrence Erlbaum Associates, pp. 1–28.

Lewis, M. (1991), *Shame: The Exposed Self.* New York: Free Press.

_____ Stanger, C. & Sullivan, M. (1989), Deception in 3-year-olds. *Devel. Psychol.*, 25:439–443.

Lichtenberg, J. (1981a), The testing of reality from the standpoint of the body self. *J. Amer. Psychoanal. Assn.*, 26:357–385.

_____ (1981b), The empathic mode of perception and alternative vantage points for psychoanalytic work. *Psychoanal. Inq.*, 1:329–356.

_____ (1983a), *Psychoanalysis and Infant Research.* Hillsdale, NJ: The Analytic Press.

_____ (1983b). An application of the self-psychological viewpoint to psychoanalytic technique. *Reflections on Self Psychology*, ed. J. Lichtenberg & S. Kaplan. Hillsdale, NJ: The Analytic Press, pp. 163–186.

_____ (1983c), The influence of values and value judgments on the psychoanalytic encounter. *Psychoanal. Inq.*, 3:647–664.

_____ (1983d), A clinical illustration of construction and reconstruction in the analysis of an adult. *Psychoanal. Inq.*, 3:279–294.

_____ (1984), The empathic mode of perception and alternative vantage points for psychoanalytic work. In: *Empathy II*, ed. J. Lichtenberg, M. Bornstein, & D. Silver. Hillsdale, NJ: The Analytic Press. pp. 113–136.

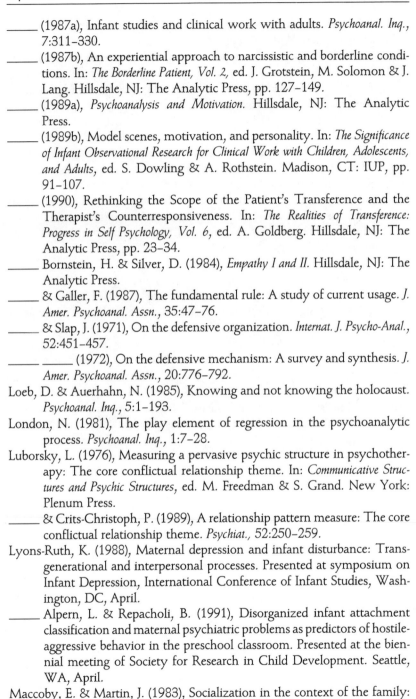

_____ (1987a), Infant studies and clinical work with adults. *Psychoanal. Inq.*, 7:311–330.

_____ (1987b), An experiential approach to narcissistic and borderline conditions. In: *The Borderline Patient, Vol. 2*, ed. J. Grotstein, M. Solomon & J. Lang. Hillsdale, NJ: The Analytic Press, pp. 127–149.

_____ (1989a), *Psychoanalysis and Motivation.* Hillsdale, NJ: The Analytic Press.

_____ (1989b), Model scenes, motivation, and personality. In: *The Significance of Infant Observational Research for Clinical Work with Children, Adolescents, and Adults*, ed. S. Dowling & A. Rothstein. Madison, CT: IUP, pp. 91–107.

_____ (1990), Rethinking the Scope of the Patient's Transference and the Therapist's Counterresponsiveness. In: *The Realities of Transference: Progress in Self Psychology, Vol. 6*, ed. A. Goldberg. Hillsdale, NJ: The Analytic Press, pp. 23–34.

_____ Bornstein, H. & Silver, D. (1984), *Empathy I and II.* Hillsdale, NJ: The Analytic Press.

_____ & Galler, F. (1987), The fundamental rule: A study of current usage. *J. Amer. Psychoanal. Assn.*, 35:47–76.

_____ & Slap, J. (1971), On the defensive organization. *Internat. J. Psycho-Anal.*, 52:451–457.

_____ _____ (1972), On the defensive mechanism: A survey and synthesis. *J. Amer. Psychoanal. Assn.*, 20:776–792.

Loeb, D. & Auerhahn, N. (1985), Knowing and not knowing the holocaust. *Psychoanal. Inq.*, 5:1–193.

London, N. (1981), The play element of regression in the psychoanalytic process. *Psychoanal. Inq.*, 1:7–28.

Luborsky, L. (1976), Measuring a pervasive psychic structure in psychotherapy: The core conflictual relationship theme. In: *Communicative Structures and Psychic Structures*, ed. M. Freedman & S. Grand. New York: Plenum Press.

_____ & Crits-Christoph, P. (1989), A relationship pattern measure: The core conflictual relationship theme. *Psychiat.*, 52:250–259.

Lyons-Ruth, K. (1988), Maternal depression and infant disturbance: Transgenerational and interpersonal processes. Presented at symposium on Infant Depression, International Conference of Infant Studies, Washington, DC, April.

_____ Alpern, L. & Repacholi, B. (1991), Disorganized infant attachment classification and maternal psychiatric problems as predictors of hostile-aggressive behavior in the preschool classroom. Presented at the biennial meeting of Society for Research in Child Development. Seattle, WA, April.

Maccoby, E. & Martin, J. (1983), Socialization in the context of the family:

Parent-child interaction. In: *Handbook of Child Psychology*, ed. P. H. Mussen. New York: Wiley.

Mahler, M. S. (1968), *On Human Symbiosis and the Vicissitudes of Individuation*. New York: IUP.

_____ Pine, F. & Bergman, A. (1975), *The Psychological Birth of the Human Infant*. New York: Basic Books.

Main, M. & Goldwyn, R. (1992), Adult attachment classification system. In: *A Typology of Human Attachment Organization: Assessed in Discourse, Drawings, and Interviews*, ed. M. Main. New York: Cambridge University Press.

_____ & Solomon, J. (1990), Procedures for identifying infants as disorganized-disoriented during the Ainsworth Strange Situation. In: *Attachment in the Preschool Years: Theory, Research and Intervention*, ed. M. Greenberg, D. Cicchetti & E. M. Cummings. Chicago: University of Chicago Press, pp. 121-160.

Major, R. & Miller, P. (1984), Empathy, antipathy, and telepathy in the analytic process. In: *Empathy II*, ed. J. Lichtenberg, M. Bornstein & D. Silver. Hillsdale, NJ: The Analytic Press, pp. 227-248.

Marohn, R. & Wolf, E. (1990). The "corrective emotional experience" revisited. *Psychoanal. Inq.*, 10:285-458.

Masterson, J. (1987), Borderline and narcissistic disorders: An integrated developmental object-relations approach. In: *The Borderline Patient, Vol. 1*, ed. J. Grotstein, M. Solomon & J. Lang, Hillsdale, NJ: The Analytic Press, pp. 205-218.

Mayer, E. L. (1991), Towers and enclosed spaces: A preliminary report on gender differences in children's reactions to block structures. *Psychoanal. Inq.*, 11:480-510.

McKinnon, J. (1979), Two semantic forms: Neuropsychological and psychoanalytic descriptions. *Psychoanal. Contemp. Thought*, 2:25-76.

McLaughlin, J. (1978), Primary and secondary process in the context of cerebral hemispheric specialization. *Psychoanal. Quart.*, 47:237-266.

_____ (1982), Issues stimulated by the 32nd Congress. *Internat. J. Psycho-Anal.*, 63:229-240.

Meissner, W. (1983), Values in the psychoanalytic situation. *Psychoanal. Inq.*, 3:577-598.

_____ (1991), A decade of psychoanalytic praxis. *Psychoanal. Inq.*, 11:30-64.

Meltzoff, A. & Borton, R. (1979), Intermodal matching by human neonates. *Nature*, 282:403-404.

Miller, J. & Post, S., ed. (1990), *How Theory Shapes Technique: Perspectives on a Self-Psychological Clinical Presentation. Psychoanal. Inq.*, 10(4).

Morrison, A. (1989), *Shame: The Underside of Narcissism*. Hillsdale, NJ. The Analytic Press.

Nathanson, D. (1987), *The Many Faces of Shame*. New York: Guilford Press.

Nelson, K. (1986), *Event Knowledge.* Hillsdale, NJ: Lawrence Erlbaum Associates.

Noy, P. (1979), The psychoanalytic theory of cognitive development. *The Psychoanalytic Study of the Child,* 34:169–216. New Haven, CT: Yale University Press.

Ogden, T. (1982), *Projective Identification and Psychotherapeutic Technique.* New York: Aronson.

Olds, D. (1992), Consciousness: A brain-centered, informational approach. *Psychoanal. Inq.* 12:419–444.

Olinick, S. (1984), A critique of empathy and sympathy. In: *Empathy I,* ed. J. Lichtenberg, M. Bornstein & D. Silver. Hillsdale, NJ: The Analytic Press, pp. 137–166.

Ornstein, A. (1974), The dread to repeat and the new beginning: A contribution to the psychoanalysis of the narcissistic personality disorders. *The Annual of Psychoanalysis,* 2:231–248. New York: IUP.

_____ (1984), Psychoanalytic psychotherapy: A contemporary perspective. In: *Kohut's Legacy,* ed. P. Stepansky & A. Goldberg. Hillsdale, NJ: The Analytic Press, pp. 171–181.

Ornstein, P. (1990). A self-psychological view. *Psychoanal. Inq.,* 10:478–497.

_____ & Ornstein, A. (1985), Clinical understanding and explaining: The empathic vantage point. In: *Progress in Self Psychology, Vol. 1,* ed. A. Goldberg. New York: Guilford Press, pp. 43–61.

Papousek, H. (1986), Intuitive parenting: A didactic counterpart to the infant's precocity in integrative capacities. In: *Handbook of Infant Development,* ed. J.D. Osofsky. New York: Wiley, pp. 669–720.

_____ & Papousek, M. (1975), Cognitive aspects of preverbal social interaction between human infant and adults. In: *Parent-Infant Interaction* (Ciba Foundation Symposium). New York: Associated Scientific Publishers.

Parens, H. (1979), *The Development of Aggression in Early Childhood.* New York: Aronson.

_____ (1991), A view of the development of hostility in early life. *J. Amer. Psychoanal. Assn.,* 39:75–108.

Peirs, G. & Singer, M. (1953), *Shame and Guilt.* Springfield, IL: Charles C. Thomas.

Piaget, J. (1969), The intellectual development of the adolescent. In: *Adolescence: Psychosocial Perspectives,* ed. G. Kaplan & S. Lebovici. New York: Basic Books.

_____ (1932), *The Moral Judgment of the Child.* New York: Free Press, 1965.

Piontelli, A. (1987), Infant observation from before birth. *Internat. J. Psycho-Anal.,* 68:453–464.

Poland, W. (1992), Transference: "An original creation." *Psychoanal. Quart.,* 61:185–205.

Porder, M. (1987), Projective identification: An alternative hypothesis. *Psychoanal. Quart.*, 56:431–451.

Pulver, S. (1987), ed. *How Theory Shapes Technique: Perspectives on a Clinical Study. Psychoanal. Inq.* 7(2).

Putnam, F. W. (1988), The switch process in multiple personality disorder and other state-change disorders. *Dissociation*, 1:24–32.

Rapaport, D. (1960), *The Structure of Psychoanalytic Theory (Psychological Issues*, Monogr. 6). New York: IUP.

Robinson, J. & Birigen, Z. (in press). Gender and emerging autonomy in development. *Psychoanal. Inq.*

Roiphe, H. & Galenson, E. (1981), *Infantile Origins of Sexual Identity*. New York: IUP.

Rosenblatt, A. (1984), The psychoanalytic process: Systems and information processing model. *Psychoanal. Inq.*, 4:9–86.

_____ & Thickstun, J. (1977), *Modern Psychoanalytic Concepts in a General Psychology (Psychological Issues*, Monogr. 42/43). New York: IUP.

Ross, D. (1991), ed. *Multiple Personality Disorder. Psychoanal. Inq.*, 12(1).

Sameroff, A. (1983), Developmental systems: Context and evolution. In: *Mussen's Handbook of Child Psychology, Vol. 1*, ed. W. Kessen. New York: Wiley.

Sander, L. (1975), Infant and caretaking environment: Investigation and conceptualization of adaptive behavior in a system of increasing complexity. In: *Explorations in Child Psychiatry*, ed. E. J. Anthony. New York: Plenum, pp. 129–166.

_____ (1980), Investigation of the infant and its caregiving environment as a biological system. In: *The Course of Life, Vol. 1*, ed. S. I. Greenspan & G. Pollock. Rockville, MD: NIMH, pp. 177–202.

_____ (1983), To begin with–reflections on ontogeny. In: *Reflections on Self Psychology*, ed. J. Lichtenberg & S. Kaplan. Hillsdale, NJ: The Analytic Press, pp. 85–104.

_____ (1986), The inner experience of the infant: A framework for inference relevant to development of the sense of self. Presented to Mahler Symposium, Paris.

Sandler, J. (1976), Countertranference and role-responsiveness. *Internat. Rev. Psycho-Anal.*, 3:43–47.

_____ (1988), *Projection, Identification, Projective Identification*. London: Karnac.

_____ & Sandler, A. M. (1984), The "second censorship," the 'three box model' and some technical implications. *Internat. J. Psycho-Anal.*, 64:413–426.

Schafer, R. (1976), *A New Language for Psychoanalysis*. New Haven, CT: Yale University Press.

Schore, A. (1991), A psychoneurobiological model of the development of emotional self regulation. Unpublished manuscript.

Schwaber, E. (1981), Empathy: A mode of analytic listening. *Psychoanal. Inq.*, 1:357–392.

_____ (1983), Psychoanalytic listening and psychic reality. *Internat. Rev. Psycho-Anal.*, 10:379–392.

_____ (1987), Models of the mind and data gathering in clinical work. *Psychoanal. Inq.*, 7:261–176.

Shane, M. (1989), The challenge posed by infant observational research to traditional psychoanalytic formulations: A discussion of the papers. In: *The Significance of Infant Observational Research for Clinical Work with Children, Adolescents, and Adults*, ed. S. Dowling & A. Rothstein. Madison, CT: IUP, pp. 134–155.

Shapiro, T. (1970), Interpretation and naming. *J. Amer. Psychoanal. Assn.*, 18:399–421.

Shweder, R. (1990), In defense of moral realism: Reply to Gabennesch. *Child Devel.*, 61:2060–2067.

Silverman, L., Lachmann, F. & Milich, R. (1982), *The Search For Oneness.* New York: IUP.

Silverman, M. (1987), Clinical material. *Psychoanal. Inq.*, 7:147–166.

Simon, B. (1984), Confluence of visual image between patient and analyst: Communication of failed communication. In: *Empathy II.* Hillsdale, NJ: The Analytic Press, pp. 261–278.

Skinner, J. (1984), Discussion. In: *Empathy II,* ed. J. Lichtenberg, M. Bornstein & D. Silver. Hillsdale, NJ: The Analytic Press, pp. 279–288.

Slap, J. & Slap-Shelton, L. (1991), *The Schema in Clinical Psychoanalysis.* Hillsdale, NJ: The Analytic Press.

Spence, D. (1982), *Narrative Truth and Historical Truth: Meaning and Interpretation in Psychoanalysis.* New York: Norton.

Spitz, R. (1957), *No and Yes.* New York: IUP.

_____ (1959), *A Genetic Field Theory of Ego Formation.* New York: IUP.

Sterba, R.F. (1934), The fate of the ego in analytic therapy. *Internat. J. Psycho-Anal.*, 15:117–126.

Stern, D. (1985), *The Interpersonal World of the Infant.* New York: Basic Books.

_____ (1988), Affect in the context of the infant's lived experience. *Internat. J. Psycho-Anal.*, 69:233–238.

_____ (1990), *Diary of a Baby.* New York: Basic Books.

Stoller, R., (1975), *Perversion.* New York: Pantheon.

Stolorow, R. (1986), Critical reflections on the theory of self psychology: An inside view. *Psychoanal. Inq.*, 6:387–402.

_____ & Atwood, G. (1989), The unconscious and unconscious fantasy: An intersubjective-developmental perspective. *Psychoanal. Inq.*, 9:364–374.

_____ & _____ (1992), *Contexts of Being: The Intersubjective Foundations of Psychological Life.* Hillsdale, NJ: The Analytic Press.

_____ Brandchaft, B., & Atwood, G. (1987), *Psychoanalytic Treatment: An Intersubjective Approach.* Hillsdale, NJ: The Analytic Press.

_____ & Lachmann, F. (1980), *Psychoanalysis of Developmental Arrests.* New York: IUP.

_____ _____ (1984/85), Transference: The future of an illusion. *The Annual of Psychoanalysis,* 12/13:19–38. New York: IUP.

Stone, L. (1961), *The Psychoanalytic Situation.* New York: IUP.

Teti, D. & Gelfand, D. (1991), Behavioral competence among mothers of infants in the first year: The mediational role of maternal self-efficacy.*Child Devel.,* 62:918–929.

Tolpin, M. (1971), On the beginnings of a cohesive self: An application of the concept of transmuting internalization to the study of the transitional object and signal anxiety. *The Psychoanalytic Study of the Child,* 26:316–354. New Haven, CT: Yale University Press.

Tomkins, S. (1962), *Affect, Imagery, Consciousness, Vol. 1: The Positive Affects.* New York: Springer.

_____ (1963), *Affect, Imagery, Consciousness, Vol. 2: The Negative Affects.* New York: Springer.

_____ (1987), Shame. In: *The Many Faces of Shame,* ed. D. Nathanson. New York: Guilford, pp. 133–161.

Trevarthan, C. (1980), The foundations of intersubjectivity: Development of interpersonal and cooperative understanding in infants. In: *The Social Foundation of Language and Thought: Essays in Honor of Jerome S. Bruner,* ed. D. R. Olson. New York: Norton, pp. 316–341.

Ulman, R. & Paul, H. (1990), The addictive personality disorder and "addictive trigger mechanisms" (ATMs): The self psychology of addiction and its treatment. In: *The Realities of Transference: Progress in Self Psychology, Vol. 6,* ed. A. Goldberg. Hillsdale, NJ: The Analytic Press, pp. 129–156.

Wachtel, T. F. (1980), Transference schema assimilation: The relevance of Piaget to the psychoanalytic theory of transference. In: *The Annual of Psychoanalysis,* 8:59–76. New York: IUP.

Wallerstein, R. (1986), *Forty-Two Lives in Treatment.* New York: Guilford.

Weiss, J. & Sampson, H. (1986), *The Psychoanalytic Process.* New York: Guilford.

Werner, H. & Kaplan, B. (1963), *Symbol Formation.* New York: Wiley.

Wilkin, K. (1991), *Caro,* ed. J. Barker. Munich, Germany: Prestel.

Winnicott, D. (1956), Primary maternal preoccupation. In: *Collected Papers.* London: Tavistock, 1958, pp. 300–305.

_____ (1958), The capacity to be alone. In: *The Maturational Processes and the Facilitating Environment.* New York: IUP, 1965, pp. 29–36.

Wolf, E. (1980), On the developmental line of selfobject relations. In: *Advances in Self Psychology,* ed. A. Goldberg. New York: IUP, pp. 117–132.

_____ (1982), Adolescence: Psychology of the self and selfobjects. *Annals of the American Society for Adolescent Psychiatry,* pp. 171–181.

_____ (1988), *Treating the Self.* New York: Guilford.

Woolf, V. (1927), *To the Lighthouse.* New York: Harcourt, Brace, 1955.

Wurmser, L. (1981), *The Mask of Shame.* Baltimore, MD: Johns Hopkins University Press.

Zahn-Waxler, C., Cummings, M., McKnew, D. & Radke-Yarrow, M. (1984), Altruism, aggression and social interactions in young children with a manic-depressive parent. *Child Devel.,* 55:112–122.

_____ Kochanska, G., Krupnick, J. & McKnew, D. (1990), Patterns of guilt in children of depressed and well mothers. *Devel. Psychol.,* 26:51–59.

_____ & Radke-Yarrow, M. (1982), The development of altruism: Alternative research strategies. In: *The Development of Prosocial Behavior,* ed. N. Eisenberg. New York: Academic Press, pp. 109–138.

_____ _____ & King, R. (1979). Child rearing and children's prosocial initiations toward victims of distress. *Child Devel.,* 50:319–330.

Zetzel, E. R. (1956), Current concepts of transference. *Internat. J. Psycho-Anal.,* 37:369–376.

Zuriff, G. (1992), Theoretical inference and the new psychoanalytic theory of infancy. *Psychoanal. Quart.,* 611:18–36.

Index

237

Sampson, H., 12, 32, 49, 55, 73, 74, 141
Sander, L., 37, 39, 40, 69, 70, 203
Sandler, A.M., 61, 86
Sandler, J., 61, 65, 86
Satiety, 143
Scanning, 50–51
Schafer, R., 64, 152
Schemata, coherent, 208
Schore, A., 185
Schwaber, E., 65, 154, 199, 210, 232
Screen memories
  analysis of, 10
  model scenes and, 9–11
  types of, 9
Script representations, 206
Secondary process, 92
Security
  sense of, infant's elicitation of, 45
  unavailable, 142
Seduction, 10
Self, 36, 57, 159
  child abuse and, 168
  cohesive state of, 75
  conceptualization of, 6
  core, 131
  depletion of, 134
  developing, 204
  emergent, 75
  grandiose, 136
  as hierarchical superordinate, 57–59
  infants' differentiation of, 131
  narcissistic, 137
  organizing and integrating capacities of, 57–58, 92
  reciprocal relationship with motivation, 3
  relatedness to others, 206
  reorganization of, 22
  revised approach to, 197
  sense of, 2, 4, 22, 74, 82–83
    development of, 35, 205
    emerging, 81
    gaps in, 127
    intensified, 211
    shame connected to, 187
    symptomatic alterations in, 200
  technique based on, 33

theory of, self psychology and, 198–205
use of selfobjects, 127
vitality of, 132
  restoration of, 89, 131
Self-affirming experience, re-creation of, 69
Self-agency, sense of, 69
Self-amusement, 125
Self-awareness, expansion of, 87
Self-cohesion, 4, 6, 75, 132, 211
  adaptation in service of, 211
  analyst as contributor to, 134
  background supports for, 138
  disturbances in, 123, 188
  experiences providing, 142
  fragmented, 166
  loss of, 134
  preservation of, 171
  restoration of, 126, 132, 145
Self-criticism, 159
Self-deception, 155
Self-esteem
  disturbances in, shame and, 47, 186, 188
  restoration of, 126
Self-experience
  regulation of, disturbed, 165
  selfobject and, 128
  validation of, 218
Self-feeding, 125
Self-functional capacity, infants' gaining of, 132
Self-identification, 82
Self-interest, 159
Self-narrative creation, 165
Self-organization, 36, 57, 161
  development of, 59
Self-organizing motivation, 35, 36, 37–38
Self-other regulation, 41
Self-preoccupation, 85
Self-preservation, 111
Self-protection, use of idealization for, 116
Self-protective idealization, diminished, 108
Self psychology, 89, 94, 134

Stoller, R., 54, 61, 62
Stolorow, R., 10, 12, 32, 61, 62, 64, 84,
117n, 119, 120n, 121, 128, 133,
134, 136, 138, 158, 212, 221
selfobject view, 128
Stone, L., 25, 195
Story world, discourse organized in
form of, 23–24
Stranger anxiety, 44, 46
Stress trauma, 25
Structure, absent, 161
Structured motivation, 218
psychoanalytic models of, 203
Subject, 4, 124
Subjective experience
selfobject in terms of, 128
states as aspect of, 75–76
Subjective world, illumination of, 117
Subjectivity, 5, 62, 96
Success, 54
Sucking, fetal, 38
Sullivan, M., 29
Superego, 3, 171 , 210
origins and functions of, 171
Survivors' guilt, 171, 172
Symbolic functioning, toddler's, 47
Symbolic mentation, 207, 213
conscious, 74
unconscious, 67, 74–80
Symbolic period, templates of funda-
mental unconscious mentation
for model scenes of, 68
Symbolic play, 207
Symbolic representation, 92, 134, 165
coding in form of, 92–93
development of, 2
lived experience and, 69
psychic phenomena coded in, 91
reorganization of, 22, 32, 146
System model, development in, 203
System orientation, 209

T

Technique, 198
empathic mode of perception and,
199–200

goals of, 217
theory of, 1, 96, 197–219
historical perspective, 198–205
laying the foundation for, 205–214
"user-friendly" technique, 214–218,
219
Telepathy, 65
Telescoping, 11–12, 92
Television, development of values and,
180–181
Temper tantrum, 54
Tension, dialectic, *See* Dialectic tension
Terminology, common, theory using,
216
Teti, D., 72
Thalamus, 82
Theoretical models, 3
Theory, 198
analyst's knowledge of, 12
formulations of, differences in, 202
Therapeutic ambience, 134
Therapeutic exchange, *See also* Analytic
exchange
concept of selfobject experience applied to, 144–148
quality of, therapist's understanding
of, 130
Therapeutic reaction, negative, 94
Therapy, sensual aspects of, 144–145
Thickstun, J., 36
Things-of-contemplation, 45
Thought(s)
awareness of, 86
reasoned, 214
separation from feelings, 151
verbal expression of, 94
waking, 82
Three-box theory, 86
Tisak, M., 180, 226
Toddler, *See also* Child
aversive motivational system in, 175
dialectic tension in, 46
exploratory-assertive motivational
system, 47
gradient of awareness in, 82
Tolpin, M., 125, 160
Tomkins, S., 75, 142, 183, 187, 211